COLORADO NONPROFIT MANAGEMENT: UNDERSTANDING THE LEGAL ISSUES

by

Marjorie J. Long, Esq. & Elise M. Burton, Esq.

BRADFORD PUBLISHING COMPANY
Denver, Colorado

DISCLAIMER

This book is intended to provide general information with regard to the subject matter covered. It is not meant to provide legal opinions or to offer advice, nor to serve as a substitute for advice by licensed, legal or other professionals. This book is sold with the understanding that Bradford Publishing Company and the authors, by virtue of its publication, are not engaged in rendering legal or other professional services to the reader.

Bradford Publishing Company and the authors do not warrant that the information contained in this book is complete or accurate, and do not assume and hereby disclaim any liability to any person for any loss or damage caused by errors, inaccuracies or omissions, or usage of this book.

Laws, and interpretations of those laws, change frequently, and the subject matter of this book can have important legal consequences that may vary from one individual to the next. It is therefore the responsibility of the reader to know whether, and to what extent, this information is applicable to his or her situation, and if necessary, to consult legal, tax, or other counsel.

Library of Congress Cataloging-in-Publication Data

Long, Marjorie J.
Colorado nonprofit management : understanding the legal issues / by Marjorie J. Long & Elise M. Burton.
p. cm.
Includes bibliographical references and index.
ISBN 1-883726-96-4
1. Nonprofit organizations--Law and legislation--Colorado. 2. Nonprofit organizations--Management. I. Burton, Elise M. II. Title.

KFC2011.L66 2004
346.788'064'068--dc22

2004008040

Colorado Nonprofit Management: Understanding the Legal Issues
ISBN: 1-883726-96-4
Cover design by Brent Beltrone

Published 2004 by Bradford Publishing Company
1743 Wazee Street, Denver, Colorado 80202
www.bradfordpublishing.com

DEDICATION

To those who have chosen to work in this mission-driven sector—whatever drives you. The world is better for the time, effort, and inspiration you bring with you to life and to work every day.

CONTENTS

FOREWORD

As the nonprofit sector has gained an increasing share of the United States' Gross Domestic Product, the laws regulating nonprofits have likewise increased. Today, nonprofits are governed by many local ordinances, state and federal statutes, administrative agency regulations, and a growing number of court decisions. Understanding the sources of law and the organization's responsibilities under the law helps to minimize a nonprofit's risk of fines, penalties, excise taxes, loss of tax-exempt status, and substantial litigation costs. These losses can seriously jeopardize the nonprofit's assets and its ability to continue delivering its mission. Nevertheless, legal advice is costly and may likewise deplete precious assets as well. Unfortunately, ignorance of the law is not a defense. This book was developed to help nonprofit organizations manage and minimize these risks and better understand when legal counsel is needed.

It was also developed to introduce executive directors and board members of nonprofit organizations, primarily those with 501(c)(3) status, to some of the more common legal issues nonprofits may face in their operation and delivery of services. It is not an exhaustive legal reference, but a compilation of basic information presented in a brief manner, designed to inform, not advise. This allows the user to identify many issues quickly and helps the user determine whether legal advice or further research may be necessary. It is essential, however, that the user understands the limitations of legal information. Legal information is NOT the same as legal advice. This publication does not give legal advice, nor is it intended as a substitute for legal advice. It provides only general information, which may not be applicable to a particular situation. Unless otherwise specified, the information given pertains to 501(c)(3) nonprofit organizations.

Nothing in this publication constitutes legal advice. All users are advised to consult with an attorney for questions about specific fact situations.

PREFACE

This work evolved out of the authors' personal needs as attorneys who, individually, after practicing law for a number of years, returned to school to obtain Masters degrees in Nonprofit Management. Independently, the authors realized that despite years of experience in the private practice of law and as legal advisors and advocates in the nonprofit sector, they were frustrated by the number of legal issues faced by nonprofit managers on a daily basis. More disconcerting was the overall lack of awareness of legal issues pertaining to and affecting the nonprofit sector by key personnel of these organizations, including executive directors and board members.

To address some of the confusion regarding legal issues in the nonprofit sector, and in completion of the requirements for her Masters degree from Regis University, Elise Burton redesigned the elective course "Legal and Government Issues for Nonprofits" in 1998, and began teaching the course both online and in the classroom at Regis. Marjorie "Peg" Long registered to take a classroom-based version of this class taught by Elise in the year 2000.

Peg noted that while there were existing resources for nonprofit managers who wished to acquire in-depth knowledge about the legal aspects of a specific subject, there was no reference tool for basic information about the myriad laws and regulations that apply to Colorado nonprofits. Thus the idea for this book was born. With Elise as her faculty advisor, in 2001, Peg created the outline on which this book is based and submitted three scaled down chapters of this book in fulfillment of her graduation requirements.

By sharing research and writing since that time, the authors have created what they hope will become a valuable tool for managers of third sector organizations in Colorado.

It is important to note that this book was not created as a self-help book nor as a substitute for legal advice. It is intended solely as a reference tool designed to create an awareness of legal issues where none might have existed previously. Every legal situation involves unique facts and circumstances that must be considered before determining the appropriate legal advice or strategy. As a result, the reader is strongly cautioned to seek legal advice regarding specific situations facing his or her organization, its members, employees or volunteers.

The information provided is, of necessity, general and may or may not apply to the facts of a given situation. Nevertheless, the authors are hopeful that this book may become a useful tool to alert nonprofit managers and board members of potential legal risks and issues, and, consequently, to protect the resources necessary for promoting the missions and viability of Colorado nonprofit organizations.

Peg Long & Elise Burton
May 2004

ABOUT THE AUTHORS

Marjorie "Peg" Long is an attorney and currently serves as the executive director of companion 501(c)(3) and 501(c)(4) Colorado nonprofit organizations. She is an affiliate faculty member with the Masters in Nonprofit Management program at Regis University where she earned her Masters in Nonprofit Management. Ms. Long also holds a B.A. in English from the University of Colorado at Boulder and a J.D. degree from the University of Colorado School of Law. She is the author of several booklets on disability rights and special education law as well as numerous legal articles. Ms. Long practiced law in the private sector for 6 years and in the nonprofit sector for 12 years before becoming an executive director. She has extensive experience in public policy and advocacy.

Elise Burton is also an attorney. She is a consultant with Higher Education Executive Associates in Castle Rock, Colorado, and is an affiliate faculty member with the Masters in Nonprofit Management program at Regis University. She has extensive experience in higher education and nonprofit legal issues with a focus on higher education policy, compliance and governance. She received her A.B. in Political Science from Barnard College; holds a Masters in Nonprofit Management from Regis University, which she obtained as Fellow of The Colorado Trust; and a J.D. from the University of Virginia School of Law.

ACKNOWLEDGEMENTS

We would both like to thank our supportive families and friends, the entire team at Bradford publishing, and the many members of the Colorado nonprofit sector who took the time to read and comment on various drafts of this book. Our special thanks go to Brad Shefrin, Esq. of Zupkus & Angell, P.C.; Marnie Walsh, Esq. of Hale Hackstaff Friesen, LLP; L. William Schmidt, Jr., Esq.; and Colleen O'Laughlin, Esq. for their substantive and editorial contributions to this text.

We also gratefully acknowledge the Regis University Department of Nonprofit Management, where we both learned a tremendous amount as students and where we are now both honored to teach.

Peg would especially like to thank Todd Lowther of the Arc in Jefferson County for his encouragement and mentorship.

Elise owes a special debt of thanks to The Colorado Trust for the financial support that allowed her to transition to work in the nonprofit sector, and to Thomas A. Emmet of Higher Education Executive Associates who has been an extraordinary mentor, teacher, and friend.

INTRODUCTION

An understanding of legal information as it applies to nonprofit corporations requires an introduction to the various sources of law that may be applicable to a given situation or entity. For many, this means a refresher on basic civics, beginning with the three branches of government. The **legislative branch** is responsible for enacting or passing laws and exercising taxing and spending powers. The **executive branch** is charged with implementing the laws passed by the legislative branch. This is done through the promulgation of agency rules and regulations, through attorney general opinions, and through budgetary decision making. The **judicial branch** is responsible for interpreting the laws, regulations, the state and U.S. constitutions, and constitutional amendments. Thus, each branch is responsible for generating a particular type of law. The chart at the end of this section shows each branch of government at the local, state and federal level, and describes the kind of law—statute, regulation, or case law—involved.

The laws passed by Congress and the Colorado General Assembly are called statutes. This body of law is called statutory law. Statutes are grouped by subject matter or titles, with further subgroups of articles. They are bound into a set of volumes. Federal laws are contained in the bound series called the United States Code (U.S.C.). The 13-volume bound set of Colorado Revised Statues (C.R.S.) is available at any Colorado law library or online by accessing the Colorado General Assembly Web page. Specific statutes may sometimes be obtained from the administrative agency itself. Administrative agencies, when authorized by Congress or the state legislature, promulgate or issue rules and regulations to implement statutory law. These are referred to as regulatory law. Federal regulations are found in the multi-volume, bound Code of Federal Regulations (C.F.R.) and are available online. State administrative agency regulations are found in the Colorado Code of Regulations (C.C.R.) and online through the agency's website. Both federal and state regulations may be found at a Colorado law library. Statutes and regulations may be changed or repealed by the legislature or agency on a regular basis. Accordingly, it is critical to ensure that the most current version of the applicable statutes or regulations is being consulted.

Administrative agencies may also have internal, quasi-judicial dispute resolution processes that are similar to trials in the judicial system. In many cases, a complaining party may be required to use or "exhaust" all administrative remedies or procedures first before filing a lawsuit in court. This means that one must proceed through all of the administrative dispute resolution steps before filing an action in a court of law. Rulings or decisions made by administrative agencies are frequently published for the public to read. They are available from the administrative agency and may be available online.

The various courts interpret statutes, constitutional issues, and bodies of law that have evolved through public policy such as contract or tort law. This body of law is called **common law** or **case law.** Trial courts hear evidence from the parties to a dispute, and a judge issues a ruling based upon the evidence and the applicable law. In cases heard by a jury, the jury decides the outcome of the case based on the evidence presented and the applicable law as given to it through jury instructions or other directives of the judge. Cases in the Colorado state courts that end at the trial court level, whether decided by a judge or a jury, are not usually published or distributed beyond the parties to the case. When a trial court's decision is appealed to a higher, appellate court by one of the parties, and the appellate court issues a written opinion, the case may be published or "reported." Whether to publish a case is discretionary in federal trial courts, and at the Colorado Court of Appeals and the United States Court of Appeals. Generally, the Colorado Supreme Court and U.S. Supreme Court publish all of their opinions. Appellate courts, whether at the state or federal level, do not hear evidence from the parties, but review the record of the lower court's proceedings and, in some cases, may permit oral argument on the issues to be presented by the parties' attorneys, or the party, if proceeding without an attorney.

Decisions of appellate courts are published in bound volumes, called "reporters." These are grouped by level of appellate court and geographic region, *e.g.*, Colorado Reporter, Pacific Reporter, U.S. Supreme Court Reporter, and are generally available in any law library. Some published decisions may also be available online through www.Findlaw.com or by inputting the name of the case through an Internet search engine. Appellate court opinions are only binding within the geographic jurisdiction of the court. For example, an opinion from the Colorado Court of Appeals or the Colorado Supreme Court must be followed by all state (but usually not federal) trial courts throughout Colorado; but it has no binding effect in Kansas. However, a case decided by the federal Tenth Circuit Court of Appeals applies in the six states under its jurisdiction—which are Colorado, Kansas, New Mexico, Oklahoma, Utah, and Wyoming—but not in New York or California. Rulings by the United States Supreme Court, on the other hand, must be followed in all 50 states.

SOURCES OF LAW BY BRANCH OF GOVERNMENT

LEGISLATIVE (Statutory law)	**EXECUTIVE (Administrative law)**	**JUDICIAL (Common law)**
FEDERAL: U.S. Congress has taxing and spending powers; passes federal laws, *e.g.*, Age Discrimination in Employment Act. Laws passed are recorded in the United States Code (U.S.C.) or United States Code Annotated (U.S.C.A.).	Administrative agencies are charged with implementing the laws passed by Congress by adopting rules and regulations, *e.g.*, Internal Revenue Service, Department of Labor; they may also conduct quasi-judicial administrative hearings, *e.g.*, the Equal Employment Opportunity Commission (EEOC), IRS. Regulations or rules are promulgated by the federal administrative agency and recorded in the Code of Federal Regulations (C.F.R.).	The courts interpret the laws and regulations; those having jurisdiction in Colorado include the following appellate courts: U.S. Supreme Court, 10th Circuit Court of Appeals; and the federal district court, a trial court. Court opinions are recorded in the U.S. Supreme Court Reporter (U.S.), Federal Supplement Reporter (F. Supp., F. Supp. 2d) (U.S. District court opinions), or in Federal Reporter (F., F.2d, or F.3d) (U.S. Court of Appeals opinions).

LEGISLATIVE (Statutory law)	**EXECUTIVE (Administrative law)**	**JUDICIAL (Common law)**
STATE: Colorado General Assembly passes state laws, *e.g.*, Colorado Revised Nonprofit Corporation Act. Laws are recorded in bound volumes called Colorado Revised Statutes (C.R.S.).	Administrative agencies are charged with implementing the laws passed by the General Assembly by promulgating rules and regulations, *e.g.*, Division of Civil Rights, Colorado Department of Labor; they may also conduct quasi-judicial administrative hearings, *e.g.*, Industrial Claims Commission. Attorney General's opinions provide guidance to the Governor and administrative agencies. Regulations are recorded in Colorado Code of Regulations (C.C.R.).	Courts interpret laws and regulations. They include appellate courts (Colorado Supreme Court, Colorado Court of Appeals), and trial courts (state district courts), small claims courts, and specialized courts, such as probate and juvenile. Published court opinions are recorded in the Colorado Reporter, or the Pacific Reporter (P., P.2d, or P.3d) as a state supreme court opinion (Colo.), or Court of Appeals opinion (Colo. App.).
LOCAL: City council, county commissioners, which pass laws in the form of city ordinances, local taxes, etc.	Mayor's or City Manager's office; administrative bodies, *e.g.*, water department, department of public safety, special districts.	Trial courts only: county courts, municipal courts, and small claims courts. These court opinions are not officially published.

Colorado Nonprofit Management: Understanding the Legal Issues references all sources of law, with emphasis on statutes and regulations. Case law is mentioned only when a court opinion has clarified an important issue not directly resolved through a simple reading of the applicable statute or regulation. The **Tip** section within each topic focuses on information that, if heeded, can assist the organization in further implementing good risk management. The authority for the tip may be a statutory requirement, regulation, or reported court opinion. In some cases, the tip may be based upon Generally Accepted Accounting Procedures (GAAP), an Internal Revenue Service Letter Ruling on the subject, or simply current information or "best practice" suggestions identified by the authors during their research and discussions with nonprofit managers.

CHAPTER 1: BOARD OF DIRECTORS

1.01

LEGAL SUBJECT: The Fiduciary Duties: Care, Loyalty, and Obedience

STATEMENT OF ISSUE: A board of directors has significant power, while an individual director has little. Nevertheless, the individual director is still individually, legally accountable for board actions in certain circumstances. In carrying out their functions, all directors are required to abide by these principles: the Duty of Care, the Duty of Loyalty, and the Duty of Obedience. Failure to perform in accordance with these duties may subject an individual director to removal from the board or to a lawsuit and potential individual liability. Therefore, it is essential that each director understands what a director should do, is expected to do, should not do, and may do as described below.

CONCERNS/RISKS/ EXPOSURE: The Duty of Care requires a director to be reasonably informed; to participate in decisions unless a conflict exists; to act independently and in good faith, with the care that an ordinarily prudent person would under the same circumstances. Such duties encompass regular attendance at board meetings (the Colorado Revised Nonprofit Corporation Act permits *members* to vote by proxy, but does not permit directors to vote by proxy unless the bylaws specifically so permit, C.R.S. § 7-128-205(4); *see also* C.R.S. § 7-128-202 regarding board actions without a meeting); careful review of all financial, corporate and other documents provided to the director; the exercise of independent judgment; the collection and review of information sufficient to make informed decisions, including awareness of applicable laws and regulations; and adherence to procedures, rules, bylaws, and articles of incorporation. A director should make certain that funds raised further the mission and that any restrictions on donations are consistent with the organization mission prior to their acceptance. The Duty of Loyalty requires directors to execute their responsibilities in the best interests of the nonprofit corporation, not in their personal best interests or the interests of another person or entity. The Duty of Obedience requires that board members ensure that the organization remains true to its mission and central purposes as described in the articles of incorporation and bylaws. Such duties encompass:

- The identification and disclosure of actual or potential conflicts of interest, as conflicts reflect on the integrity of the board as a whole, even though they may not be illegal.
- Full disclosure of any opportunities of which a director is aware, in which the director may participate, or from which the director may benefit, prior to any participation on the director's or organization's part.
- Treatment of all corporation business and confidential matters as confidential unless and until there has been public disclosure of the information through the designated spokesperson, or unless the information is a matter of public record, or is common knowledge.
- Periodic review of the organization's mission and central purposes, and comparison of these to the organization's programs and activities.

Board members must use the same reasonable care that *an ordinarily prudent person would exercise in a like position and under similar circumstances* when acting as a trustee of the nonprofit. Board members must apply the standard of "best interests of the organization" when making decisions affecting the organization and cannot put personal interests, family interests or business interests above the interests of the organization. *See* Section 2.09, Private Inurement, for a discussion of conflicts of interest. The assets of the organization should be protected in the same manner that an individual's assets would be protected by a trustee. Finally, board members have a duty to see that the organization remains true to its mission or purpose as described in the organization's articles of incorporation, bylaws, or other governing documents. Both the nonprofit and the board members as individuals may be sued by persons or entities claiming that the organization or its directors have breached one or more of these duties, or who claim some sort of injury or harm caused by dealings with the corporation or its board of directors. Board members who disagree with a particular board action should make sure that their positions on the action are clearly reflected in the board or committee minutes or other record of the action taken. This may allow the board member to minimize personal liability for board actions the board member voted against.

> ***TIP:*** These responsibilities derive from a century of litigation involving business corporations and have been deemed applicable to nonprofit corporation directors. A director exercising good faith judgment in the areas described above generally will be protected from liability to the nonprofit corporation or its members under the Business Judgment Rule. This rule provides directors of publicly traded companies immunity from liability if their actions were executed in good faith, using sound business judgment and with reasonable care. The rule will not protect a director who has breached these duties, *e.g.*, fraud, bad faith, or criminal activity. BLOCK, BARDIN AND RADIN, THE BUSINESS JUDGMENT RULE (3rd ed. 1989); KURTZ, BOARD LIABILITY (1988) 49-59. OLSEN AND HATCH, DIRECTOR AND OFFICER LIABILITY (1991), Section 11.02[1][b]; KNEPPER AND BAILEY, LIABILITY OF CORPORATE OFFICERS AND DIRECTORS (4th ed., 1988), Section 13.04.

RESOURCES: Guidebook for Directors of Nonprofit Corporations (1993), Chicago, IL; American Bar Association; to order, call (800) 285-2221.

J.C. Leifer & M.B. Glomb, The Legal Obligations of Nonprofit Boards: A Guidebook for Board Members (1999). National Center for Nonprofit Boards. Available from the Colorado Association of Nonprofit Organizations (CANPO).

Governance for Nonprofits: A Summary of Organizational Governance Principles and Resources for Directors of Nonprofit Organizations; http://www.ascs.org/governnfp/hints.shtml.

L. Runquist, *Responsibilities and Duties of a Director of a Nonprofit Organization* (1991), http://www.runquist.com/article_director.htm.

1.02

LEGAL SUBJECT: Risk Management Issues for Directors

STATEMENT OF ISSUE: A risk management program helps a nonprofit further its mission, programs, operations, and reputation and safeguard its financial assets.

CONCERNS/RISKS/ EXPOSURE: Nonprofit directors should make sure they are informed about the organization's risk management efforts. Effective risk management identifies potential threats, prevents or minimizes losses, protects against unauthorized uses of funds, assures legal compliance, and sets aside funds or purchases insurance sufficient to cover claims that may arise. Although risk management encompasses liability and indemnification, it is a much broader topic that extends to employment issues, the primary reasons nonprofits are sued, and use of the Internet, *e.g.*, copyright and trademark infringement, interstate solicitation of funds, and defamation. Nonprofits exist to benefit the welfare of individuals and communities, but they are not immune to risks, including lawsuits that may cost thousands of dollars to defend or settle. In order to protect the organization's assets, including its human resources, a nonprofit must develop a sound risk management plan to evaluate and identify the risks, prioritize risks, choose appropriate risk management tools such as Directors and Officers (D&O) insurance, and periodically evaluate risk management practices and strategies.

Upon assuming the position, a director should review organizational documents such as bylaws and articles of incorporation to become aware of the stated purpose and mission of the organization. All decisions and actions of the board should be made in accordance with these documents and in the best interests of the organization, even if the director's personal interests may not be served. A director should review the general liability coverage, professional liability coverage (for professionals who counsel or treat clients), if any, and the directors' and officers' liability insurance policy to verify adequate coverage to protect the organization's mission and the director's own personal liability. A director's homeowners' insurance policy may cover activities such as service on a board, or additional protection may be purchased under a homeowners' insurance umbrella policy for an additional premium. *See also* Section 1.04, Indemnification, and Chapter 5, Risk Management Issues, generally.

> ***TIP:*** In discharging duties, a director is entitled to rely on information, opinions, reports or statements, including financial statements, if prepared and presented by an officer or employee of the corporation who is reasonably believed to be reliable and competent in the matters presented; by legal counsel, a public accountant or other person within the scope of that person's professional or expert competence; religious authorities who are believed to be reliable and competent; or a committee of the board of which the director is not a member if the director reasonably believes the committee merits confidence. C.R.S. § 7-128-401(2). A useful practice is conducting a periodic, thorough legal audit to identify potential problem areas and allow for their correction before trouble arises. It is preferable to have such a review conducted by legal counsel, but an organization can go a long way to protect itself from potential risk through an internal review as well. Suggested areas for review include: Governance Documents and Required Filings, Volunteer Management Practices, Financial Management Practices, Employment and Personnel Policies, Insurance Coverage (Directors' and Officers' (D&O), professional and general liability), and Contractual Relationships. Such an audit is also a

> useful way to assure potential funders that the nonprofit is a well-run and responsible organization. STARTING AND MANAGING A NONPROFIT ORGANIZATION: A LEGAL GUIDE, *(see Resources, below)* pp. 268-279.

RESOURCES: Nonprofit Risk Management Center, 1001 Connecticut Avenue, NW, Washington, D.C. 20036; (202) 785-3891, fax: (202) 296-0349. http://www.nonprofitrisk.org/. E-mail: info@nonprofitrisk.org.

Nonprofit CARES (Computer Assisted Risk Evaluation System). A CD-ROM based tool that guides the user through six modules, each with a series of questions about the nonprofit's organization, practices, and policies. Upon completion, the program develops a risk management profile and generates a report containing recommendations for addressing any risk management issues detected. Available from the Nonprofit Risk Management Center (see above).

B. Hopkins, STARTING AND MANAGING A NONPROFIT ORGANIZATION: A LEGAL GUIDE (3rd ed.), John Wiley & Sons, New York, NY (2001).

1.03

LEGAL SUBJECT: The Lawyer on the Board

STATEMENT OF ISSUE: Ethical questions arise when a lawyer serves on the board as a director. Both the lawyer and the organization should understand the functions and limitations of such an arrangement.

CONCERNS/RISKS/ EXPOSURE: Many nonprofits seek to have a lawyer on the board for several reasons: (1) it may afford the board access to free legal advice; (2) it may assist the board and executive director in the identification of potential legal issues; (3) it allows the organization to review and keep control over legal fees paid to outside counsel; and (4) the organization may benefit from the lawyer's contacts in the legal community. But may a lawyer serve on the board of an organization that is also the lawyer's client? Judges, lawyers, legal scholars, and bar associations have pondered the propriety of this arrangement, questioning whether a lawyer can ethically wear both hats. The complexity of laws and application of them has increased dramatically, requiring most lawyers to specialize in a few areas. A lawyer on the board may have little actual knowledge of the legal subject raised at a board meeting or otherwise. Rule 1.1 of the Colorado Rules of Professional Conduct states:

> A lawyer shall provide competent representation to a client. Competent representation requires the legal knowledge, skill, thoroughness and preparation reasonably necessary for the representation.

It is important that both the lawyer-director and the organization fully understand the nature of the relationship. Nonprofits contemplating the service of a lawyer as a director should understand the lawyer's specific areas of expertise, as well as the limits of that expertise, and should document, in writing, the scope of the lawyer's responsibilities, if any, as counsel to the nonprofit. All lawyers on the board need to realize that they probably have an attorney-client relationship with the organization if they elect to fill the dual role. It is very difficult for a lawyer to refrain from giving legal advice when sitting on the board. The fact that the lawyer is not paid does not negate the existence of an attorney-client relationship. Areas that pose particular problems include:

- Confidentiality—a lawyer is required to maintain confidentiality of client information; this may become an issue if the organization seeks court protection of discussions involving the attorney, but the court cannot distinguish between business advice and legal advice.
- Conflicts of interest—a lawyer-director may be faced with a conflict if fees are paid for services, particularly in light of the private inurement and excess benefit rules (*see* Section 2.09, Private Inurement, and Section 2.10, Excess Benefits Transactions and Intermediate Sanctions); issues may arise that prevent the lawyer-director from zealously representing the client-organization or require the lawyer to be called as a witness, necessitating termination of the relationship.
- Relationships with the lawyer's firm—because the knowledge and actions of one lawyer are imputed to all of the lawyers in a firm, and ethical rules prevent lawyers within the same firm from representing clients in conflict with one another, the lawyer-director cannot file suit on behalf of the organization against another client of the firm or defend an action brought by one of the firm's clients against the nonprofit; other problems may arise if the organization seeks a large donation from one of the firm's clients.
- Conflicts between board and organization—the legal positions of the board of directors and the nonprofit corporation are not necessarily identical; in some situations the board or a subset of the board may

need to obtain legal counsel of its own as the organization's lawyer may be obligated to assert claims on the organization's behalf against the directors.

Lawyers on boards should always list the organization as a client for purposes of conflicts checks. To be fully protected, a lawyer should obtain malpractice insurance that covers board service, even though no specific claim has ever involved legal advice, so that the lawyer-director's actions do not fall between the organization's directors' and officers' policy and the firm's malpractice insurance. Most likely, the insurer excludes actions outside the scope of a typical director's responsibility, as legal advice is not a responsibility of board members. It is essential that issues regarding this dual role be acknowledged and understood so that neither the lawyer nor the organization will be put at risk. Both the lawyer and the organization should seriously consider the question of whether the benefits outweigh the potential risks.

TIP: Like doctors, lawyers typically specialize. Generally speaking, a banking lawyer knows as much about filing nonprofit tax forms as an allergist knows about cardiology. While it might seem to be a great opportunity, electing a lawyer to serve on a nonprofit board of directors with the thought that the lawyer (as a lawyer) might be an asset to a nonprofit organization is NOT always a good idea. When a board member who is an attorney acts in the capacity of attorney for the organization, whether paid or volunteer, the lawyer-board member's conduct is not covered under the organization's Directors' and Officers' liability insurance. Legal malpractice insurers may specifically exclude claims that arise when an attorney is acting in the capacity of an officer or director of an organization unless the individual is specifically named as covered by the policy. This is not to say that lawyers cannot or should not become valued nonprofit board members. However, both the attorney board member and the nonprofit board should understand and clearly establish that the attorney board member is not a legal adviser to, or advocate for, the nonprofit. Any real or potential conflicts of interest should be disclosed in writing, and the attorney board member should refrain from providing legal advice to the nonprofit. This is important from a liability perspective for both the nonprofit and the individual attorney board member and his/her firm. In addition, appropriate insurance for all parties should be obtained. Colorado Rules of Professional Conduct, Rule 1.1, Competence.

RESOURCES: Nonprofit Issues at: http://www.nonprofitissues.com.

GUIDEBOOK FOR DIRECTORS OF NONPROFIT CORPORATIONS (1993), Chicago, IL; American Bar Association. Order at (800) 285-2221.

Colorado Rules of Professional Conduct, found in Volume 12 of Colorado Revised Statutes.

1.04

LEGAL SUBJECT: Indemnification

STATEMENT OF ISSUE: A nonprofit organization may indemnify its directors in the event of a lawsuit in which the board members are individually named as defendants.

CONCERNS/RISKS/ EXPOSURE: Board members may face personal liability for actions taken in the performance of their duties as board members. Indemnification means that the organization promises to pay a director's legal costs, court-ordered judgments, settlements and attorney's fees for claims that result from the board member's service. This is usually stated in the organization's bylaws. Indemnification is permitted under state law, but it is the organization's bylaws that detail the particulars of indemnification coverage. Adequate indemnification is only as reliable as the organization's finances and assets, regardless of the scope of the indemnification language. To fully protect its directors, the organization should also purchase a directors' and officers' (D&O) insurance policy, which is an indemnification policy rather than a liability policy. Indemnification protects a board member from an individual judgment in a lawsuit. Liability insurance provides for defense of the organization and payment of a settlement or court award in the event of a lawsuit. Generally, D&O insurance does not cover fines and penalties imposed by law, libel and slander, personal profit, dishonesty, failure to obtain or maintain insurance, bodily injury and property damage claims, pollution claims and suits by one board member against another. Prior to committing to serve on a nonprofit board, a potential board member should examine a copy of the organization's bylaws and its directors' and officers' insurance policy to make certain that the governance document provides for indemnification and that there is adequate insurance coverage. Insurance is particularly important where the nonprofit's assets may not be adequate to cover potential liability. *Guidebook for Directors of Nonprofit Corporations. See also* Section 1.07, Directors' and Officers' Insurance, and Section 5.05, Directors' and Officers' Insurance.

> ***TIP:*** A nonprofit corporation may indemnify a director against liability in a legal proceeding if the director acted in good faith; the director reasonably believed that the conduct performed in an official capacity was in the nonprofit corporation's best interests; and the conduct was not opposed to the best interests of the nonprofit corporation; or, in the case of a criminal proceeding, that the director had no reasonable cause to believe that the conduct was unlawful. C.R.S. § 7-129-102(1).

RESOURCES: J.C. Leifer & M.B. Glomb, LEGAL OBLIGATIONS OF NONPROFIT BOARDS: A GUIDEBOOK FOR BOARD MEMBERS (1999), National Center for Nonprofit Boards, available from NCNB: (800) 883-6262.

GUIDEBOOK FOR DIRECTORS OF NONPROFIT CORPORATIONS (1993), Chicago, IL; American Bar Association. Order at (800) 285-2221.

Nonprofit Risk Management Center, 1001 Connecticut Avenue NW, Suite 410, Washington, D.C. 10036-5504; (202) 785-3891; http://www.nonprofitrisk.org/.

1.05

LEGAL SUBJECT: Sarbanes-Oxley Act of 2002

STATEMENT OF ISSUE: This federal act, passed in 2002, contains governing and auditing principles designed to hold for-profit board members to higher standards of ethics in the performance of their duties. It amends several existing federal statutes, including the Securities Exchange Act of 1934 and the Responsibility in Federal Contracts Act. In at least one state (New York), the attorney general's office has called for legislation extending the act's principles to the financial accountability of nonprofits and their boards.

CONCERNS/RISKS/ EXPOSURE: The Sarbanes-Oxley Act was targeted at publicly-traded corporations primarily to prevent a repeat of the Enron debacle. It is not yet determined whether Sarbanes-Oxley will apply to nonprofits, or whether the Colorado legislature will enact similar laws for nonprofits. Some believe that nonprofits and their boards are obligated to make their operations as transparent as possible to their donors, potential donors, recipients of services, and the public sector when public sector funds support nonprofit services. Chief executive officers of the organization would be required to certify financial reports and the adequacy of internal controls and demonstrate the independence of audit committees that certify financial statements. There are at least three Sarbanes-Oxley Act provisions with which tax-exempt organizations should do their best to comply.

(1) The act contains a new federal prohibition on document manipulation and destruction, or what is called spoliation. All nonprofit organizations, including

charities, that provide information to the federal government, should develop a comprehensive document management, retention and destruction policy, training for staff on the policy, and records to show that the policy is enforced. If interpreted broadly in conjunction with other federal statutes, the Sarbanes-Oxley Act may apply to virtually any federal financial reporting obligations, even if reports are not actually made. Destruction of documents that are later required to be produced by subpoena or otherwise, even if unintentional, may expose a nonprofit to spoliation charges and penalties.

(2) There is a new "whistleblower" protection provision that prohibits any person from retaliating against anyone who provides information to federal authorities concerning a possible violation of several federal laws, even if the whistleblower is ultimately shown to have been mistaken. Nonprofits should review their personnel and supervisory policies to ensure compliance with the new rules. Penalties for violation of this provision are criminal and may result in jail sentences up to ten years and a commensurate fine.

(3) Charities that have federal contracts subject to government auditing standards should be aware that the Government Accounting Office (GAO) promulgated new "independence" standards modeled after Sarbanes-Oxley, which may change their auditing and financial reporting behavior.

TIP: Whether Sarbanes-Oxley is ultimately determined to apply fully to nonprofits or not, it is important for all nonprofits to examine the principles espoused in the act and incorporate them to the greatest extent possible. To demonstrate their attention to financial matters, nonprofits with the resources could insist that the audit committee of the board hire the independent auditors and review the results of the audit, could require that the president of the board sign the management letter prepared by the auditors, and could use an accounting firm to assist in the preparation of year-end closing activities and to prepare their records for the audit. Sarbanes-Oxley Act of 2002.

RESOURCES: The text of the Sarbanes-Oxley Act of 2002 (Pub. L. 107-204) may be viewed or downloaded in Adobe Acrobat (PDF) format from the Government Printing Office website, http://www.gpoaccess.gov/plaws/search.html, by searching "Sarbanes-Oxley" under the 107th Congress.

Braun, D., "The Sarbanes-Oxley Act of 2002"; http://www.michbar.org/business/pdfs/braun.pdf.

New York Attorney General Seeking to Apply Sarbanes-Oxley Act, The NonProfit Times, March 1, 2003; http://www.nptimes.com/Mar03/npt2.html.

Sarbanes-Oxley Changes the Rules on Document Retention from Bowne & Co., Inc.; http://www.bowne.com/newsletters/newsletter.asp?storyID=631.

Prohibition on Contracting with Companies Without Financial Reports/Certifications; http://www.theorator.com/bills108/hr746.html.

1.06

LEGAL SUBJECT: Tax Liability Issues

STATEMENT OF ISSUE: Nonprofits may benefit from a number of favorable tax exemptions depending on the type of nonprofit and the activity involved. However, violations of the Internal Revenue Code may jeopardize the organization's tax-exempt status and may cause individual board members to incur taxes and penalties.

CONCERNS/RISKS/ EXPOSURE: The Internal Revenue Service recognizes more than 20 types of 501(c) tax-exempt nonprofit organizations. See Appendix 1. They do not automatically qualify for exemption from federal income tax just because they are nonprofits. A board member should have a general understanding of tax status and requirements and fully understand that exemption from federal income taxes does not necessarily mean that donors may deduct gifts to the nonprofit. Such gifts are only deductible to the donor if the organization is a recognized 501(c)(3) nonprofit. While the other types of 501(c) nonprofits may seek recognition of their tax-exempt status from the IRS, most 501(c)(3) nonprofits *must* obtain recognition of tax-exempt status. They continue to hold that status only as long as such recognition is in effect. In order to maintain 501(c)(3) status, an organization must comply with specific Internal Revenue Code restrictions. These include limitations on lobbying and political activity, on unrelated business income, on private benefit and private inurement, and on self-dealing. These terms, requirements and penalties for violation are more fully explained in Chapter 2, Tax and

Administrative Requirements, and Chapter 10, Lobbying, Political Activity and Advocacy.

> ***TIP:*** The articles of incorporation and any amendments thereto must reflect the restrictions on the 501(c)(3) organization's purposes, activities, use and disposition of assets. Board members should bear this in mind when considering amendments to the articles of incorporation and in the fulfillment of their duties as board members. IRS Publication 557, *Tax Exempt Status for Your Organization;* Guidebook for Directors of Nonprofit Corporations; C.R.S. § 7-121-401(2).

RESOURCES: Internal Revenue Service Publication 557, available at http://www.irs.gov/pub/irs-pdf/p557.pdf.

GUIDEBOOK FOR DIRECTORS OF NONPROFIT CORPORATIONS (1993), Chicago, IL; American Bar Association. Order at (800) 285-2221.

1.07

LEGAL SUBJECT: Directors' and Officers' Insurance

STATEMENT OF ISSUE: Directors and officers of nonprofit corporations may be personally liable for intentional actions taken, which someone else believes are wrong. This exposure may be a disincentive to serve in a volunteer capacity.

CONCERNS/RISKS/ EXPOSURE: Board members are exposed to two types of risk: (1) liability to third parties for injury or property damage arising from acts or omissions in performance of their duties on behalf of the organization; and (2) liability to the organization itself for failure to fulfill the required fiduciary duties. Directors' and officers' (D&O) insurance coverage is essential to protect board members from foreseeable hazards. Generally, D&O insurance covers "wrongful acts" and claims, *e.g.*, alleged acts, errors and omissions, misleading statements, neglect, and breach of duty, but may contain significant exclusions from coverage. Most often, these wrongful acts involve employment-related claims. The policy may be an "occurrence" policy, which means that any claim filed *during the time the policy is in effect* will be covered. Or it may be a "claims-made" policy, which requires that the incident giving rise to the claim *occurred during the policy coverage period.* Although there is no distinct advantage or disadvantage to either type of policy, directors should know which type of coverage is provided prior to its activation. It is important to note that D&O insurance does *not* cover: fines and penalties imposed by law; libel and slander; dishonesty; failure to maintain or procure insurance;

bodily injury and property damage claims; pollution claims; and suits by one board member against another. The need for D&O insurance is even greater for larger organizations and wealthier board members. Some policies may be expanded to include other volunteers and employees in addition to board members. Because D&O coverage can be fairly expensive, small organizations may wish to inquire about limited coverage or larger deductibles. A "Duty to Defend" policy may be added to define the insurer's obligation to pay for defense costs, *e.g.*, attorney fees and court costs, as they are incurred rather than reimbursing costs after resolution. Some policies allow the organization to choose counsel and direct the defense; others require the insured to waive the right to choose counsel and/or control the defense. It is always wise to have a proposed policy reviewed by an insurance professional other than the one selling the policy.

> ***TIP:*** In its articles of incorporation, a nonprofit organization may restrict or eliminate the personal liability, for monetary damages, of a director towards the nonprofit corporation or its members, except when liability is based upon breach of fiduciary duties. C.R.S. § 7-128-402(1). Directors should ask to review the extent of such coverage prior to joining a nonprofit board.

RESOURCES: *Some Legal Considerations for Board Members, Management Assistance Program for Nonprofits;* http://www.mapnp.org/library/legal/lgl_thot.htm.

Directors Often Fear Risks of Personal Liability, Don Kramer's Nonprofit Issues Ready Reference #30; http://www.nonprofitissues.com/public/features/ready/2000janrr.html.

C. McNamara, *Insurance Against Liability, Management Assistance Program for Nonprofits;* http://www.mapnp.org/library/legal/lia_inrs.htm.

What are the Essential Components of Nonprofit D&O Policy?, Nonprofit Risk Management Center; http://www.allianceonline.org/FAQ/risk_management/what_are_essential_components.faq.

CHAPTER 2: TAX & ADMINISTRATIVE REQUIREMENTS

2.01

LEGAL SUBJECT: Articles of Incorporation

STATEMENT OF ISSUE: Articles of incorporation are essential for obtaining nonprofit corporate status and should be carefully drafted.

CONCERNS/RISKS/ EXPOSURE: Qualifications for nonprofit corporation status are determined by state law. Ordinarily, a nonprofit organization must file its articles of incorporation with the secretary of state along with a filing fee in order to operate as a corporate entity within the state. Changes in existing articles of incorporation, *e.g.*, name, address, or registered agent, are more difficult to make than bylaws changes. Any changes in articles must be filed with the secretary of state and must similarly be accompanied by a filing fee. For this reason, it is advisable to include in the articles of incorporation only the minimum information required by law.

Organizations that filed their articles of incorporation in Colorado prior to July 1, 1998, should review their articles of incorporation to ensure compliance with the Colorado Revised Nonprofit Corporation Act (CRNCA) which became effective July 1, 1998. C.R.S. § 7-122-102 lists the elements that must be included in a Colorado nonprofit organization's articles of incorporation. Additional elements are required by federal legislation if tax-exempt status is desired. A number of provisions of the CRNCA are operative "unless otherwise provided in the articles of incorporation." The creators of an organization should determine whether they want these or other provisions to apply. *See, e.g.*, C.R.S. §§ 7-129-103, 105, and 107. In order to ensure that the articles of incorporation contain all of the elements that will enable the organization to accomplish its objectives and to minimize the number of amendments to the articles, it is advisable to consult with legal counsel before filing articles of incorporation or amendments to articles with the secretary of state. *See also* Section 2.02, Bylaws.

> ***TIP:*** A § 501(c)(3) organization must be "organized" exclusively for one or more exempt purposes. This is accomplished only if the articles of incorporation: (i) limit the purposes of the organization to one or more exempt purposes; (ii) do not empower the organization to engage in activities that are not in furtherance of these exempt purposes; and (iii) dedicate the organization's assets to a § 501(c)(3) purpose on dissolution. Treas. Reg. § 1.501(c)(3)-1(b)(1)(i) and § 1.501(c)(3)-1(b)(4).

RESOURCES: Colorado Secretary of State, 1560 Broadway, Suite 200, Denver, CO 80203; (303) 894-2251; http://www.sos.state.co.us/ for forms and information.

Colorado Association of Nonprofits (CANPO), (303) 832-5710; (800) 333-6554; http://www.canpo.org/.

The Colorado Revised Nonprofit Corporation Act, with Commentary by the Revision Committee, published by Continuing Legal Education in Colorado, Inc., 1900 Grant St., Suite 300, Denver, CO 80203-4301, (303) 860-0608; (888) 860-2531; http://www.cobar.org/cle/.

Colorado Revised Nonprofit Corporation Act, C.R.S. §§ 7-121-101 through 7-137-301.

Publication 557, "Tax-Exempt Status for Your Organizations," Internal Revenue Service; http://www.irs.gov/pub/irs-pdf/p557.pdf.

2.02

LEGAL SUBJECT: Bylaws

STATEMENT OF ISSUE: Bylaws, like articles of incorporation, must comply with the laws of the state of incorporation. Bylaws may contain specific provisions that permit a nonprofit to operate in ways that differ from default provisions in the statutes, depending on the nonprofit's unique needs or operations.

CONCERNS/RISKS/ EXPOSURE: Bylaws are the organization's operating rules and cover such topics as the membership; meetings of members and directors; titles and duties of directors; election, qualifications and terms of directors; titles and duties of officers; procedures for removing directors or filling a vacancy; duties of committees; procedures for amending the bylaws; and indemnification of directors and officers. In Colorado, if the organization's bylaws are silent with respect to a specific topic or action, the Colorado Revised Nonprofit Corporation Act (CRNCA) will generally apply, so it is important to know and understand the act. A number of provisions of the CRNCA are operative "unless otherwise provided in the Bylaws." The creators of an organization should determine whether they want these or other provisions to be operative. *See, e.g.*, C.R.S. §§ 7-128-104, 7-128-105, and 7-134-102. Bylaws do not have to be filed with the secretary of state, but must be filed with the IRS if the organization seeks § 501(c)(3) status. Many start-up nonprofits draft their own bylaws without the benefit of legal counsel or legal review and end up in trouble. Bylaws must be consistent with the articles of incorporation. They are usually not easily changed, so great care should be taken in their drafting and any subsequent amendment. It is advisable to obtain a review of the bylaws by competent legal counsel prior to adoption or amendment of the bylaws.

> ***TIP:*** Most financial institutions will require a nonprofit organization's taxpayer identification number before establishing an account in the name of the organization. A nonprofit organization may now obtain a taxpayer identification number by filing Form SS-4, Application for Employer Identification Number, online at: https://sa1.www4.irs.gov/sa_vign/newFormSS4.do. (**Note:** the online application form will not accept any form of punctuation.)

RESOURCES: *The Colorado Revised Nonprofit Corporation Act, with Commentary by the Revision Committee,* published by Continuing Legal Education in Colorado, Inc., 1900 Grant St., Suite 300, Denver, CO 80203-4301, (303) 860-0608; (888) 860-2531; http://www.cobar.org/cle/.

Colorado Revised Nonprofit Corporation Act, C.R.S. §§ 7-121-101 through 7-137-301.

The Center for Community Change has a template for bylaws; http://www.communitychange.org.

Colorado Association of Nonprofit Organizations (CANPO), (303) 832-5710; (800) 333-6554; http://www.canpo.org/.

Consult an attorney who represents tax-exempt organizations or the attorney retained by the nonprofit organization.

2.03

LEGAL SUBJECT: Unincorporated Nonprofit Associations

STATEMENT OF ISSUE: Some smaller nonprofit organizations that do not generate much revenue or do not have employees may choose to operate outside of a corporate structure as an unincorporated nonprofit association.

CONCERNS/RISKS/ EXPOSURE: Before a small nonprofit chooses to operate as an unincorporated entity, it should understand the differences between the two formats. In Colorado, an unincorporated nonprofit association requires at least two members who have a common interest, much like a business partnership. Unincorporated nonprofits are regulated by Colorado's Uniform Unincorporated Nonprofit Association Act (CUUNAA), which does not require the formalities of creation and operation that the Colorado Revised Nonprofit Corporation Act does. The organization is typically formed by adopting a constitution rather than filing articles of incorporation. The constitution serves essentially the same function as the nonprofit corporation's bylaws. The CUUNAA is not confined to nonprofits with tax-exempt status under § 501(c)(3), (4), or (6), but covers unincorporated philanthropic, educational, scientific, and literary clubs, unions, trade associations, political organizations, cooperatives, churches, hospitals, condominium associations, neighborhood associations and all other unincorporated nonprofit associations. The CUUNAA confers the status of legal entity and describes an organization's authority to acquire, hold and transfer property, especially real property; the authority to sue and be sued as an entity; and the contract and tort liability of officers and members of the association.

> ***TIP:*** Unlike an incorporated nonprofit organization, the unincorporated nonprofit association form does not shield individuals against certain forms of liability. A group that wishes to avoid prohibitions on certain corporate activities might use the structure of the unincorporated nonprofit association to accomplish its purposes.

RESOURCES: Uniform Unincorporated Nonprofit Association Act, C.R.S. §§ 7-30-101 through 7-30-119.

Colorado Association of Nonprofits (CANPO), (303) 832-5710; (800) 333-6554; http://www.canpo.org/.

For choice of legal entity, it is recommended that the nonprofit organization consult with an attorney who specializes in tax exempt organizations.

2.04

LEGAL SUBJECT: § 501(c)(3) Public Charity or Private Foundation?

STATEMENT OF ISSUE: In making choice of entity decisions, a charitable nonprofit organization should contemplate not only corporate status but also status as either a public charity or a private foundation.

CONCERNS/RISKS/ EXPOSURE: The IRS assigns certain privileges and responsibilities to an organization that qualifies for exemption under § 501(c)(3) according to whether it is a public charity or private foundation. A private foundation is a charitable organization that receives the majority of its funding from a small number of contributors, as opposed to broad public support. A public charity is a charitable organization that is supported by the public. Computation of sources of support is made on IRS Form 990, Return of Organization Exempt from Income Tax, and the IRS averages these amounts over a four-year period. The IRS will take into consideration that new organizations often rely on a single source for a large percentage of start-up funds but will expect diversification of funding sources thereafter.

Private foundation status means substantial burdens and disadvantages. Excise taxes are imposed on the net investment income of a private foundation. The tax must be reported on IRS Form 990-PF, Return of Private Foundation, and must be paid annually at the time for filing the return. Other receipts of a private foundation will be taxable to the foundation, and contributions will not be deductible to the donor, unless the foundation's governing document contains the following: 1) restrictions on self-dealing between a private foundation and its substantial contributors and other disqualified persons; 2) requirements that the foundation annually make a qualifying distribution of its minimum investment return (generally 5 percent of the fair market value of all non-charitable assets of the foundation) for charitable purposes; 3) limits on foundation holdings in private business; 4) provisions that investments held may not jeopardize the carrying out of the exempt purposes; and 5) provisions to assure that expenditures further exempt purposes. Violations of these provisions give rise to taxes and penalties against the corporate entity and, in some situations, against its managers, contributors and related persons.

A § 501(c)(3) organization will be considered a public charity only if it (1) falls within one of the categories excluded from the definition of private foundation (relating to public support) and (2) gives timely notice to the IRS that it is not a private foundation. To avoid treatment as a private foundation, the burden is on the organization to "prove" that it meets a public support test under Internal Revenue Code § 509: (1) a substantial portion of support comes from government units or from direct or indirect contributions by the general public or a combination of both these sources, or (2) at least one-third of its support comes from governmental units, direct or indirect contributions by the general public, other public charities, and receipts that are related to the organization's exempt functions, and no more than one-third of its support comes from investments and unrelated business income. *See* Section 2.11, Unrelated Business Income Tax (UBIT).

> ***TIP:*** A charitable nonprofit corporation may be subject to income tax on all of its receipts including gifts, grants, and membership fees if it fails the public support tests and fails to include certain restrictions, limits, and requirements in its articles of incorporation. Of particular concern to both charities and the foundations that fund them is the concept of "tipping." This occurs when a grant to a charity is so large that the charity might not meet the public support test and is in danger of "tipping" into status as a private foundation. (*See* Foundation News and Commentary; Legal Brief: Tipping, http://www.foundationnews.org/CME/article.cfm?ID=193.)

RESOURCES: Colorado Association of Nonprofit Organizations (CANPO), (303) 832-5710 (800) 333-6554; http://www.canpo.org/, which has numerous publications and may offer technical assistance.

P. Nagel, *Starting a Nonprofit Corporation: Incorporation and Tax Exemption* (1996), published by Metro Volunteers, 225 E. 16th Ave., Suite 200, Denver, CO 80203, (303) 894-0103.

IRS Publication 578, "Tax Information for Private Foundations and Foundations Managers," Internal Revenue Service; http://www.irs.gov/pub/irs-pdf/p578.pdf, also available by calling (800) 829-3676.

Publication 557, "Tax-Exempt Status for Your Organization," Internal Revenue Service; http://www.irs.gov/pub/irs-pdf/p557.pdf.

"Private Foundations," Internal Revenue Service; http://www.irs.gov/charities/charitable/article/0,,id=96114,00.html.

R. Shoemaker and B. Brockner, "Public Charity Classification and Private Foundations Issues: Recent Emerging Significant Developments," Internal Revenue Service; http://www.irs.gov/pub/irs-tege/topicp00.pdf.

2.05

LEGAL SUBJECT: § 501(c)(3) Federal Exemption Application Process

STATEMENT OF ISSUE: All § 501(c)(3) organizations are exempt from federal income tax; however, not all nonprofits qualify for § 501(c)(3) status.

CONCERNS/RISKS/ EXPOSURE: Organization at a state level as a nonprofit corporation or association does not automatically confer federal tax-exempt status on the organization. The procedure for obtaining federal tax exemption is set forth at the federal level. In fact, the IRS may recognize an organization as exempt from tax regardless of whether the state requirements for nonprofit corporations are met. Federal tax laws and treasury regulations determine whether the organization meets the criteria to operate as a charity or tax-exempt organization.

Although the application process for tax-exempt status is beyond the scope of this publication, the process is initiated with the filing of IRS Form 1023, Application for Recognition of Exemption, with the IRS. In reviewing a Form 1023 for approval, the IRS analyzes a number of considerations or "tests." These tests include, but are not limited to, (1) the "organizational test" that requires that an entity be organized exclusively for one or more acceptable exempt purposes, (2) an "operational test" that requires the entity to operate primarily toward the accomplishment of one or more of the exempt activities for which it was organized, and (3) the "primary purpose test" that requires the entity to operate primarily for its exempt purpose in order to remain exempt. (Hopkins, Bruce R., The Law of Tax Exempt Organizations, Eighth Ed., John

Wiley & Sons, Inc., 2003 pp. 69-91.) The organizational test can be satisfied most easily by ensuring that the articles of incorporation (or the unincorporated organization's creating and governing documents) comply with the applicable federal regulations. The operational and primary purpose tests will only be satisfied if the actual activities of the organization benefit the public.

Benefits of federal tax-exempt status include: exemption from corporate federal income taxes; ability to solicit tax-deductible donations; greater ease in applying for exemption from sales taxes from state and local jurisdictions; the potential for qualification to mail at nonprofit standard A rates; and the potential to own real property free of real property taxes. However, with the granting of § 501(c)(3) status come a host of burdens, including a number of specific reporting and disclosure requirements and limitations on lobbying activities. *See* Section 2.07, Form 990 and Disclosure Requirements.

> ***TIP:*** The form provided by the Colorado Secretary of State to incorporate as a Colorado nonprofit corporation does not contemplate all of the language required by the IRS for the granting of § 501(c)(3) status under the various tests it applies. Accordingly, obtaining technical assistance (preferably the advice of qualified legal counsel) from the start is essential. To do otherwise may require a nonprofit to amend its Articles of Incorporation or other creating document after obtaining recognition by the State of Colorado as a nonprofit organization in order to comply with federal requirements and obtain recognition as a § 501(c)(3) organization.

RESOURCES: Assistance with the application process for § 501(c)(3) status may be obtained from the Colorado Association of Nonprofit Organizations (CANPO), (303) 832-5710; (800) 333-6554, http://www.canpo.org/, which has several publications and offers technical assistance.

P. Nagel, *Starting a Nonprofit Corporation: Incorporation and Tax Exemption* (1996), published by Metro Volunteers!, 225 E. 16th Ave., Suite 200, Denver, CO 80203, (303) 894-0103.

Treas. Reg. § 1.501(c)(3)-1.

Rev. Rul. 72-369, 1972-2 C.B. 245.

The entire IRS Form 1023 package may be obtained from the IRS by calling (800) 829-1040 or by writing: Internal Revenue Service, Employee Plans and Exempt Organizations, P.O. Box 192, Covington, KY 41012-0192, or online from http://www.irs.gov/pub/irs-pdf/k1023.pdf.

Publication 557, "Tax-Exempt Status for Your Organization," Internal Revenue Service; http://www.irs.gov/pub/irs-pdf/p557.pdf.

Publication 4220, "Applying for 501(c)(3) Tax-Exempt Status," Internal Revenue Service; http://www.irs.gov/pub/irs-pdf/p4220.pdf.

Publication 4221, "Compliance Guide for 501(c)(3) Tax-Exempt Organizations," Internal Revenue Service; http://www.irs.gov/pub/irs-pdf/p4221.pdf.

2.06

LEGAL SUBJECT: Other Kinds of Tax-Exempt Organizations

STATEMENT OF ISSUE: Nonprofit organizations that have been granted § 501(c)(3) status are not the only organizations that are exempt from federal income tax.

CONCERNS/RISKS/ EXPOSURE: There are over 25 distinct classifications of tax-exempt organizations described in § 501(c) of the Internal Revenue Code. These include such diverse organizations as federal credit unions, § 501(c)(1); social clubs, § 501(c)(7); cemetery companies, § 501(c)(13); black lung benefit trusts, § 501(c)(21); and veterans organizations, § 501(c)(23). Classification in one category or another can make a significant difference in an organization's responsibilities and compliance concerns. With a few exceptions, only § 501(c)(3) "charitable" organizations are eligible to receive donations that are tax-deductible to the donor. A list of all types of organizations exempt from federal income tax under § 501(c) is provided in Appendix 1. Organizations seeking recognition of exemption from tax under § 501(c), other than § 501(c)(3), file applications using IRS Form 1024, Application for Recognition of Exemption Under Section 501(a).

A tax-exempt nonprofit need not be a corporation; it can also operate as an unincorporated association (*see* Section 2.03, Unincorporated Nonprofit Associations) or in the form of a charitable trust. A charitable trust does not provide the same level of protection from personal liability to its trustees and an unincorporated association cannot receive grants from most foundations. Consequently, the nonprofit corporation (and in some cases a nonprofit LLC) is the most commonly used form of entity. (Establishing a Nonprofit Organization; The Foundation Center, http://fdncenter.org/learn/classroom/establish/page01.html.)

> ***TIP:*** There are instances in which it may not be necessary to become a § 501(c)(3) organization, as in the case of social and recreational clubs pursuant to § 501(c)(7) that do not expect to benefit from the tax deductibility of donations. Also, a § 501(c)(3) can form a related § 501(c)(4) social welfare organization that is not subject to as many restrictions on lobbying and public advocacy. Solicitations for contributions or other payments by certain organizations exempt from tax under § 501(c) must include a conspicuous and easily recognizable statement that payments are not deductible as charitable contributions for federal income tax purposes.

RESOURCES: B.R. Hopkins, THE LAW OF TAX EXEMPT ORGANIZATIONS (8th ed. 2003), John Wiley & Sons, Inc.; http://www.wiley.com/WileyCDA/WileyTitle/productCd-0471268208.html.

Internal Revenue Service, "Charities & Nonprofits"; http://www.irs.gov/charities/index.html.

Publication 557, "Tax-Exempt Status for Your Organization," Internal Revenue Service; http://www.irs.gov/pub/irs-pdf/p557.pdf.

2.07

LEGAL SUBJECT: Form 990 and Disclosure Requirements

STATEMENT OF ISSUE: Subsequent to June 1999, tax-exempt organizations are required to file either Form 990, Return of Organization Exempt from Income Tax, or Form 990EZ, Short Form Return of Organization Exempt from Income Tax, on an annual basis. They must make these forms available to the public upon request. They must also comply with disclosure and substantiation rules with respect to contributors.

CONCERNS/RISKS/ EXPOSURE: Form 990, Return of Organization Exempt from Income Tax, is an annual information return required by the IRS if gross annual receipts of a tax-exempt organization exceed $25,000. An organization with annual gross receipts under $25,000 may elect to file an information return, but it is not mandatory. Form 990 reporting requirements include: (1) the five highest compensated employees paid over $50,000; (2) the total number of employees paid over $50,000; (3) the compensation paid for professional services over $50,000 and the total number of persons paid this amount of compensation; (4) a description of any legislative or political campaign activities (actual expenditures must be reported on another IRS form); (5) an explanation of any acts of self-dealing between the organization and its directors or officers; (6) information concerning certain legislative activities if the organization has elected to come under special lobbying rules; (7) information on direct or indirect transfers to and relationships with tax-exempt organizations other than charitable ones; (8) the identification of revenue sources (but not the names and addresses of private donors), allocation of expenses, accounting method used, and similar information. Form 990 is due on or before the fifteenth day of the fifth month following the close of the organization's fiscal year. Failure to timely file a Form 990 may give rise to a $20 per day penalty, up to a maximum of $10,000 for organizations with gross revenue below one million dollars. The per day penalty for organizations with gross revenue above one million dollars is $100, up to a maximum of $50,000.

Every nonprofit organization with gross revenue greater than $25,000 must make its Form 990 or 990-EZ (990-PF in the case of private foundations) available for public inspection without charge at its place of business during office hours and must provide a copy without charge for mailing costs, but may charge a reasonable reproduction fee, to any individual who requests a copy in person or in writing. The organization has 30 days to respond to requests in writing. What constitutes a reasonable fee has for a long time meant $1.00 for the first page and fifteen cents for each additional page. At the time of this writing, proposed treasury regulations would change the "reasonable charge" to conform to the twenty cent per page requirement under the IRS's Freedom of Information Act. Failure to comply with the disclosure and public inspection requirements may lead to penalties imposed on the organization.

While the form and schedules must be disclosed, certain information on the schedules, such as the names and addresses of contributors listed on Schedule B, need not be shared. Nonetheless, an organization required to disclose Form 990 ought to take the time to ensure that the information included in the form is accurate and consistent with the positions of the organization expressed to the press or the public. Board members need not list home addresses in Part V of the Form 990. If the organization makes its information return easily and readily available on the World Wide Web, this may satisfy the public inspection requirement. Guidestar, the National Database of Nonprofit Organizations, has registered almost 70,000 U.S. public charities.

Charities that are exempt from taxation under § 501(c)(3) must provide timely disclosure statements to contributors who make "quid pro quo" contributions of more than $75 and must provide contemporaneous written acknowledgments to contributors of at least $250. A quid pro quo contribution is a payment made up of a charitable contribution, or donative, element and a payment for goods or services provided to the contributor. Failure to provide disclosure statements may result in penalties of $10 per contribution, up to $5,000. If a contributor does not have substantiation of charitable contributions, the contributor will not be allowed to take a charitable contribution deduction.

> ***TIP:*** Although churches and nonprofits with gross revenues below $25,000 are not required to file a Form 990, many foundations and other grantors require one to three years of Form 990s as part of their grant application process. One concern grantors may have with small budget organizations is that a single grant may constitute such a significant portion of the nonprofit's revenue that it could jeopardize the organization's status as a § 501(c)(3) by making it look more like a foundation. (*See* also the Tip provided in Section 2.11, Unrelated Business Income Tax.)

RESOURCES: "IRS Form 990: An Illustrated Tutorial," GuideStar: The National Database of Nonprofit Organizations; http://www.guidestar.org/learn/tutorial/990_0intro.jsp.

National Center for Charitable Statistics; http://nccsdataweb.urban.org/NCCS/Public/.

J. Blazek, 990 HANDBOOK: A LINE-BY-LINE APPROACH (2001), John Wiley & Sons, (800) 225-5945; http://www.wiley.com/WileyCDA/WileyTitle/productCd-0471417815.html.

Internal Revenue Service; http://www.irs.gov/.

Colorado Association of Nonprofit Organizations (CANPO), (303) 832-5710; (800) 333-6554; http://www.canpo.org/.

Publication 557, "Tax-Exempt Status for Your Organization," Internal Revenue Service; http://www.irs.gov/pub/irs-pdf/p557.pdf.

"Instructions for Form 990 and Form 990-EZ, Return of Organization Exempt from Income Tax and Short Form Return of Organization Exempt from Income Tax," Internal Revenue Service; http://www.irs.gov/pub/irs-pdf/i990-ez.pdf.

2.08

LEGAL SUBJECT: Change in Mission or Other Material Change

STATEMENT OF ISSUE: A material change in the organization's mission, purpose or operational status (*e.g.*, unincorporated to incorporated) must be reported to the Internal Revenue Service.

CONCERNS/RISKS/ EXPOSURE: Some changes, if they substantially alter the organization's mission, purpose, or operational structure, may cause the IRS to modify or revoke the organization's tax-exempt status. For example, an organization that was formed to educate the community about health care issues lost its tax-exempt status when it conducted a fundraising campaign to send medical supplies overseas. Changes contemplated should be carefully reviewed for impact on the organization's tax-exempt status before being adopted. It is advisable to include language in the mission statement and organizational documents that allows broader charitable purposes, *e.g.*, "... and all other charitable purposes and activities related to the promotion of community health."

> ***TIP:*** If the change is not material—as when the wording, but not the intent, of a mission statement is changed—an organization can simply disclose the change by attaching the amended statement or organizational document to its Form 990, Return of Organization Exempt from Income Tax.

RESOURCES: An attorney who represents tax-exempt organizations or is very familiar with the Internal Revenue Code may advise on the likelihood that the proposed change is material and whether it would generate a review by the I.R.S.

Colorado Association of Nonprofit Organizations (CANPO), (303) 832-5710; (800) 333-6554; http://www.canpo.org/, has publications and may offer technical assistance.

2.09

LEGAL SUBJECT: Private Inurement

STATEMENT OF ISSUE: The existence of private inurement within a tax-exempt organization may result in IRS sanctions or revocation of the organization's tax-exempt status.

CONCERNS/RISKS/ EXPOSURE: The IRS grants tax-exempt status to a nonprofit organization only if "no part of ... [its] net earnings ... inures to the benefit of any private shareholder or individual." (*See* Internal Revenue Code of 1986, as amended, § 501(c) (3)). Private inurement occurs when there is a payment or diversion of a nonprofit organization's assets to an insider for less than fair market value. The individual with a private interest does not have to be a person with control or influence over the organization. It may be an employee who has a personal interest due to an employment relationship with the organization. A finding of private inurement can be the basis for the revocation of tax-exempt status as well as excise taxes. Also, private inurement may constitute imputed income to the recipient, resulting in unexpected employment tax liabilities.

Private inurement is not, in and of itself, sanctionable. Only when the compensation or value received is not reasonable or varies from fair market value is the transaction prohibited. While many private inurement concerns arise in the context of executive compensation, the concept is not limited to salary levels but also includes (1) the purchase, lease or sale of property or services to or from an insider, (2) lending or borrowing money to or from an insider, (3) the rendering of services, and (4) entering into joint ventures with insiders.

Executive compensation has become a particularly scrutinized area. Determining whether an executive's compensation package is "reasonable" depends on many factors. These may include the size and complexity of the organization and its operations, the experience and qualifications of the individual, and the compensation package as a whole, including all fringe benefits. The IRS has developed a three-part test for determining whether a compensation arrangement results in prohibited inurement to private interests:

- Is the compensation arrangement consistent with exempt purposes?
- Is the compensation arrangement the result of arm's length bargaining?
- Does the compensation arrangement result in reasonable compensation?

The IRS has ruled that there is no "de minimis" test, *i.e.*, even seemingly insubstantial economic benefit may be subject to scrutiny. *See also* Section 2.10, Excess Benefits Transactions and Intermediate Sanctions.

Some private benefits are deemed merely incidental to the exempt purpose of the organization and accordingly do not constitute private inurement. Such private benefit must be both quantitatively (insubstantial in the context of the exempt activity) and qualitatively (necessary to achieving the overall exempt activity) incidental to the exempt purpose of the organization. Accordingly a physician who establishes a nonprofit medical clinic can be employed by the clinic at a reasonable salary since the physician's salary is necessary to achieving the exempt purpose of running a clinic and the mere payment of a salary is insubstantial in the context of the activity of providing community medical services. GCM 39598 (January 23, 1987); *Truth Tabernacle, Inc. v. Commissioner of Internal Revenue,* T.C. Memorandum (1989-451). The private benefits conferred upon the patients of such a clinic are also incidental to the exempt purpose of the organization and do not amount to prohibited private inurement.

> ***TIP:*** There is a difference between private inurement and a "conflict of interest" that can be confusing. A conflict of interest exists when an individual has a direct or indirect financial interest in certain affairs of the organization (such

as an ownership or investment interest in an entity with which the organization has a transaction or arrangement; a compensation arrangement with an entity or individual with whom the organization has a transaction or arrangement; or a potential ownership or investment interest with an entity or individual with whom the organization is negotiating a transaction or arrangement). A person with a "financial interest" is generally defined as one who has a financial interest in the affairs listed above directly or indirectly through business investment or family, including spouses, siblings, spouses of siblings, ancestors, children, grandchildren and great-grandchildren and the spouses of children, grandchildren, and great-grandchildren. The existence of a conflict of interest is not necessarily illegal but should be disclosed to the Board of Directors. The Board should then make an official determination regarding the acceptability of conflict or the potential conflict (deliberating without the interested party present).

RESOURCES: The Internal Revenue Service; http://www.irs.gov/.

"Private Benefit and Inurement," Chapter 5, The Texas A&M University System Tax Manual; http://sago.tamu.edu/soba/TaxManual/Prvinur.html.

"Executive Compensation: Nonprofit Organizations Face Unique Problems," Kern, DeWenter & Viere Consulting; http://www.kdv.com/executive.html.

B.R. Hopkins, Starting and Managing a Nonprofit Organization: A Legal Guide (3rd ed. 2000), John Wiley & Sons, Inc.; http://www.wiley.com/WileyCDA/WileyTitle/productCd-047139727X.html.

2.10

LEGAL SUBJECT: Excess Benefits Transactions and Intermediate Sanctions

STATEMENT OF ISSUE: If a tax-exempt organization engages in an excess benefits transaction with a disqualified person, the disqualified person may be subject to an excise tax of up to 200 percent of the excess benefit, and a manager of the organization may be subject to an excise tax of up to $10,000.

CONCERNS/RISKS/ EXPOSURE: Following a stream of negative publicity that revealed exploitation of tax-exempt organizations by individuals for private gain, the IRS added IRC § 4958, permitting the assessment of intermediate sanctions in cases where public charities engage in excess benefit transactions. Intermediate sanctions are penalties that are between the most drastic—termination of an organization's tax-exempt status—and no penalty at all. An excess benefit transaction is any transaction in which a § 501(c)(3) or § 501(c)(4) organization provides an economic benefit, either directly or indirectly, to a disqualified person, and the value given exceeds the value received by the organization. Private foundations have similar sanctions in the form of a rule against "self-dealing." *See* I.R.C. § 4941. Until the adoption of the Intermediate Sanctions Regulations, the only previously authorized sanction the IRS had for public charities was revoking the exemption of the charity.

A disqualified person means any officer, director, trustee, highly compensated employee, manager, major donor, or anyone else in a position to exert substantial influence over the organization within five years prior to the transaction. It includes relatives and entities in which the disqualified person has a 35 percent or greater interest. Transactions that involve the assets, income or property of the tax-exempt organization such as excessive salary or severance payments, property transfers, and payment of luxury expenses or expenses for relatives of disqualified persons may qualify as excess benefits transactions. *See* I.R.C. §§ 4946 and 4947. The key is determining the value of the benefit. If the value exceeds the fair market value (FMV) of the benefit received by the organization or is not similar to benefits paid by comparable tax-exempt organizations, the transaction will be characterized as an excess benefit transaction, triggering excise taxes. For this reason, it is important to obtain a fair market evaluation and to disclose, explain, and document any discrepancy between FMV and the amount of the transaction.

The disqualified person may be charged a 25 percent excise tax on the excess portion of the benefit. If the excess benefit is not repaid or reversed before the IRS imposes the first tax, the disqualified person is charged an additional tax of 200 percent of the excess benefit. The managers, officers, directors, trustees, or others who "knowingly" approve the transaction and are in a position of power may each be subject to a ten percent tax on the excess benefit, up to a maximum of $10,000 for each transaction. If an excess benefit transaction is corrected prior to an audit, the IRS may waive the taxes. Mitigation may occur if (1) there is full advance disclosure of the facts of the transaction; (2) any insider with a conflict of interest removes himself or herself from the discussion and action; (3) there is documented consideration of the fair market value of the transaction and its comparability features; and (4) there is complete documentation of the facts and the underlying decision. An organization may also obtain a "reasoned opinion of legal counsel," *i.e.*, a memo in a particular format, drafted and signed by an attorney qualified to represent tax-exempt organizations.

> ***TIP:*** Compensation arrangements are presumed to be reasonable if: (i) they are approved in advance by an authorized body made up of individuals entirely without a conflict of interest; (ii) appropriate data as to comparability was obtained and relied upon; and (iii) the authorized body adequately documented the basis for its determination. Treas. Reg. § 53.4958-6.

RESOURCES: B. Zall, "How to Comply with 'Intermediate Sanctions' Regulations," http://www.nonprofits.org/npofaq/18/13.html.

L.M. Brauer and L.J. Henzke, "Intermediate Sanctions (I.R.C. 4958) Update," Internal Revenue Service; http://www.irs.gov/pub/irs-tege/eotopice03.pdf.

Publication 557, "Tax-Exempt Status for Your Organization," Internal Revenue Service; http://www.irs.gov/pub/irs-pdf/p557.pdf.

2.11

LEGAL SUBJECT: Unrelated Business Income Tax (UBIT)

STATEMENT OF ISSUE: Organizations that are exempt from federal income tax may be subject to taxes on earned income that: 1) comes from a trade or business; 2) is regularly carried on; and 3) is unrelated to its mission.

CONCERNS/RISKS/ EXPOSURE: Organizations that are exempt from federal income tax may earn unlimited income on business activities that are related to their mission without incurring income tax liability. However, they are subject to taxes on earned income from business activities that are regularly carried on and do not relate directly to the mission of the organization. Unrelated business income tax (UBIT) will apply if all of the following factors exist: 1) the activity is a "trade or business;" 2) the activity is "regularly carried on;" and 3) the activity is not "substantially related" to the organization's exempt purposes. A trade or business is defined as "any activity carried on for the production of income from the sale of goods or provision of services." Treas. Reg. § 1.513-1(b). The sale or distribution of goods with a nominal cost to the organization ($5.00) and nominal value ($25.00) (indexed for inflation since 1986) are excluded. When substantially all of the work has been done by volunteers, *e.g.*, a gift shop; the activity is carried on for the convenience of members, customers or employees, *e.g.*, a museum lunchroom; or substantially all of the merchandise is received as contributions, *e.g.*, a thrift store, the activity will not be considered unrelated business income. In order to be "regularly carried on," the activity must be frequent, continuous, or generally similar to commercial activities of nonexempt organizations.

Merely applying the proceeds of the activity to the organization does not make it mission-related. The activity itself must contribute in an important way to the charitable purpose for which the organization has been granted tax-exempt status. The seasonal sales of Girl Scout cookies have been determined not to be an activity generating UBIT. The year-round operation of a restaurant training and employing people with developmental disabilities has been deemed subject to UBIT. Membership dues are not subject to UBIT. The manner in which the business activity is operated also impacts its relatedness. Passive income, *e.g.*, investment income, royalties and certain types of rental income, are generally excluded from the category of unrelated business income. If the IRS determines that the charitable organization has too much unrelated business income, it may revoke the organization's tax exemption. Organizations that earn over $1000 in gross receipts as result of unrelated business activities must file a Form 990-T, Exempt Organization Business Income Tax Return.

TIP: In 2003 the Internal Revenue Service (IRS) shortened the automatic extension granted to exempt organizations that request additional time to file Form 990 returns, from six months to three. Organizations that need additional time must file a second request with a justification for an additional three months. As of this writing, Form 8868, Application for Extension of Time to File an Exempt Organization Return (the form used for requesting an extension for a Form 990-T filing), had not been revised to conform with this broader change. Pending clarification, organizations requesting an extension of their 990-T filing should confer with their accountant and/or obtain updates at http://www.irs.gov/charities/article/0,,id=113424,00.html.

RESOURCES: Don Kramer's Nonprofit Issues, Inc., P.O. Box 1002, Dresher, PA 19025, (212) 542-7547, (888) 674-7783; see the Ready Reference pages available for downloading, some for a small fee; http://www.nonprofitissues.com/public/indices/byfeature/ready.html.

B.R. Hopkins, STARTING AND MANAGING A NONPROFIT ORGANIZATION: A LEGAL GUIDE (3rd ed. 2000), John Wiley & Sons, Inc.; http://www.wiley.com/WileyCDA/WileyTitle/productCd-047139727X.html.

S. Ruth and C. Barrett, "UBIT: Current Developments," Internal Revenue Service; http://www.irs.gov/pub/irs-tege/topicn.pdf.

Publication 598, "Tax on Unrelated Business Income of Exempt Organizations," Internal Revenue Service; http://www.irs.gov/pub/irs-pdf/p598.pdf.

Form 8868, "Application for Extension of Time To File an Exempt Organization Return," Internal Revenue Service; http://www.irs.gov/pub/irs-pdf/f8868.pdf.

2.12

LEGAL SUBJECT: Sponsorship Payments and UBIT

STATEMENT OF ISSUE: Sponsorship payments received in conjunction with a fundraising event may be either nontaxable charitable contributions or unrelated advertising income, triggering unrelated business income tax (UBIT).

CONCERNS/RISKS/ EXPOSURE: Section 513(i) provides that "qualified sponsorship payments" will not be subject to the UBIT if there is no expectation of any substantial return benefit other than an acknowledgment. The acknowledgment may include use of the sponsor's name, logo or product, and is not considered advertising unless it contains qualitative or comparative language, price information, indications of savings or value, or a solicitation to use or buy the product or service. If a sponsor makes a combined payment, in part for sponsorship and in part for advertising, the payment should be allocated so that each is treated as a separate transaction. Nonqualifying sponsorship payments and advertising payments are subject to UBIT if the payments are from a trade or business, are regularly carried on, and are not substantially related to the charitable purpose for which the organization is tax-exempt.

> ***TIP:*** An annual fundraising event will not be considered to be regularly carried on. Advertising revenue received in connection with the event will be considered income, but will generally not be taxable. If the event takes place over several days, however, the IRS may scrutinize the advertising more closely.

RESOURCES: Don Kramer's Nonprofit Issues, Inc., P.O. Box 1002, Dresher, PA 19025, (212) 542-7547, (888) 674-7783; see the Ready Reference pages available for downloading, some for a small fee; http://www.nonprofitissues.com/public/indices/byfeature/ready.html.

"Unrelated Business Income Tax – Special Rules," Internal Revenue Service; http://www.irs.gov/charities/article/0,,id=96106,00.html.

Publication 598, "Tax on Unrelated Business Income of Exempt Organizations," Internal Revenue Service; http://www.irs.gov/pub/irs-pdf/p598.pdf.

2.13

LEGAL SUBJECT: Endorsements and Taxes

STATEMENT OF ISSUE: When an organization that is exempt from federal income tax endorses a vendor's product or service to its members and nonmembers and is compensated for its endorsement, the compensation may be taxable to the organization.

CONCERNS/RISKS/ EXPOSURE: Revenue derived from the endorsement of products or services may generate unrelated business income tax (UBIT), *i.e.* income from a business activity that is regularly carried on and not substantially related to the organization's mission or exempt purpose. Unrelated business income is generally taxable unless the income fits into one of several exclusions. One such exclusion is royalty income, *i.e.*, payments received for the use of a trademark, trade name, copyright, facsimile signature or name.

If an organization endorses a vendor's product or service, but does not actually market the product or service, often called an "affinity" arrangement, the action could be viewed as an exclusive licensing of the organization's name, logo, or mailing list. If the organization is compensated for the exclusive licensing, the payments may be royalties and be tax-free. However, if the organization actually markets the product or service or provides administrative services, the tax issues are considerably more complicated. For example, if an environmental organization manufactured tee-shirts with its own logo on them, the income would be taxable. If the same organization created nature designs to be screened on tee-shirts by a vendor in exchange for a fee, the income would likely constitute a tax-free royalty. *See also* Section 2.11, Unrelated Business Income Tax.

> ***TIP:*** When determining royalty payments, calculate them as a percentage of gross sales of the endorsed product or service to reduce the chance that the payments will be taxable. A contract for a percentage of net profits is a joint venture which may result in taxable unrelated business income.

RESOURCES: J.S. Tennebaum, "Association Endorsements: The Current State of the Tax Law"; http://www.venable.com/publication.cfm?publication_type_ID=2&publication_ID=452.

2.14

LEGAL SUBJECT: Postal Regulations for Nonprofits

STATEMENT OF ISSUE: The United States Postal Service (USPS) regulations for determining qualifications for the discounted "Nonprofit Standard (A)" rate for certain mailings differ considerably from the IRS tax-exemption rules.

CONCERNS/RISKS/ EXPOSURE: Preferred postal rates for nonprofits do exist. The application process for these is entirely separate from the § 501(c)(3) application process. The USPS has special regulations that restrict nonprofit mailings at preferred rates. The regulations contain several types of restrictions: content-based; qualified mailings; substantially-related mailings; cooperative mailings jointly with commercial businesses and others. The postal service looks at every mailing that the nonprofit brings it, even when the Standard A rate permit and nonprofit indicia appear on it. What matters to the USPS is the content of the mailing. If the material contains advertising, for instance, the organization will have to pay the nonpreferred, higher postal rate for each piece. Special rules apply to mailed products, which must be low-cost (indexed for inflation, around $8.00 at present) or items donated or contributed to the mailing organization. Familiarity with the postal regulations regarding mailing may save the organization both time and money.

> ***TIP:*** The words "sponsored by" are a red flag to the USPS. Material that promotes travel, insurance, or bankcard sales may also trigger a nonpreferred rate. "What About Getting a Nonprofit Bulk Mail Permit?"; http://www.nonprofits.org/npofaq/02/06.html.

RESOURCES: "U.S. Postal Service Regulations for NPOs," Online Compendium of Federal and State Regulations for U.S. Nonprofit Organizations; http://www.muridae.com/nporegulation/postal.html.

Alliance for Nonprofit Mailers: http://nonprofitmailers.org/.

"What About Getting a Nonprofit Bulk Mail Permit?" Internet Nonprofit Center; http://www.nonprofits.org/npofaq/02/06.html.

United States Postal Service; http://www.usps.com/.

U.S. Postal Service Publication 417: Nonprofit Standard Mail Eligibility; http://pe.usps.gov/cpim/ftp/pubs/Pub417/Pub417.pdf.

DMA Nonprofit Federation; http://www.the-dma.org/nonprofitfederation/index.shtml.

2.15

LEGAL SUBJECT: Other Tax Considerations

STATEMENT OF ISSUE: Nonprofits that have obtained exemption from federal income taxes may need to comply with additional requirements of state or local law to obtain exemption from state or local income, sales, or property taxes.

CONCERNS/RISKS/ EXPOSURE: Organization at a state level as a nonprofit corporation or association does not automatically confer exemption from taxation by the state or local municipalities. Recognition of exemption from federal income tax may not automatically confer exemption at the state or local level either. In Colorado, however, organizations that are exempt from federal income tax are also exempt from state income tax. Also, organizations that are subject to unrelated business income tax at the federal level are subject to Colorado income tax on the same unrelated business income.

Colorado allows charitable organizations an exemption from state-collected sales tax for purchases made in conducting their regular charitable functions and activities. C.R.S. § 39-26-114(1)(a)(II). Nonprofit charitable organizations that qualify under the Emergency Retail Sales Tax Act of 1935 (C.R.S. § 39-26-101) may apply for sales tax exemption by submitting Form DR 0715, "Application for Sales Tax Exemption for Colorado Organizations" to the Colorado Department of Revenue. If the Department of Revenue approves the application, it will issue a "Certificate of Exemption" that authorizes the purchase of goods and services without paying state sales tax and state-administered local sales tax. Refer to

DRP 1002, "Colorado Sales/Use Tax Rates," for information about state-administered local tax exemptions. Contact the local jurisdiction directly to determine the appropriate procedures to follow to obtain exemption from local taxes collected directly by the jurisdiction.

Charitable organizations may also be exempt from collecting state sales taxes for fundraising events if they have § 501(c)(3) qualification letters and Colorado exemption certificates and if their sales meet duration and total income limitations set forth in the statute. C.R.S. § 39-26-114(18). Governmental entities and schools that sell tangible personal property must obtain a sales tax license and collect all applicable state and local taxes on purchases.

In Colorado, property tax exemptions are determined on an annual basis, based on the use of the property in each tax year. Real and personal property may be exempt from property tax if it is owned and used solely and exclusively for religious, certain educational, or charitable purposes and not for private gain or corporate profit. An application for exemption from real or personal property tax must be accompanied by $150 and must contain the following: (1) the legal description and address of the property, (2) the name and address of the owner, (3) the name and telephone number of any agent, (4) the date the owner acquired the property, (5) the date the property is first used for charitable purposes, (6) a complete list of how the property is used by third parties during the previous 12 months, (7) the total gross income and the total gross rental income derived from any unrelated trade or business and from any rental for unrelated purposes in the previous 12 months, (8) the total number of hours the property was used for unrelated purposes in the previous 12 months, and (9) if applicable, a declaration of the religious mission and religious purposes of the owner. The property owner must also pay $53 and file a report containing similar information on or before April 15 of each year.

> ***TIP:*** Note that exemption from state sales tax does not mean that donations to the organization are tax deductible for federal income tax purposes. In addition, donors completing state income tax forms should refer to the requirements and guidelines for deductibility under state income tax laws.

RESOURCES: Colorado Income Tax statutes; C.R.S. §§ 39-3-101 through 39-3-136.

Colorado Sales and Use Tax statutes; C.R.S. § 39-26-101 through 39-26-211.

"Sales Tax Exemption for Charitable Organizations: Application Requirements," Colorado Department of Revenue; http://www.revenue.state.co.us/fyi/html/sales02.html.

2.16

LEGAL SUBJECT: Colorado-Specific Tax Credits

STATEMENT OF ISSUE: Nonprofits providing child care, housing or services to the homeless or "jobless" and operating within 16 identified enterprise zones in Colorado may be able to offer their donors a 25 percent tax credit in addition to the tax deductibility of the donation.

CONCERNS/RISKS/ EXPOSURE: The Urban and Rural Enterprise Zone Act, C.R.S. §§ 39-30-101 through 39-30-109, creates 16 enterprise zones in the State of Colorado. Nonprofits operating within these identified geographic zones and providing child care, housing or services to the homeless or "jobless" can be deemed to be promoting the implementation of the "economic development plan." The advantage to § 501(c)(3) nonprofits is that they can offer their donors a tax credit in addition to the tax deductibility of the donation.

This tax credit is currently 25 percent of the amount of a cash contribution and 12.5 percent for in-kind contributions. C.R.S. § 39-30-103.5(7).

Those claiming the credit must file the Department of Revenue tax form "Certification of Qualified Enterprise Zone Contributions" (DR Form 0075) with their tax return. The taxpayer must also obtain certification from the enterprise zone administrator that the nonprofit is an organization approved to receive direct contributions. This can be done directly on the Colorado Department of Revenue Form 0075. If the tax credit is more than $250, the form has to be filed with the tax return; otherwise the taxpayer just needs to keep it as a tax record in the event of an audit.

> ***TIP:*** Donors have been eligible for the tax credit since 1999. Eligible nonprofits that have received substantial donations may want to notify their donors that they may wish to consider amending their tax returns.

RESOURCES: Urban and Rural Enterprise Zone Act, C.R.S. §§ 39-30-101 through 39-30-109.

Colorado Department of Revenue; http://www.taxcolorado.com.

"General Information About Colorado Enterprise Zones," Colorado Department of Revenue; http://www.revenue.state.co.us/fyi/html/generl06.html.

Colorado Office of Economic Development and International Trade, 1625 Broadway, Room 1700, Denver, CO 80202; (303) 892-3840; http://www.state.co.us/oed/edc/e_zone.cfm.

2.17

LEGAL SUBJECT: Dissolution—Voluntary, Administrative and Judicial

STATEMENT OF ISSUE: Voluntary dissolution of a nonprofit corporation requires specific actions similar to those of initial incorporation. Nonprofits may also be dissolved through administrative or judicial action.

CONCERNS/RISKS/ EXPOSURE: In Colorado, members may vote to dissolve the nonprofit corporation and distribute its assets in accordance with the Colorado Revised Nonprofit Corporation Act (CRNCA) and the organization's articles of incorporation and/or bylaws. In the absence of members, the directors or trustees may vote to dissolve the organization in accordance with the CRNCA and the organization's articles of incorporation and/or bylaws. Dissolution is officially recorded when articles of dissolution are delivered to the secretary of state's office. A nonprofit may revoke its dissolution within 120 days after the effective date of the dissolution. Despite dissolution, a nonprofit continues its corporate existence, but may not conduct any activities other than liquidating its assets and closing out its affairs. A dissolved nonprofit must maintain a registered corporate agent for the purpose of service of process in the event any claims are filed against the organization.

The IRS requires that a § 501(c)(3) organization's assets be dedicated to charitable purposes. The articles of incorporation of an organization seeking exemption from federal income tax must include dissolution provisions restricting the distribution of the organization's assets. Upon dissolution, the assets must be distributed to one or more charitable, tax-exempt organizations or to the local, state or federal government for public purposes.

A nonprofit organization may also be dissolved through administrative action by the secretary of state if it is determined that one or more grounds exists, *e.g.*, nonpayment of taxes, fees or penalties; failure to deliver a corporate report to the secretary of state when due; or failure to maintain a registered agent or report a change in registered agent. A nonprofit may be dissolved through a judicial proceeding brought by the attorney general's office if, among other things, there is evidence of fraud, if the organization exceeded its authority under the law, if the directors are deadlocked in the management of the organization's operations and irreparable injury is likely, or if corporate assets are being misapplied or wasted. A creditor of the organization also may bring an action to dissolve the nonprofit. In such cases, the court will generally appoint a receiver to manage the disposal of assets and payment of creditors.

> ***TIP:*** The bylaws of an organization should clearly state the type of organization to which a nonprofit's assets should be distributed in the event of dissolution. An entity that serves the homeless would want to state that any assets should, to the extent possible, be distributed to another organization that also serves the homeless in perhaps the same geographic area. It is acceptable to use a generic statement that, in the event of dissolution, any remaining assets will go to another nonprofit closely allied with the mission of the dissolved nonprofit. This directive will assist those charged with distributing assets and will help ensure that the organizational mission (and the money of those who gave with the intent of furthering that mission) does not go toward a wholly unrelated purpose. C.R.S. §§ 7-134-101 through 7-134-501.

RESOURCES: Colorado Revised Nonprofit Corporation Act, sections on dissolution, C.R.S. §§ 7-134-101 through 7-134-501.

IRS Form 1023, "Application for Recognition of Exemption Under Section 501(c)(3) of the Internal Revenue Code"; http://www.irs.gov/pub/irs-pdf/k1023.pdf.

CHAPTER 3: EMPLOYMENT ISSUES

3.01

LEGAL SUBJECT: Employee Handbook or Personnel Manual

STATEMENT OF ISSUE: Development of an employee handbook requires time and resources, including legal fees for review before implementation. Employers fear that putting their policies in writing will create opportunities for employee dissatisfaction and litigation rather than prevent them.

CONCERNS/RISKS/ EXPOSURE: Employers are not required to have an employee handbook. Nonprofit culture may discourage such handbooks as destructive of the feelings of informality and freedom within which nonprofits believe they operate. Nevertheless, employee handbooks provide important information to both employees and the organization, and, in some cases, may shield an organization from liability. An employee handbook generally addresses such operational policies as working hours; overtime; holiday, vacation, personal and sick leave; employee benefits such as health insurance and retirement; orientation periods and performance review procedures; employee discipline and termination procedures; and any other relevant office policies. It is important that an employee handbook comply with all state and federal laws applicable to employees and the workplace. In some cases, employee information may be communicated through a third party. For example, retirement benefits may be offered by an employer, but the terms and details of the program are often provided by a third party insurance company or other entity that administers the plan and invests the employees' funds. The handbook should contain language clearly stating the employer's "at will" policy so that employees are informed that no employment contract exists. *See* Section 3.02, Employment at Will. The employer's anti-discrimination policies should be included along with a description of the procedure for pursuing a harassment complaint against anyone involved with the organization. An employer should have written policies prohibiting other forms of harassment as well, *e.g.*, on the basis of race, age, disability, sexual orientation, ethnic origin, religion, military status, etc. The U.S. Supreme Court held that if an employer has a written policy prohibiting sexual harassment, and the employer follows its policy, the employer might be immunized from liability. *Farragher v. City of Boca Raton,* 524 U.S. 775 (1998).

Although model or sample personnel policy handbooks are available from a number of sources, it is important that the organization ensure that the handbook reflects the organization's actual practices and that it complies with all board policies, bylaws and any other governing documents. As a result, many model or sample handbooks will not contain all the information a particular organization needs. Once a handbook is in place, the organization should ensure that the policies and procedures outlined in the handbook are referred to and utilized, and applied to each employee consistently. Employees should be given a personal copy of the employee handbook and should be asked to sign a statement acknowledging that they received a copy, have reviewed it, and understand that their employment is strictly at will. This will assist the organization in defeating an employee's subsequent claim that s/he was not aware of a particular policy.

> ***TIP:*** An employer's failure to follow procedures in its employer-created handbook may negate the at-will nature of the employment. In one case, the employment manual provided for a hearing, if one was requested, by any managerial employee who was discharged. When the employee was discharged, he was denied a hearing. He sued for breach of contract. The Colorado Supreme Court concluded that, under certain conditions, a promissory statement by an

employer may constitute an offer and demonstrate a willingness on the employer's part to enter into a bargain in a manner that justifies an employee's belief that continued employment constituted an acceptance of the employer's offer. The court reasoned that existence of the offer and acceptance, along with the consideration of continued employment, created a contractual relationship between the employer and the employee. *Continental Air Lines, Inc. v. Keenan,* 731 P.2d 708 (Colo. 1997). *See also* Section 3.02, Employment at Will.

RESOURCES: S. Galpern, Editor, *Hiring and Firing Within the Law* (1999), available from Colorado Association of Nonprofit Organizations (CANPO), 225 E 16th Avenue, Suite 1060, Denver, CO 80203; (303) 832-5710; (800) 333-6554; http://www.canpo.org/.

L. Bernstein, BEST PRACTICES: THE MODEL EMPLOYEE HANDBOOK FOR CALIFORNIA NONPROFITS (1998), available from Jossey-Bass, (800) 956-7739 or http://www.josseybass.com/.

Continental Air Lines, Inc. v. Keenan, 731 P.2d 708 (Colo. 1997) (employer failed to follow its own disciplinary procedures before terminating an employee).

J.W. Hunt & P.K. Strongin, THE LAW OF THE WORKPLACE: RIGHTS OF EMPLOYERS AND EMPLOYEES (3rd ed. 1994), Washington, D.C., Bureau of National Affairs.

3.02

LEGAL SUBJECT: Employment at Will

STATEMENT OF ISSUE: An employment relationship that may be terminated by either the employer or the employee at any time for any reason, or no reason, is called *employment at will.*

CONCERNS/RISKS/ EXPOSURE: In Colorado, an employee who is not hired for either a specific amount of time or until the occurrence of a specific event is considered to be an "at-will" employee and may be terminated "at will," meaning with or without cause, at any time as long as the termination is not based upon prohibited forms of discrimination. "At-will" employment is a legal term that may be altered by certain actions or representations on the part of the employer. To preserve at-will status, an employer should avoid any references to duration of employment, statements regarding employment through the completion of a specific project, or for a probationary period. Employer policies should never refer to a position as being "permanent." It is better to call a probationary period an orientation period to avoid creating a contract for employment. Employers should also avoid requiring or requesting a period of notice, such as two weeks' notice, when an employee resigns. Some courts have ruled that language in an employee handbook could be reasonably relied upon by an employee challenging the employer's actions for termination at will. Because Colorado is an at-will state, there is no cognizable claim for "wrongful termination" unless the employee establishes that the termination violated public policy. For example, Colorado prohibits termination of an employee for refusing to perform illegal acts if requested by the employer, as a matter of public policy. *See* C.R.S. § 24-34-402.5. Discharge for exercising an employee right, *e.g.*, filing a workers' compensation claim, protesting the employer's handling of overtime pay, or serving on jury duty, has also been held by courts to constitute wrongful termination in violation of public policy.

> ***TIP:*** An employer should include in its employment manual a highly visible statement that nothing in the manual is intended to construe a promise, contract or agreement between the organization and the employee, but that it is offered for the purposes of information and guidance only, and does not change the nature of the employment-at-will relationship. *See also* Section 3.01, Employee Handbook or Personnel Manual. Employers must also avoid termination as a response to an employee's grievance or an employee's undertaking of a protected activity.

RESOURCES: J.W. Hunt & P.K. Strongin, THE LAW OF THE WORKPLACE: RIGHTS OF EMPLOYERS AND EMPLOYEES (3rd ed. 1994), Washington, D.C., Bureau of National Affairs.

S. Galpern, Ed., *Hiring & Firing Within the Law in Colorado* (1999), Denver, CO: Colorado Association of Nonprofit Organizations (CANPO).

N. Davidovich, *Employers: Can You Reduce the Risk of Lawsuits for Wrongful Termination by Inclusion of Internal Grievance Procedures in Employee Handbooks?* http://www.talk-law.com/grievance.shtml.

N. Davidovich, *Public Policy and Employment at Will in Colorado;* http://www.talk-law.com/pubpol.shtml.

3.03

LEGAL SUBJECT: Colorado Wage Claim Act

STATEMENT OF ISSUE: Colorado's Wage Claim Act was passed to ensure timely payment of wages and to provide judicial relief when wages are not paid when due. In addition to corporate liability, the act also imposes personal liability for wages on corporate officers. The statute underwent significant amendments and renumbering of sections in 2003.

CONCERNS/RISKS/ EXPOSURE: The Colorado Wage Claim Act applies to all Colorado employers with one or more employees, but does not apply to counties, cities, school districts, quasi-municipal organizations and some special district entities. It covers employer obligations for payment of earned wages, which are defined as all amounts earned, vested and determinable. Wages include bonuses, commissions and earned vacation pay, but do not include sick leave. The act also provides for the immediate payment of wages upon involuntary discharge. C.R.S. § 8-4-109(1). The Director of the Colorado Division of Labor has jurisdiction over administrative claims for wages. A plaintiff may also bring an action in a Colorado civil court that has jurisdiction over the parties to the wage dispute. An employee may bring suit under both the Colorado Wage Claim Act and the Fair Labor Standards Act (discussed in Section 3.05, Fair Labor Standards Act) simultaneously. The winning party is entitled to recover attorney fees and costs. Under the Colorado Act, penalties in the form of *per diem* fines (*i.e.*, for each day the employer is in violation of the law) may be assessed against an employer for failure to pay wages in addition to back wages. Because accrued employee vacation and personal leave may constitute a significant sum of money, it is important for a nonprofit to identify the total amount of its obligation for these as liabilities on its balance sheet. The Wage Claim Act does, however, permit employers to withhold or offset from a separating employee's final paycheck any money owed to the employer for unreturned property or other reasons when there is a pre-existing agreement to do so. C.R.S. § 8-4-109(2).

Employers should also be aware of Wage Claim Order 23, which outlines in detail those circumstances and categories of employees requiring the payment of overtime and other conditions of employee work hours and compensation. Wage Order 23 was being drafted as this publication went to press and will supercede Wage Order 22. It should soon be available online at the address below. Even if an employer is exempt from payment of overtime under this Order, the employer may still be liable for overtime under the terms of the federal Fair Labor Standards Act (FLSA). Where state law and the FLSA conflict, employers must follow the provision that is more favorable to the employee. *See* Section 3.05, Fair Labor Standards Act.

> ***TIP:*** In Colorado, employer "use-it-or-lose-it" policies regarding accrued vacation or annual leave are illegal and unenforceable. At the time of job separation, the employer must pay an employee for accrued but unused vacation or personal leave if the employee is unable to take the leave prior to an identified deadline and the employment policy does not permit carry-over of accrued leave. C.R.S. § 8-4-101(8)(a)(III) (2003), which codifies *Thompson v. Cheyenne Mountain School District,* 844 P.2d 1235 (Colo. App. 1992) and *Hartman v. Freedman,* 591 P.2d 1318 (Colo. App. 1979). To avoid making significant payouts at the time of an employee's separation, an employer's policy should cap the maximum amount of vacation an employee may accrue. Nonprofit officers and directors are not, in general, personally liable for employees' claims of unpaid wages or

compensation. *Leonard v. McMorris,* 63 P.3d 323 (Colo. 2003) (employees of bankrupt corporation could not seek wages from corporate officers and directors).

RESOURCES: Colorado Wage Claim Act, C.R.S. §§ 8-4-101 through 123.

Colorado Division of Labor and Employment, 1515 Arapahoe, Tower 2, Suite 400, Denver, CO 80202, (303) 318-8000.

Colorado Minimum Wage Order Number 22; http://www.coworkforce.com/LAB/WageOrder22.pdf.

Fair Labor Standards Act, 29 U.S.C. §§ 201 through 219.

3.04

LEGAL SUBJECT: Exempt vs. Nonexempt Employee Status

STATEMENT OF ISSUE: Nonexempt employees who believe their Fair Labor Standards Act (FLSA) rights have been violated may file a wage claim against the employer, and the employer may face fines of up to $10,000 for each violation, as well as actual, liquidated damages and attorney fees and costs.

CONCERNS/RISKS/ EXPOSURE: The FLSA covers only nonexempt employees with respect to overtime compensation and minimum wage, so knowing the difference between an exempt and nonexempt employee is important. *Nonexempt* employees are typically service employees and others who are compensated hourly for no less than the federal minimum wage. They may be paid a salary or by piecework or commission, with their hourly rate determined by dividing their weekly compensation by the number of hours worked in a week. Overtime pay is then calculated at one and one-half times their hourly rate. *Exempt* employees are those "exempt" from the minimum wage and overtime provisions of the FLSA. Exempt employees are generally determined by job duties and salary. They include those who perform primarily executive, administrative or professional duties that require supervision of two or more employees, the exercise of independent judgment or discretion, the practice of a profession (law, medicine, teaching), the performance of managerial work, the performance of work requiring specialized knowledge acquired through specialized instruction, or work requiring invention or talent in a recognized artistic field. In short, an exempt employee receives the same pay regardless of the quantity or quality of the work. A case-by-case analysis may be required in some job categories to determine whether a particular employee is exempt or nonexempt under the FLSA. *See also* Section 3.05, Fair Labor Standards Act.

> ***TIP:*** When an employee is employed a portion of the time by an exempt business and a portion of the time during the same workweek in a position not exempt from the FLSA, *i.e.*, doing work covered by the act, the employee is considered nonexempt for any part of that workweek. 29 C.F.R. § 780.723.

RESOURCES: Fair Labor Standards Act and amendments, 29 U.S.C. §§ 201 through 219.

U.S. Department of Labor, Wage and Hour Division, 1801 California St., Suite 935, Denver, CO 80202, (303) 844-4405; http://www.dol.gov/.

Fair Labor Standards Act Explained—A Wage-Hour Guidebook (1997), CCH Inc.; http://www.cch.com, (800) 449-9525.

3.05

LEGAL SUBJECT: Fair Labor Standards Act

STATEMENT OF ISSUE: The Fair Labor Standards Act (FLSA) covers employers with revenues over $500,000 and those engaged in interstate commerce. It distinguishes between exempt and nonexempt employees in its protections and contains mandatory provisions for minimum hourly wage and overtime.

CONCERNS/RISKS/ EXPOSURE: The federal FLSA applies to employers with revenues over $500,000 or who engage in interstate commerce, with this requirement being very liberally interpreted to include practically every public and private employer in the United States. The act exempts certain categories of employees from minimum wage requirements and mandatory overtime pay; thus, all nonexempt employees must be paid for work in excess of 40 hours in a workweek. The categories of exempt employees are: (1) professionals, whose duties require consistent exercise of discretion and judgment using advanced knowledge acquired by specialized instruction or specialized knowledge of the computer field, invention or artistic imagination, or the practice of a profession; (2) executives whose duties consist of management of departments or subdivisions of a company and who supervise two or more employees; and (3) administrators whose duties require performance of nonmanual work related to management policies, general business operations and require the exercise of discretion and independent judgment. Some examples of jobs that are exempt include, but are not limited to: doctors, lawyers, nurses, teachers; highly skilled workers in computer-related occupations; employees of seasonal or recreational establishments; family members of the owner; outside sales people meeting minimum earning requirements; and employees of motion picture theaters. Undocumented aliens, who are prohibited from working legally in the United States, are nevertheless covered under the FLSA. They may be entitled to back wages as a matter of public policy, as it is the employer who violates the Immigration Control and Reform Act by not verifying or by ignoring the employee's work status. Additionally, the act requires gender-neutral pay, *e.g.*, equal pay for equal work. Failure to comply with the act's provisions subjects an employer to claims for up to two years of back wages, liquidated damages, civil and criminal sanctions that may involve fines of up to $10,000 for each violation, and a prevailing employee's reasonable attorney fees and costs.

Unless specifically exempt in the statute, employees must be compensated at no less than one and one-half times their hourly rate for each hour worked in excess of 40 hours in a seven-day workweek, which is defined as any seven consecutive, twenty-four-hour periods, not necessarily a calendar week. For example, if an employee's normal workweek is 37.5 hours, no overtime pay is required until the employee works more than 40 hours in a seven-day consecutive period. The act contains other provisions regarding workers who are full-time students (exempt from minimum wage), under the age of 18 (restricts hours and types of work), or who receive tips as part of their compensation.

The FLSA also contains several exemptions that may be applicable to some nonprofit organizations. For example, a hospital or residential child care facility may pay overtime based on a 14-day work period rather than a workweek. Job descriptions may be helpful to an employer in distinguishing between exempt and nonexempt employees. An employer must keep accurate wage and hour records to prove exemption and to defend a claim. It is a violation of the act for an employer to fire or discriminate against an employee for filing a complaint or participating in a legal proceeding under the act. The FLSA is enforced by the Wage and Hour Division of the U.S. Department of Labor through investigators who gather data on hours worked and wages earned as well as other conditions of employment. Penalties for violations include civil penalties of up to $1,000 for each violation, penalties of $10,000 for violation of the child labor provisions, and criminal prosecution, including fines up to $10,000 and imprisonment, for willful violations. The act covers employees in all sectors—public, private and nonprofit. *See also* Section 3.04, Exempt vs. Nonexempt Employees and Section 3.03, Colorado Wage Claim Act.

> ***TIP:*** Where state minimum wage or overtime provisions conflict with the FLSA, employers must apply the provision most favorable to the employee. 29 U.S.C. § 218(a). The FLSA does not require an employer to pay overtime rates for work on a Saturday, Sunday or holiday, unless the hours worked on those days are in excess of the 40 hours in the employee's workweek.

RESOURCES: Fair Labor Standards Act and amendments, 29 U.S.C. §§ 201 through 219.

U.S. Department of Labor, Wage and Hour Division, 1801 California St., Suite 935, Denver, CO 80202, (303) 844-4405; http://www.dol.gov/.

Fair Labor Standards Act Explained-A Wage-Hour Guidebook (1997), CCH Inc.; available from: http://www.cch.com, (800) 449-9525.

J.W. Hunt & P.K. Strongin, THE LAW OF THE WORKPLACE: RIGHTS OF EMPLOYERS AND EMPLOYEES (3rd ed. 1994), Washington, D.C., Bureau of National Affairs.

3.06

LEGAL SUBJECT: State Reporting Requirements for New Hires

STATEMENT OF ISSUE: Within the first 20 days of a new employee's hire, the employer must submit a copy of the employee's W-4 Form, or a document providing similar information, to the State Directory of New Hires.

CONCERNS/RISKS/ EXPOSURE: Employers are required to assist the child support collection activities of the State of Colorado and the federal Office of Child Support Enforcement by reporting the following information on all new hires, as well as rehires after 30 days' lapse. The fine for failure to report new hires is $25.00 per unreported employee.

- Employee's name.
- Employee's Address.
- Employee's Social Security Number.
- Employer Name.
- Employer Address.
- Federal Employer Identification Number (FEIN).

If reporting electronically or magnetically, also include:

- Employee Date of Hire.
- Employee Date of Birth.
- Employer Payroll Address (if different from employer address).

This information may be mailed to the State Directory at P.O. Box 2920, Denver, CO 80201-2920, faxed to the State Directory at (303) 297-2595, or it may be submitted electronically at: https://www.conewhire.com/.

> ***TIP:*** Employers must not only report this information, but may be required to withhold child support from an employee's paycheck and remit it to the county child support enforcement office. Personal Responsibility and Work Opportunity Reconciliation Act of 1996. 42 U.S.C. § 653.

RESOURCES: Federal Directory of New Hires liaison: Barbara Brown, (202) 401-9270; (202) 401-5647 fax, e-mail: bbrown1@acf.hhs.gov.

3.07

LEGAL SUBJECT: Prohibited Pre-Employment Inquiries

STATEMENT OF ISSUE: Federal and state employment laws regulate, through statutory anti-discrimination statutes and others, the types of questions and information that employers may legally ask on an employment application or in a job interview.

CONCERNS/RISKS/ EXPOSURE: Compliance with both state and federal laws regulating the employment application and interview process is critical if a tax-exempt organization wishes to avoid defending a state or federal administrative complaint or civil litigation. Inquiries that are not permissible include:

1. *Do you have a physical or mental impairment?* The Americans with Disabilities Act (ADA) prohibits this question and any information designed to elicit such information. Employers may set forth the *essential* functions of the position and ask whether the applicant would have any problem meeting the requirements. For example, an employer may tell an applicant that an essential function of a position is to lift and carry 25-pound loads and may ask the applicant whether s/he can meet the requirements.

2. *Have you ever filed a workers' compensation claim?* This question is permissible only after the employee has been hired and then only for the purpose of establishing a pre-existing condition for a subsequent work-related injury.

3. *What is your birth date, date of graduation, etc.?* The Age Discrimination in Employment Act (ADEA) prohibits any question that is designed to disclose an applicant's age. An employer may ask if the applicant is over the age of 18 and whether the applicant has graduated from high school or college. If the application process requires provision of transcripts from all applicants to verify the awarding of a diploma or degree, and this is information relevant to the position, collection of graduation information is permissible. Once an applicant has commenced employment, the birth date may be requested for purposes of benefits.

4. *Have you ever been arrested for a crime?* Questions regarding arrest records are not permissible. Questions regarding *convictions*, however, are permissible, and an affirmative response may be grounds for rejection of an applicant if such conviction adversely impacts the position and the employer has considered the nature/gravity of the offense and the time lapsed since the conviction.

5. *Are you a U.S. citizen?* The Immigration Reform Control Act (IRCA) prohibits pre-employment questions regarding citizenship or green card status, although an employer may advise an applicant that verification of employment eligibility under the IRCA will be required upon acceptance of a job offer.

6. *Do you have a car? Valid driver's license?* Questions regarding ability to drive or possession of a valid driver's license are not permissible unless the position requires driving a vehicle as an essential function of the position, *e.g.*, a truck driver delivering products. In such a case, it is a better practice to list driving as an essential function of the position and ask the applicant whether s/he can meet the essential functions.

7. *Do you have children? Are you married?* Questions to elicit personal information such as marital status or children should not be asked during the application process but may be requested once an offer of employment has been made and the employee commences work. Such an inquiry may be construed as gender discrimination.

> ***TIP:*** Although an employer may not ask a potential employee's religious background, Title VII requires employers to make "reasonable accommodations," even "for a prospective employee's religious observance," unless it causes "undue hardship." Title VII, Civil Rights Act of 1964, 42 U.S.C. § 2000e, 29 CFR § 1607. Thus an employer may need to reschedule an interview for a prospective employee if the interview falls on a day of religious observance and should not discriminate against the prospective employee for making such a request.

RESOURCES: S. Galpern, Editor, *Hiring and Firing Within the Law* (1999), available from Colorado Association of Nonprofit Organizations (CANPO), 225 E 16th Avenue, Suite 1060, Denver, CO 80203; (303) 832-5710; (800) 333-6554; http://www.canpo.org/.

W.J. Liszka, *Job Interviews: The Unknown Minefield* (1997), W & P Virtual Library; http://www.w-p.com/page.asp?type=articles&id=119.

3.08

LEGAL SUBJECT: Pre-Employment Background Checks of Employees and Volunteers

STATEMENT OF ISSUE: Hiring an employee who works with children or other vulnerable groups or with substantial sums of money, without conducting a background check, may increase an organization's risk of civil liability as well as the risk to people with whom the employee works.

CONCERNS/RISKS/ EXPOSURE: Pre-employment background checks of potential employees' and volunteers' criminal records, driving records and other relevant information may reduce liability and safety risks. The Colorado Bureau of Investigation (CBI) will conduct a background check for $10 per search. Since 2002, online background checks have been available from the CBI for $5.00 per search. Although volunteer organizations must perform background checks only when required by statute or regulation, organizations that need to conduct frequent background checks, *e.g.*, child care centers, may wish to purchase screening or background check software or subscribe to a service that conducts checks for them. These checks are usually required to protect vulnerable persons such as minors, the elderly, and those with diminished mental capacity. Software should be endorsed by reputable organizations such as the National Association of Independent Private Investigators, police organizations, or the Federal Bureau of Investigation. It is also possible to do a basic public records search on the Internet or use specific background check vendors. Planned Parenthood of the Rocky Mountains has an excellent form for use with volunteers. A polygraph test may not be administered prior to employment. *See also* Section 3.25, Polygraph Testing, and Section 8.07, Special Issues When Clients Are Vulnerable.

> ***TIP:*** An employer may make direct pre-employment inquiries of the applicant regarding convictions, but not arrests. The safest approach is obtaining a job applicant's written consent to conduct a background check that includes contacting previous employers, obtaining criminal and motor vehicle records, and checking other sources as appropriate, such as the Colorado Department of Human Services' Trails database for child abuse records. The employer should act as required by law or as appropriate to the job and best practice. If a position requires the applicant to drive a company vehicle, or the employee's personal vehicle, for company business, the employer should obtain information regarding the applicant's recent traffic record to defend against any claims regarding negligent supervision and entrustment in an automobile accident situation. Note: If the nonprofit has commercial motor vehicles, it may also be subject to federal department of transportation drug and alcohol testing and pre-employment inquiry requirements.

RESOURCES: Title VII, Civil Rights Act of 1964, 42 U.S.C. § 2000e.

Colorado Bureau of Investigation, Colorado Department of Public Safety; (303) 239-4400, 700 Kipling St., #1000, Denver, CO 80215; http://www.cdpsweb.state.co.us/.

Background Check Guide software (Net Detective); information and instant download available; http://www.background-check-guide.com/.

Planned Parenthood of the Rocky Mountains Volunteer Application, which includes permission for background check, confidentiality agreement and verification of health insurance coverage; http://www.pprm.org/pprm/volunteer.html#Application.

3.09

LEGAL SUBJECT: Sexual and Other Forms of Harassment

STATEMENT OF ISSUE: Sexual harassment, a form of discrimination, is prohibited under Title VII of the Civil Rights Act of 1964, as amended. The federal prohibition applies to employers with 15 or more employees. Colorado's Anti-discrimination Act applies to employers of one or more employees.

CONCERNS/RISKS/ EXPOSURE: Sexual harassment claims have increased dramatically. Sexual harassment is defined as:

> unwelcome sexual advances, requests for sexual favors, and other verbal or physical conduct of a sexual nature ... when (1) submission to such conduct is made either explicitly or implicitly a term or condition of an individual's employment, (2) submission to or rejection of such conduct is used as a basis for employment decisions, or (3) such conduct has the purpose or effect of unreasonably interfering with an individual's work performance or creating an intimidating, hostile or offensive working environment. 29 C.F.R. § 1604.11(a).

Violations may occur in the form of continuing offensive jokes, sexual conduct or assaults. Furthermore, employers may be vicariously liable for employees and volunteers who commit sexual harassment in the workplace. Damages include compensatory and punitive damages. Avoidance is critical as large jury awards are not uncommon. The employer is responsible for developing and enforcing a written sexual harassment/discrimination policy taking a "zero tolerance" stand. The policy should be reviewed with each employee who should then sign it to acknowledge receipt. The employer may mitigate liability by demonstrating (usually through documentation) that it took reasonable steps to prevent or correct sexual harassment and that the employee unreasonably failed to take advantage of preventative or corrective opportunities provided by the employer. Procedures for filing complaints should be included in the policy, with employees having several options for lodging the complaint (*e.g.*, going to a male or female supervisor and procedures to follow when the alleged harasser is the supervisor).

The Equal Employment Opportunity Commission (EEOC) and the Colorado Civil Rights Division (CCRD) have an agency-sharing agreement that permits an aggrieved person to take a sexual harassment claim to either agency. The CCRD has a 180-day time limit from the date of the last violation; whereas, the EEOC permits filing a claim within 300 days of the last violation if, as in Colorado, there is a state anti-discrimination statute. Both have initial jurisdiction over complaints. The CCRD process usually requires less time to resolve claims. The aggrieved person must first file a complaint with the employer. If the employer does not resolve the complaint, the employee may then file a formal complaint with either the EEOC or CCRD. If the complaint is filed with the CCRD, it will notify the employer and file the complaint with the EEOC as well to protect the complainant's federal rights. Prior to conducting a full investigation, the CCRD may schedule an expedited resolution meeting with the complainant and the respondent in an attempt to resolve the complaint. An unsuccessful expedited resolution will be followed by a full investigation that may take up to 270 days. If the investigation finds that no probable cause exists to substantiate discrimination or unfair employment practice, the CCRD will dismiss the complaint, ending the administrative process. If the investigation reveals probable cause, the parties must enter into compulsory mediation, which may be followed by an administrative hearing. A complainant may file a lawsuit in court only after the administrative resolution process has been completed.

The EEOC notifies the employer upon receipt of a complaint filed by an employee. The charge may be assigned for priority investigation if the initial facts appear to support a violation, or may be assigned for follow up investigation is the evidence is less strong. The EEOC can seek to settle the charges or schedule mediation at any stage of the investigation if the charging party and the employer express an interest in doing so. A charge may be dismissed at any point in the investigation if the EEOC believes further investigation will not establish a violation of law. Upon notice of dismissal of a charge, the charging party has 90 days in which to file a lawsuit. If the EEOC finds a violation, it will attempt conciliation with the employer to develop a remedy for the discrimination. If settlement of the charge is achieved, neither the EEOC nor the charging party may go to court unless the settlement or mediation is not honored. If the EEOC is unsuccessful in achieving resolution, it may bring a suit in federal court. It may also decide to close the case and issue the charging party a right to sue letter, giving the charging party 90 days within which to file a suit in court. Just as is the case with the CCRD, a complainant must use all available EEOC administrative remedies for resolution before filing a suit in court.

TIP: An employer may be responsible for the acts of non-employees (*e.g.*, volunteers or board members) with respect to the workplace when the employer, its agents or supervisors knew or should have known of the sexual harassment conduct and failed to take action. 29 C.F.R. § 1604.11(e); *Farragher v. City of Boca Raton,* 524 U.S. 775 (1998); *Burlington Industries Inc. v. Ellerth,* 524 U.S. 742 (1998). Even if the harassment involved an isolated incident, an employer may still be liable for "assault." Therefore, an employer should not ignore a harassment claim for the reason that the conduct failed to meet the "persistent, continuous or pervasive" requirement for sexual harassment.

RESOURCES: *Questions and Answers on Sexual Harassment;* GSA Office of the EEOC; http://lalabor.com/main/id/151.html.

Sexual Harassment;
http://www.employer-employee.com/sexhar1.htm.

Sexual Harassment: FAQ's;
http://www.courttv.com/legalcafe/work/sex_harass/sexual_background.html.

Colorado Civil Rights Division complaint process, C.R.S. § 24-34-306.

3.10

LEGAL SUBJECT: Discrimination on the Basis of Race, Color, Religion, National Origin, and Sex.

STATEMENT OF ISSUE: Titles VI and VII of the federal Civil Rights Act of 1964, as amended, and the Colorado Civil Rights Act, prohibit discrimination in employment on the basis of race, color, sex, religion or national origin. Some cities and counties also prohibit discrimination on the basis of sexual orientation.

CONCERNS/RISKS/ EXPOSURE: Title VI applies to any program or activity that receives federal assistance, *e.g.*, grants. Title VII applies to any employer that has more than 15 employees at any location. *See also* Section 3.09, Sexual and Other Forms of Harassment and Section 3.12, Termination for Activities Outside the Workplace and Discriminatory Actions, Including Discrimination Based on Sexual Orientation, for a discussion of potential discrimination based on sexual orientation. Both titles prohibit discrimination in the recruiting, hiring, promoting, demoting, firing, pay or benefits and apply to any employer who engages in or affects interstate commerce. A 1978 amendment also prohibits discrimination based on an applicant's pregnancy and requires that pregnancy be treated as any other illness for purposes of employee sick leave, the Family and Medical Leave Act, vacation leave, health and other benefits. The liberal interpretation of interstate commerce makes it difficult to claim exclusion as not participating in/affecting interstate commerce.

Title IX of the Equal Rights Act of 1964 prohibits discrimination on the basis of sex in any academic, extracurricular, research, occupational training or other education program operated by an organization or agency that receives or benefits from federal education aid, preschool through postgraduate school. It is the program itself that must be in compliance, not the institution as a whole. *Grove City College v. Bell,* 465 U.S. 555 (1984). Among the activities exempt from this prohibition are membership policies of the Girl and Boy Scouts, the YMCA and the YWCA, Campfire Girls and other single-sex, tax-exempt youth service organizations whose members are typically under the age of 19. In enforcing Title IX, the U.S. Department of Education will follow the procedures outlined in Title VI. These include filing within 180 days of the alleged discrimination, a prompt investigation, voluntary compliance attempts if discrimination is found to exist, an administrative hearing, and sanctions such as termination of financial assistance. The Department of Education can also refer a complaint to the Department of Justice for federal prosecution or to the Colorado Civil Rights Division for local action.

Both the Equal Employment Opportunity Commission (EEOC) and the Colorado Civil Rights Division (CCRD) have jurisdiction over complaints against employers based on Title VII. Colorado's Anti-Discrimination Act, administered by the CCRD, also prohibits discrimination on the basis of race, creed, color, gender, age, national origin, ancestry or disability and covers any Colorado employer with one or more employees. C.R.S. § 24-34-402. A complainant may file with either the EEOC or the CCRD. *See* Section 3.09, Sexual and Other Forms of Harassment, for a full discussion of the complaint process under the CCRD and EEOC. The CCRD requires a complaint to be filed within 180 days of the date of the last violation; whereas the EEOC permits filing within 300 days of the last violation. The CCRD process usually requires less time to resolve claims.

Occasionally an employee will file a companion charge of *constructive discharge* with a complaint alleging discrimination based on one of these prohibited categories. Constructive discharge simply means a situation created by an employer that makes continued employment so intolerable that an employee resigns. It requires proof that the employee suffered an adverse employment action committed by the employer. The courts use an objective test to determine the existence of constructive discharge. The question is not whether the job became so intolerable that the employee had to quit, but rather whether it had become so intolerable that a reasonable person would have felt that there was no other choice but to resign. Proving a case of constructive discharge is extremely difficult for an employee. *Duffy v. Paper Magic Group, Inc.*, 265 F.3d 163 (3rd Cir. 2001).

> ***TIP:*** The Civil Rights Act of 1991 amends several sections of Title VII to provide for the recovery of compensatory and punitive damages in cases of intentional violations of Title VII. 42 U.S.C. § 1981. Colorado's counterpart statute provides for similar penalties and an employee has the option of seeking a remedy from either the federal or state antidiscrimination agency. Colorado law prohibits discrimination in hiring or discharging an employee based on the fact that the employee is married to another employee. C.R.S. § 24-34-402(1)(h).

RESOURCES: Title VII, Civil Rights Act of 1964, 42 U.S.C. § 2000e.

Colorado Anti-Discrimination Act, C.R.S. §§ 24-34-401 through 406.

J.W. Hunt & P.K. Strongin, THE LAW OF THE WORKPLACE: RIGHTS OF EMPLOYERS AND EMPLOYEES (3rd ed. 1994), Washington, D.C., Bureau of National Affairs.

S. Galpern, Ed., *Hiring & Firing Within the Law in Colorado* (1999), available from: Colorado Association of Nonprofit Organizations (CANPO).

Equal Employment Opportunity Commission, 303 East 17th Avenue, Suite 510, Denver, CO 80203-9634.

Colorado Civil Rights Division, 1560 Broadway, Suite 1050, Denver, CO 80203, (303) 894-2297.

3.11

LEGAL SUBJECT: Age Discrimination in Employment Act

STATEMENT OF ISSUE: The federal Age Discrimination in Employment Act (ADEA) and Colorado's Anti-Discrimination Act protect workers between the ages of 40 through 70 from discrimination in hiring, promotion, compensation and termination.

CONCERNS/RISKS/ EXPOSURE: Although employers may advertise that a position requires a college degree, it may not lawfully advertise a position as requiring "a recent college graduate" or use any other age specification unless it is a necessary qualification of the job, *e.g.*, an actor in a youthful role or an airline pilot. Hiring a younger job applicant solely because the person is younger than a more qualified older applicant could be deemed a violation of the ADEA, which applies to employers (including state and federal government employers) of 20 or more employees. However, the Colorado Anti-Discrimination Act applies to employers of *one* or more employees. Several Colorado companies have been ordered to pay large sums of money to older workers who were passed over for promotions given to younger workers and who were fired and replaced with younger workers at lower wages or because a younger worker's health insurance premiums were lower. As in most states, the complaint process in Colorado is commenced by filing an administrative complaint with the federal Equal Employment Opportunity Commission (EEOC) or with the Colorado Civil Rights Division (CCRD). Colorado plaintiffs may also proceed to filing a civil court action before exhausting (*i.e.*, using) their administrative remedies. Additionally, Colorado courts have concurrent jurisdiction with federal courts, which means that a plaintiff may commence a discrimination lawsuit in either court.

The Older Workers Benefit Protection Act of 1990 is a federal law that amended the ADEA and prohibits employers from denying benefits to older employees. An employer may reduce benefits based on age only if the cost of providing the reduced benefits to older workers is the same as the cost of providing benefits to younger workers. This same amendment allows older workers, who may be asked to forego rights under the ADEA in exchange for consideration, *i.e.*, something of value, to waive ADEA protections as long as they do so knowingly and voluntarily. Another federal law, the Older Workers Benefits Protection Act (OWBPA), governs the actions of employers who offer severance or termination benefits in exchange for a signed release. The OWBPA requires the employer to make the release language readily understandable. The release must give the employee the opportunity to consult with legal counsel and have the release reviewed. The employee must also have the opportunity to retract acceptance of the release anytime during a seven-day rescission period. Additionally, the severance offer and accompanying release must be available for consideration for at least 21 days. If the employee is part of a group separation, each employee in the group has 45 days to consider acceptance.

> ***TIP:*** The employer must ensure that a separation agreement in which the employee waives any future claims to benefits complies with all elements of the Older Workers Benefits Protection Act or the agreement will not be enforced, and the employee may still sue the employer for, among other things, a claim under the ADEA. *Oubre v. Energy Operations Inc.,* 522 U.S. 422 (1998).

RESOURCES: Age Discrimination in Employment Act, 29 U.S.C. §§ 621 through 634.

Older Workers Benefits Protection Act, 29 U.S.C. § 626(f)(1).

The Age Discrimination in Employment Act of 1967, U.S. Equal Employment Opportunity Commission; http://www.eeoc.gov/types/age.html.

The Age Discrimination in Employment Act of 1967, U.S. Department of Labor; http://www.dol.gov/oasam/regs/statutes/age_act.htm.

Employment Discrimination: An Overview, Cornell Law School; http://www.law.cornell.edu/topics/employment_discrimination.html

Colorado Anti-Discrimination Act, C.R.S. §§ 24-34-401 through 406.

Colorado Civil Rights Division, 1560 Broadway, Suite 1050, Denver, CO 80203, (303) 894-2297.

3.12

LEGAL SUBJECT: Termination for Activities Outside the Workplace and Discriminatory Actions, Including Discrimination Based on Sexual Orientation

STATEMENT OF ISSUE: Occasionally, employers are faced with terminating an employee for participation in activities outside of work. Discrimination on the basis of sexual orientation may arguably be covered in the absence of a specific city or county prohibition and is specifically addressed in some county and city ordinances.

CONCERNS/RISKS/ EXPOSURE: Colorado's Anti-Discrimination Act deems it discriminatory for an employer to terminate an employee for "engaging in any lawful activity off the premises of the employer" unless the activity meets one of two exceptions: (1) it relates to a bona fide occupational qualification (BFOQ) or is reasonably and rationally related to the employment activities and responsibilities of the employee; or (2) it is necessary to avoid a conflict of interest. Some have interpreted this type of prohibition to include discrimination on the basis of lifestyle or sexual orientation. The statute clearly does not prohibit other forms of discrimination in employment based on sexual orientation.

Several municipalities in Colorado do have ordinances prohibiting any form of discrimination in employment based on sexual orientation. These include Denver, Boulder, Aspen, Crested Butte, and Telluride. Furthermore, some foundations require their potential grantees to submit their anti-discrimination policy with the grant application. Failure to include prohibition on the basis of sexual orientation in a nonprofit's anti-discrimination policy may preclude the awarding of a grant. Off-duty religious conduct that may be contrary to an employer's interests may not always fall under the BFOQ exception, because such conduct may still be protected under other anti-discrimination statutes, or even state or federal constitutional protections.

Complaints are administered by the Colorado Civil Rights Division for the state statute and by the agency identified in the respective city ordinances. In most cases, a plaintiff does not have to exhaust all of the administrative remedies available before filing a complaint in court. City and county ordinances may differ, however.

> ***TIP:*** As with any claim brought to the Colorado Civil Rights Division, an employee is required to file an action under this statute within six months of the occurrence of the prohibited actions. *Galieti v. State Farm Mutual Auto Ins. Co.,* 840 F. Supp. 104 (D. Colo. 1993), applying C.R.S. § 24-34-403 to all actions under Part 4, Employment Practices. A claim brought before the Equal Employment Opportunity Commission (EEOC), however, may be brought as late as 300 days following the last occurrence of the discriminatory conduct.

RESOURCES: Colorado Anti-Discrimination Act, C.R.S. §§ 24-34-401 through 406, especially § 24-34-402.5.

J.W. Hunt & P.K. Strongin, THE LAW OF THE WORKPLACE: RIGHTS OF EMPLOYERS AND EMPLOYEES (3rd ed. 1994), Washington, D.C., Bureau of National Affairs.

S. Galpern, Ed., *Hiring & Firing Within the Law in Colorado* (1999), available from: Colorado Association of Nonprofit Organizations (CANPO).

Equal Employment Opportunity Commission, 303 East 17th Avenue, Suite 510, Denver, CO 80203-9634.

Colorado Civil Rights Division, 1560 Broadway, Suite 1050, Denver, CO 80203, (303) 894-2297.

3.13

LEGAL SUBJECT: Section 504 of the Rehabilitation Act of 1973

STATEMENT OF ISSUE: Like the Americans with Disabilities Act, Section 504 of the Rehabilitation Act of 1973 prohibits discrimination on the basis of disability.

CONCERNS/RISKS/ EXPOSURE: Section 504 requires that individuals with disabilities shall not be excluded from, denied access to, or be subjected to discrimination under any program or activity that either receives federal financial assistance, or is conducted by any executive agency or the U.S. Postal Service. Covered entities may include postsecondary institutions, recipients of federal grants or federal funds including those that flow through state agencies, or beneficiaries of federal support programs, such as free and reduced lunch programs. The Act applies whether the employer is involved in interstate commerce or not. Section 504 applies the same definition of disability that is used in the Americans with Disabilities Act (ADA). For employment purposes, a "qualified person" is a person with a disability who can, with or without reasonable accommodation, perform the essential functions of a job. A qualified person must have a physical or mental impairment that substantially impacts or limits one or more major life functions, such as seeing, hearing, speaking, walking, learning, working or caring for one's self. It also covers those who have a history of a disability or are regarded by the employer as if they have a disability, but it does not cover current abusers of alcohol or drugs. An employee may initiate an administrative complaint with the Department of Justice alleging violation by an employer. Investigative procedures and remedies are similar to those available under the ADA. Loss of federal funding is also a potential risk to the violating employer. *See also* Section 3.14, Americans with Disabilities Act.

> ***TIP:*** A recipient of federal funds is required to make reasonable accommodations in order to provide a qualified person equal access to jobs, programs, activities and services. Reasonable accommodations must be made unless they cause undue hardship. A determination of hardship includes the type and size of the business and the cost of the accommodation needed. 45 C.F.R. § 84.12.

RESOURCES: Section 504 of the Rehabilitation Act of 1973, 29 U.S.C. § 793.

Section 504, Department of Labor; http://www.dol.gov/oasam/regs/statutes/sec504.htm.

SECTION 504 COMPLIANCE HANDBOOK, available from Thompson Publishing Group; information and order form: http://www.thompson.com/libraries/grantmanage/hand/. Also includes a section on the ADA.

Office for Civil Rights, U.S. Department of Health and Human Services; Hotlines: (800) 368-1019 (Voice); (800) 537-7697 (TDD); E-Mail: ocrmail@hhs.gov; website: http://www.hhs.gov/ocr.

3.14

LEGAL SUBJECT: Americans with Disabilities Act

STATEMENT OF ISSUE: The Americans with Disabilities Act (ADA) prohibits discrimination on the basis of disability in order to make employment, services and public accommodations more accessible to individuals with disabilities.

CONCERNS/RISKS/ EXPOSURE: The ADA covers protected persons in several areas: Employment (Title I); Public Services (Title II); Public Accommodations (Title III); Telecommunications (Title IV); and Miscellaneous (Title V), all of which prohibit discrimination, retaliation and other actions. Although the employment provisions of the ADA apply only to employers with 15 employees or more, Colorado's anti-discrimination statute contains a counterpart policy applicable to employers of one or more employees. Moreover, the ADA's public accommodations provisions apply to all sizes of businesses, regardless of number of employees. In addition, the ADA applies to both public and private businesses and entities.

A person with a disability is one who: (1) has a physical or mental impairment, that substantially limits one or more major life activities (*e.g.*, seeing, hearing, walking, working, self-care, learning); or (2) who has a record of such an impairment (*e.g.*, someone who has had a heart attack); or (3) who is regarded as having such an impairment (*e.g.*, resides with a person who has AIDS/HIV). The term includes those with a history of drug or alcohol abuse, but does not protect those who are current, active alcohol or drug abusers. For employment purposes, a "qualified person" is a person with a disability who can, with or without reasonable accommodation, perform the essential functions of a job.

A good job description can often be very helpful in determining the essential functions of a job, and the Equal Employment Opportunity Commission (EEOC) regulations give deference (but not unfettered discretion) to the employer to determine those aspects of a particular position that are "essential functions." Employer compliance requires the provision of "reasonable accommodations." These are adjustments that the employer can provide without "undue hardship," with cost being a major factor relative to the size and ability of the employer to absorb the cost of the accommodation. A qualified person may also voluntarily provide his or her own accommodation. The Equal Employment Opportunity Commission enforces the ADA. Once a complaint is filed with the EEOC, an investigation is commenced. The EEOC will receive information from the complaining party and the organization against which the complaint was made. The EEOC may ask the organization to respond to specific questions. The organization may then provide a written response and, if appropriate, provide documents. The EEOC may also ask the parties to engage in mediation or other conciliation efforts. If the EEOC finds reasonable cause for the complainant's allegations but conciliation efforts are unsuccessful, the EEOC may issue a "right to sue letter," with or without reasonable cause, giving the employee the right to file a lawsuit in federal court. The EEOC may also issue a right to sue letter if requested by the complainant where more than six months have passed since the filing of the complaint and the EEOC has not yet completed its investigation. Because the EEOC has experienced serious budget constraints, its caseload is heavy. As a result, many investigations are not complete after six months and complainants, particularly those represented by counsel, often request the right to sue letter at the expiration of this period.

> ***TIP:*** Job descriptions should clearly state the essential functions of the job. Such descriptions should always detail the physical requirements of the position, such as "lift 50 pounds above the head" or "climb stairs." An otherwise protected person may be denied employment by "qualification standards" that are "job-related and consistent with business necessity," and which could not be cured through reasonable accommodations. This may include situations that threaten the safety of the employee as well as other employees in the workplace. *Chevron USA Inc. v. Eschazabal,* 122 S. Ct. 2045 (2002).

RESOURCES: Americans with Disabilities Act, 42 U.S.C. §§ 12101 through 12213.

Colorado Anti-Discrimination Act, C.R.S. §§ 24-34-401 through 406.

J.W. Hunt & P.K. Strongin, THE LAW OF THE WORKPLACE: RIGHTS OF EMPLOYERS AND EMPLOYEES (3rd ed. 1994), Washington, D.C., Bureau of National Affairs.

The Americans with Disabilities Act: A Brief Overview; http://www.jan.wvu.edu/links/adasummary.htm.

A Guide to Disability Rights Laws; http://www.usdoj.gov/crt/ada/cguide.htm.

3.15

LEGAL SUBJECT: Wage Discrimination on the Basis of Gender

STATEMENT OF ISSUE: Under both federal and state anti-discrimination statutes, an employer may not discriminate in the amount or rate of wages or salary paid to an employee solely on the basis of gender. The Colorado Wage Equality Act and the federal Equal Pay Act specifically prohibit discrimination in compensation or benefits based on gender.

CONCERNS/RISKS/ EXPOSURE: Employees must be given equal pay for equal work in the same business entity. The actual jobs need not be identical, but must be substantially equal as measured by skill, effort, responsibility, and working conditions. All forms of compensation are covered: salary, overtime pay, bonuses, life insurance, vacation and holiday pay, allowance for expenses, reimbursement for travel expenses and benefits. Pay systems that result in employees of one gender being paid less than the other gender for equal work are permitted if the system is actually based on a factor other than gender, such as seniority or merit. In order to sustain a wage claim based on gender, the complainant must show that gender was the sole factor for the disparity. The Equal Pay Act applies to all employees covered by the Fair Labor Standards Act (FLSA), but also extends protection to professional, executive and administrative employees who are exempt from the FLSA.

An employee may file a claim with the Equal Employment Opportunity Commission (EEOC), the Colorado Division of Labor and Employment or the Colorado Civil Rights Division (CCRD) if the employee believes that the employer has discriminated against the employee in the compensation paid based solely upon the employee's gender. The employee may also file suit in a court of law without using all available administrative remedies first, unlike some other complaints based on discrimination. The employee will be required to prove that gender was the sole basis for the discrimination in the compensation paid. *See* Section 3.09, Sexual and Other Forms of Harassment, for a complete discussion of the complaint process.

In cases where both Title VII and the Equal Pay Act apply, the Equal Pay Act offers employees two advantages: (1) the employee can file a lawsuit without using all existing administrative remedies, *i.e.*, without filing with the Department of Labor, CCRD or EEOC; and (2) the employee is not required to present proof that the employer acted intentionally, unlike in Title VII cases. When a complaint is filed with the Colorado Division of Labor and Employment, the employer will be required to make available all books, records and payrolls that are material and pertinent to the complaint. C.R.S. § 8-5-104.

A wage discrimination claim may be an element of a broader gender discrimination complaint under Title VII or Colorado's Anti-discrimination Act. If a claim is brought to the Colorado Division of Labor and Employment, an employer who violates Colorado's Wage Equality Act is liable to the employee for the amount that the employee would have received had there been no discrimination. If the director finds that the discrimination was willful, the director may impose an additional penalty upon the employer up to the amount of the difference. C.R.S. § 8-5-104. If a claim is brought in violation of Title VII of the Civil Rights Act of 1964, the employee may be eligible to recover attorney fees as well as back pay. *See* Section 3.09, Sexual and Other Forms of Harassment, for a complete discussion of the administrative complaint process for the EEOC and the CCRD.

Title IX of the Civil Rights Act of 1964 does protect employees of covered entities from gender discrimination, including discrimination in compensation. *North Haven v. Bell*, 456 U.S. 512 (1982). However the bulk of applicable case law regarding discrimination in employment based on gender still arises under Title VII and the Equal Pay Act. *See also* Section 3.10, Discrimination on the Basis of Race, Color, Religion, National Origin and Sex.

> ***TIP:*** An employer cannot rely solely on job descriptions for protection from a wage claim based upon gender. It is important to document legitimate business differences among positions and any compensation factors such as merit or seniority.

RESOURCES: Colorado Wage Equality Act, C.R.S. §§ 8-5-101 through 105.

Fair Labor Standards Act, 29 U.S.C. §§ 201 through 219.

Equal Pay Act of 1963, 29 U.S.C. §§ 206 through 262, regulations at 29 C.F.R. §§ 1614.101 through 607.

3.16

LEGAL SUBJECT: Discrimination on the Basis of Military Status

STATEMENT OF ISSUE: An employer may not discriminate against a person in the uniformed services.

CONCERNS/RISKS/ EXPOSURE: Under C.R.S § 28-3-506, an employer, its officer or agent may not refuse to hire a person, and may not discharge a person, due to the individual's military status. Neither may an employer hinder or prevent an employee from performing any military service or from enlisting in the military. The Uniformed Services Employment and Reemployment Rights Act of 1994 (USERRA), prohibits discrimination against persons because of their service in the Armed Forces Reserve, the National Guard, or other uniformed services. USERRA prohibits an employer from denying *any* benefit of employment on the basis of an individual's membership, application for membership, performance of service, application for service, or obligation for service in the uniformed services. USERRA also protects the right of veterans, reservists, National Guard members, and certain other members of the uniformed services to reclaim their civilian employment after being absent due to military service or training. An individual may be entitled to reemployment rights if military service does not exceed five years and in the absence of undue hardship to the employer.

Under the Vietnam Era Veterans' Readjustment Assistance Act of 1974 (VEVRAA), employers with federal contracts or subcontracts of $25,000 or more are prohibited from discriminating against Vietnam era veterans, special disabled veterans, and veterans who served on active duty during the war. A veteran who believes the employer has violated VEVRAA may file a complaint with the Office of Federal Contract Compliance Programs (OFCCP) or with the local Veteran's Employment Representative at the state employment service office.

> ***TIP:*** An employer who violates the state statute may be convicted of a misdemeanor punishable by a fine of up to $500. A USERRA claimant must first file a complaint with the Department of Labor's Veterans' Employment and Training Service (VETS). If VETS is unsuccessful in resolving the complaint, the claimant may request that VETS refer the complaint to the Office of Special Counsel. If the Special Counsel believes there is merit to the complaint, OSC will initiate an action before the Merit Systems Protection Board and appear on behalf of the claimant. The successful claimant is entitled to receive the employment benefits that s/he was denied as the result of the agency's violation of USERRA. Additionally, a prevailing claimant is entitled to attorney fees, expert witness fees, and other litigation expenses. C.R.S. § 28-3-506; 38 U.S.C. § 4301.

RESOURCES: C.R.S. § 28-3-506.

Uniformed Services Employment and Reemployment Rights Act of 1994, 38 U.S.C. §§ 4301 through 4333.

Vietnam Era Veteran's Readjustment Assistance Act of 1974, 38 U.S.C. § 4212.

Compliance Assistance—Uniformed Services Employment and Reemployment Rights Act (USERRA), U.S. Department of Labor; http://www.dol.gov/dol/compliance/comp-userra.htm.

3.17

LEGAL SUBJECT: Independent Contractor vs. Employee Status

STATEMENT OF ISSUE: Misclassifying workers may subject an employer to payment of back payroll taxes, benefits, and overtime, as well as penalties by the IRS.

CONCERNS/RISKS/ EXPOSURE: The distinction between an employee and an independent contractor is an important one due to the fact that employers are obligated to employees in ways they are not obligated to independent contractors. Factors to be considered when distinguishing between the two include the following. An *employee* is hired and trained by the employer, who establishes the worker's hours and provides workspace. An employee is generally compensated per unit of time (hour/week/month) and generally has the right to terminate his or her employment at any time with proper notice. The employer determines the methods or means by which the work is to be done as well as the end result expected. The employer may usually terminate the employee at any time.

Generally, an *independent contractor* has the freedom to determine how the work is to be done and is responsible to the employer only for completing the work and providing the service or product for which the employer contracted. An independent contractor may perform the same or similar work for others, *e.g.*, as a consultant. An independent contractor usually provides his or her own materials and workspace, and determines the hours the work is to be performed. In the case of an independent contractor, an employer does not have to withhold income taxes, social security or other taxes, does not have to provide employee benefits, and does not have to pay social security, workers' compensation or unemployment compensation on behalf of an independent contractor. In addition, independent contractors are not covered as employees under federal equal employment opportunity laws. The IRS has issued a checklist of 20 factors used to decide, for tax purposes, between employee and independent contractor status. These are contained in IRS Publication 15. An employer still uncertain about how to classify a worker after reviewing these factors may request an IRS ruling by filing IRS Form SS-8 or may wish to seek the advice of legal counsel.

> ***TIP:*** An individual who regularly performs work for the contractor and no one else is considered an employee of the contractor. *See* IRS Publication 15-A (Rev. Jan. 2003), http://www.irs.gov/pub/irs-pdf/p15a.pdf. When using an independent contractor, there should be a written contract describing the scope of the work to be performed, the amount to be paid, the fact that the contractor is not an agent of the employer, and a statement that the contractor is responsible for payment of his or her own state and federal taxes, F.I.C.A. withholding, insurance, and other "benefits" that might otherwise typically accrue to an employee of the organization.

RESOURCES: J.W. Hunt & P.K. Strongin, THE LAW OF THE WORKPLACE: RIGHTS OF EMPLOYERS AND EMPLOYEES (3rd ed. 1994), Washington, D.C., Bureau of National Affairs.

S. Galpern, Ed. *Hiring & Firing Within the Law in Colorado* (1999), available through the Colorado Association of Nonprofits (CANPO) online bookstore; http://www.canpo.org/bookstore_xl.htm.

Guide to the Twenty Questions; http://www.prounlimited.com/20guide.html.

Hiring Independent Contractors FAQs; follow the "Independent Contractors" link on the Nolo Law Center website at http://www.nolo.com/lawcenter/index.cfm.

D. Kramer, *Classify: Employee or Independent Contractor* (Dec. 1999), available for download (for a $5.00 fee) on Don Kramer's Nonprofit Issues "Ready Reference" pages; http://www.nonprofitissues.com/xmlNpi/RR.php.

3.18

LEGAL SUBJECT: Workers' Compensation & Unemployment Compensation

STATEMENT OF ISSUE: Nonprofit employers in Colorado are required to provide insurance coverage to employees to compensate them for permanent or temporary work-related injuries, illnesses or diseases. They are also required to make unemployment reimbursement payments to eligible employees if they have four or more employees, although some religious organizations may be exempt.

CONCERNS/RISKS/ EXPOSURE: Workers' compensation provides protection to employees injured from causes arising out of and during the course of their employment. Nonprofits must purchase workers' compensation insurance coverage from a third party insurer to cover paid employees. Volunteers, including uncompensated board members, officers and directors, and uncompensated interns are not covered by workers' compensation insurance. They may, however, be covered by the organization's general liability policy for injuries sustained during their volunteer activities. Independent contractors are likewise not covered but may be covered under the organization's general liability policy. An employer that does not have workers' compensation coverage may be subject to penalties and fines, and will be responsible for payment of medical expenses (short-term and long-term), lost wages, permanent disability, and related costs of the work-related injury. Some employers do not contract with a workers' compensation insurer but, instead, set aside funds to cover employee injury claims. This is known as "self-insuring." Employers that choose to self-insure are generally not subject to fines and penalties as long as their self-insurance is a formalized program and the employer does not exercise bad faith in the payment of injury claims. Colorado underwent tort reform in the workers' compensation area in 1990, resulting in a schedule of benefits for permanent medical impairment. Workers' Compensation Act of Colorado, C.R.S. §§ 8-40-101 through 8-47-209. Employers are advised to activate the injured worker's Family and Medical Leave Act coverage, if any, concurrent with time off for a workers' compensation injury, especially if the injury may preclude the employee from immediately returning to work. *See also* Section 3.27, Family and Medical Leave Act.

Under state and federal law, an employer may be liable for the payment of unemployment benefits to eligible employees who become involuntarily unemployed. The Federal Unemployment Tax Act (FUTA) imposes on every employer an excise tax on the total wages paid during a calendar year. The employer is allowed a credit against this excise tax in the amount contributed to the state unemployment insurance fund. Under the Colorado Employment Security Act, an employer that is a church or an organization that is primarily operated for religious purposes and is supervised, controlled or principally supported by a church is not required to pay into the state's unemployment insurance fund on behalf of its employees. C.R.S. § 18-70-140. A nonprofit that employs four or more employees for some portion of the day in at least 20 different weeks of the year, during the current or preceding year, is a covered employer and must pay into the state unemployment insurance fund. Nonprofits may comply with the unemployment reimbursement requirements in one of three ways: (1) by paying into the state unemployment insurance pool; (2) by directly reimbursing the former employee, *i.e.*, paying unemployment benefits directly when a claim is made (this is known as "self-insuring" and requires that the employer have no previous unemployment claims and that the employer post a bond); or (3) by participating in an unemployment insurance trust, *e.g.*, the National Nonprofit Unemployment Trust (NNUT) or United Services Trust (UST). C.R.S. § 8-76-110(2).

The general rule is that an employee who separates involuntarily from employment, through no fault of the employee, is entitled to collect unemployment benefits. There are also some situations in which an employee who voluntarily separates from employment may be eligible. Partial benefits for partial unemployment may be paid to an eligible employee in an amount equal to the eligible individual's weekly benefit amount for total unemployment, minus the that portion of wages payable with respect to such week which is in excess of 25 percent of the employee's weekly benefit amount, with the resulting benefit payment computed to the next lower dollar. C.R.S. § 8-73-103. Part-time employees may also be eligible for unemployment benefits depending upon the number of hours worked per week and the length of time employed. C.R.S. § 8-73-105. Employees are covered by unemployment compensation; however, independent contractors are not covered because they are not considered "employees" of the organization. *See also* Section 3.17, Independent Contractor vs. Employee Status.

> ***TIP:*** A worker traveling to and from home and the workplace is not an employee covered by workers' compensation. If an employee's travel is at the express or implied request of the employer, *e.g.*, between work sites, any disability arising from an accident during that travel is within the scope of employment and is covered under Colorado workers' compensation law. *Staff Administrators, Inc. v. Reynolds,* 977 P.2d 866 (Colo. 1999).
>
> Unemployment insurance trust payments are based upon statewide claims for all employers. Payments into an unemployment services trust are generally based upon a nonprofit's own claims experience.

RESOURCES: COLORADO EMPLOYER'S HANDBOOK, published by the Division of Employment and Training, available by calling: (303) 603-8231 or (800) 480-8299.

Contact Colorado Association of Nonprofit Organizations (CANPO) regarding the NNUT, (303) 832-5710; (800) 333-6554; http://www.canpo.org.

Contact Workers' Compensation Division, Colorado Department of Labor, employers' services at (303) 575-8874.

Colorado Department of Labor, Unemployment Compensation Division, Employer Benefit Inquiries: (303) 866-6357. Contact the Tax Section for information about reimbursement and posting of bonds.

Workers' Compensation Act of Colorado, C.R.S. §§ 8-40-101 through 8-47-209.

C.R.S. § 8-73-108(4) and (5) for a listing of circumstances in which an employee may be awarded, or disqualified from, receipt of unemployment benefits.

Colorado Employment Security Act, C.R.S. §§ 8-70-101 – 8-82-103.

3.19

LEGAL SUBJECT: Jury Duty

STATEMENT OF ISSUE: Colorado law requires employers to compensate employees serving jury duty.

CONCERNS/RISKS/ EXPOSURE: Employers are expected to support employees' obligations to perform trial and grand jury juror service. Employers who fail to compensate employees in accordance with state statute expose themselves to wage claims. An employer must pay the employee's regular wages, up to $50 per day unless mutually agreed otherwise, for each of the first three days of juror service, unless the employer and employee mutually agree otherwise. C.R.S. § 13-71-126. Beginning with the fourth day of juror service, the state compensates an employee-juror at the rate of $50 per day. C.R.S. § 13-71-129. Employees fulfilling juror service in federal court are compensated at the rate of $40 per day after the first three days. An employer may not threaten or discharge an employee who performs jury service. Every juror should prepare to serve at least three trial days in the absence of extreme hardship.

> ***TIP:*** An employer who fails to compensate an employee as required under the statute or who harasses, threatens or coerces an employee or prevents the employee from fulfilling juror service may be subject to payment of treble damages and the employee's attorney fees. The employer may also be found guilty of willful harassment of a juror under C.R.S. § 18-8-614, which is a Class 2 criminal misdemeanor punishable under C.R.S. § 18-1-106, resulting in up to 12 months imprisonment and a fine of $1,000 or both. C.R.S. § 13-71-133 and § 13-71-134.

RESOURCES: Colorado Uniform Jury Selection and Service Act, §§ 13-71-126 through 145.

3.20

LEGAL SUBJECT: Employees as Volunteers

STATEMENT OF ISSUE: Volunteer work by a nonexempt employee is a complex issue, which may lead to an employer's obligation to compensate an employee for volunteer work at triple the employee's hourly wage.

CONCERNS/RISKS/ EXPOSURE: The nonprofit sector tends to draw people who have a strong volunteer ethic. As a result, some employees may wish to volunteer their support beyond their regular work hours and position description. The federal Fair Labor Standards Act (FLSA) requires that nonexempt employees be paid for time spent at work at the employer's discretion beyond 40 hours in a seven-day consecutive period. If a nonexempt employee volunteers additional time, but there is insufficient documentation that the service is purely voluntary, the employer may be at risk for unpaid wages. Exempt employees are not compensated for overtime, thus this issue is moot as to exempt workers. *See also* Section 3.04, Exempt vs. Nonexempt Employee Status; and Chapter 8, Volunteers and Volunteer Management. Some nonprofit organizations have a labor pool of volunteers. Extra care must be taken to ensure proper treatment and segregation of such volunteers.

> ***TIP:*** Citing the FLSA, the federal Department of Labor (DOL) defines a volunteer as an individual who performs hours of service for a public agency for civic, charitable or humanitarian reasons, without promise, expectation, or receipt of compensation for services rendered. The DOL further states that an individual shall not be considered a volunteer if the individual is otherwise employed by the same public agency to perform the same type of services as those for which the individual proposes to volunteer. 29 U.S.C. § 203(e)(4)(B).

RESOURCES: Fair Labor Standards Act, 29 U.S.C. §§ 201 through 219.

U.S. Department of Labor, Wage and Hour Division, 1801 California St., Suite 935, Denver, CO 80202, (303) 844-4405; http://www.dol.gov/.

3.21

LEGAL SUBJECT: COBRA and HIPAA Provisions

STATEMENT OF ISSUE: Employers who provide group health insurance coverage must offer most employees who lose or leave their jobs the option to continue coverage under the employer's health insurance plan. Employers are also required to comply with privacy rules concerning personal health information of employees.

CONCERNS/RISKS/ EXPOSURE: Under the federal Consolidated Omnibus Budget Reconciliation Act of 1985 (COBRA), employees and their dependents may continue group health insurance coverage when they lose coverage due to termination, reduction in hours, or resignation. Under these circumstances, an eligible employee and dependents may continue coverage for up to 18 months. If an employee dies or divorces, the spouse and dependent children may elect to continue coverage for a maximum of 36 months. In order to be eligible for extended coverage the employee (1) must continue to keep all premiums current; and (2) must not be eligible for group health insurance from another source, such as a subsequent employer, unless such insurance excludes pre-existing conditions. A former employee who is eligible for Medicare will lose COBRA coverage but the employee's spouse and dependents would be able to maintain their own coverage for the duration of the 18 months. Employers have an affirmative responsibility to notify their covered employees, spouses and dependents when they become eligible to continue coverage. The former employee may be charged up to 102 percent of the average employer cost of providing the group health insurance under the group plan rate rather than the rate nominally charged to active employees, which is frequently subsidized by the employer.

The Health Insurance Portability and Accountability Act of 1996 (HIPAA) restricts the ability of health insurers to exclude pre-existing medical conditions from insurance coverage. It also requires insurance companies to issue or renew coverage for individuals who have previously been insured but no longer have access to group health insurance coverage. The purpose of HIPAA is to allow individuals to maintain health insurance regardless of changes in their employment or personal circumstances. Under HIPAA, employer-sponsored group health insurers must reduce exclusions for pre-existing conditions by one month for each month that the individual can substantiate uninterrupted health insurance coverage prior to current coverage. Colorado law also addresses limitations on pre-existing limitations coverage. New HIPAA privacy regulations, effective April 2003, govern protected health information an employer may have regarding an employee's health records. The employer must maintain any such records separate from the employee's personnel file and in a locked location.

> ***TIP:*** The Colorado Health Care Coverage Act prohibits an insurer from excluding a pre-existing condition from coverage if the losses occurred more than six months following the employee's date of enrollment in the employer-sponsored group health plan. The act contains several additional limitations regarding exclusion of pre-existing conditions, including when the employee can demonstrate previous continuous coverage. C.R.S. § 10-16-118(1)(a)(I).

RESOURCES: Colorado Health Care Coverage Act, C.R.S. §§ 10-16-101 through 104.

Employers' Guide to HIPAA Protected Health Information; http://www.thelenreid.com/articles/Employer_Guide_to_HIPAA.pdf

3.22

LEGAL SUBJECT: State and Federal Notice Posting Requirements

STATEMENT OF ISSUE: Employers are required to provide workers with a safe and fair working environment and must post notices to employees regarding a number of state and federal laws regulating employment.

CONCERNS/RISKS/ EXPOSURE: Employees have the right to know about the laws that protect employee wages, health and safety, and jobs, and that protect employees against various forms of discrimination. Depending on the number of their employees, employers may be required to post notices concerning the following federal laws: Age Discrimination in Employment Act (ADEA), the Americans with Disabilities Act (ADA), the Employer Polygraph Protection Act (EPPA), the Equal Pay Act, Equal Employment Opportunity (EEO), the Fair Labor Standards Act (FLSA), the Family and Medical Leave Act (FMLA), the Occupational Safety and Health Act (OSHA), the Rehabilitation Act of 1973, and Title VII of the Civil Rights Act of 1964 (Title VII). A complete listing of current federal posting requirements may be obtained from the U.S. Department of Labor. Employers can also obtain a list of posting requirements by completing an online set of questions. *See* Resources, below.

Colorado posting requirements include information regarding: workers' compensation; unemployment benefits; wage and hours; civil rights and notice of paydays. For a complete listing of all current state posting requirements, contact the Labor Standards Office of the Colorado Division of Labor. *See also* Appendices 2A and 2B.

> ***TIP:*** If an employer voluntarily extends benefits of a federal act that is not mandated due to the number of employees, the employer must post the notice, *e.g.*, the Family Medical Leave Act (FMLA). Even if an employer is not covered under a particular federal statute due to the number of employees, it may still be required to post a notice. For example, employers are required to post notices to all employees of their rights under the EEOC and their right to be free from retaliation for filing a complaint. A laminated Combined Labor Law Poster for Colorado, containing state, federal and OSHA requirements can be purchased from Business-Know-How at: http://www.laborposter.com/posters/index.asp. Willful violations of the federal posting requirements are punishable by a fine of up to $100 for each offense. 29 C.F.R. § 516.4 (FLSA); 42 U.S.C. § 2000e-10 (Title VII), 42 U.S.C. § 12115 (ADA); 29 C.F.R. § 1601.30 (Title VII and ADA); 29 U.S.C. § 627 (ADEA); 29 C.F.R. § 1627.10 (ADEA); 29 U.S.C. § 9, C.F.R. § 825.300 and Appendix C (FMLA); 29 U.S.C. § 657 and 29 C.F.R. § 1903.2 (OSHA); 29 U.S.C. § 2003 and 29 C.F.R. § 801.6 (EPPA).

RESOURCES: J.W. Hunt & P.K. Strongin, The Law of the Workplace: Rights of Employers and Employees (3rd ed. 1994), Washington, D.C., Bureau of National Affairs; Appendix D.

U.S. Department of Labor: http://www.dol.gov/ for general information regarding employer responsibilities.

To obtain a customized list of federal posting requirements for an employer, go to: http://www.dol.gov/elaws/asp/posters/industry.asp.

Labor Standards Office of the Division of Labor, Colorado Department of Labor and Employment at: 1515 Arapahoe St., Tower #2, Suite 375, Denver, CO 80202-2117; (303) 572-2241 or (800) 390-7936; http://www.coworkforce.com/LAB/.

3.23

LEGAL SUBJECT: Federal Record Keeping and Reporting Requirements

STATEMENT OF ISSUE: Several federal laws impose record keeping and reporting requirements on employers.

CONCERNS/RISKS/ EXPOSURE: Several major federal employment laws and regulations impose record keeping requirements specifying how long each particular type of record must be kept by the employer. These include: Age Discrimination in Employment Act (ADEA – three years); Americans with Disabilities Act (ADA – one to two years); OSHA's Bloodborne Pathogens Standard (duration of employment, up to 30 years); the Employee Polygraph Protection Act (three years from date of test); the Employee Retirement Income Security Act (ERISA – not less than six years after filing date); the Equal Pay Act of 1963 (varies depending on record); the Fair Labor Standards Act (FLSA – varies depending on record); the Family Medical Leave Act (FMLA – three years); the Immigration Reform and Control Act (three years after date of hire or one year after termination, whichever is later); the Internal Revenue Code (four years); the Social Security Act (four years from later of tax due date or payment of tax); Title VII of the Civil Rights Act of 1964 (Title VII – one year from date of record or personnel action); and the Rehabilitation Act of 1973 (one year minimum). Retention requirements may include payroll records, personnel or employment records, unemployment tax payments, training records, records of employee benefit plans, individual and collective bargaining contracts, records of employee leave, and immigration forms.

In addition to record keeping requirements, the federal government also has several reporting requirements under specified conditions. For details regarding specific reporting requirements, employers should consult the Bureau of National Affairs (BNA) Policy and Practice series. The following are addressed in the BNA series under the Tab indicated: ERISA (benefits; Compensation Tabs 339 and 343); EEOC-Title VII (Fair Employment Practices, Tabs 401, 403, 441); OSHA (safety and health, Labor Relations Tab 85, Personnel Management Tab 247); FICA (payroll, Compensation Tab 305). All employers are required to report new hires within the first 20 days of employment. *See* Section 3.06, State Reporting Requirements for New Hires.

> ***TIP:*** Employers must comply with HIPAA requirements when establishing their employee files for record keeping and reporting requirements. *See* Section 3.21, COBRA and HIPAA Provisions.

RESOURCES: J.W. Hunt & P.K. Strongin, THE LAW OF THE WORKPLACE: RIGHTS OF EMPLOYERS AND EMPLOYEES (3rd ed. 1994), Washington, D.C., Bureau of National Affairs. *See* Appendix D for a complete listing of records to be kept and length of time records should be retained.

Personnel Record Retention Requirements, SmartPros.com; http://finance.pro2net.com/x38310.xml.

BNA Policy & Practice Series, http://www.bna.com/bpp/bod_main.htm.

BNA Policy & Practice Reporting Forms, http://www.bna.com/bpp/idx_midx.htm.

3.24

LEGAL SUBJECT: Collective Bargaining

STATEMENT OF ISSUE: Organized labor disputes can have a significant impact on the flow of commerce. State and federal labor laws have been passed to minimize these effects while protecting the rights of both employers and employees.

CONCERNS/RISKS/ EXPOSURE: Colorado workers have state and federal rights to unionize and to elect representatives for the purpose of collective bargaining. The National Labor Relations (Wagner) Act (1935) established a national policy to protect non-supervisory workers' right to self-organize and to elect representatives for the purpose of collective bargaining during labor disputes. Although later amendments eroded somewhat the power of unions, the act bans any practices by employers that interfere with efforts to unionize, bring workers into the union, conduct boycotts, strike, and be represented in labor disputes and contract negotiations. Employers must also negotiate with union representatives. Additionally, the act prohibits unfair employment practices. For example, the National Labor Relations Board has ruled that all employees covered by the act are entitled to have a co-worker present during an investigatory interview that the employee reasonably believes may result in disciplinary action. The Board ruled that if an employee requests the presence of a co-worker, the employer can grant the request, deny the request and terminate the interview or inform the employee of the choice to continue without a representative or terminate the interview. *Epilepsy Foundation of Northeast Ohio,* 331 NLRB No. 134 (2000). An employer may not discharge or discipline an employee for participating in protected conduct. Violations of the act expose an employer to injunctions, fines, and penalties.

The federal Wagner Act is administered by the National Labor Relations Board, which has jurisdiction over nonprofit employers involved in interstate commerce, but does not have power over public employers, agricultural employers or domestic workers. Claims alleging either violations of union provisions or unfair labor practices may be filed with the board within six months from the date of the event or conduct that is the subject of the charge. Upon receipt of a charge of unfair labor practice, the National Labor Relations Board (NLRB) assigns an investigator. If the charge is found to have merit, the NLRB will attempt settlement with the parties. If settlement attempts are unsuccessful, the NLRB's general counsel will issue a formal complaint against the offending party and will refer the complaint to an administrative law judge. The NLRB presents the case for hearing and the union or employer, whichever is the offending party, presents its own defense. If a party objects to the ruling of the administrative law judge, the decision can be appealed to the National Labor Relations Board in Washington, D.C. Appeals after the NLRB rules must be filed with a federal appellate court.

Colorado's Labor Peace Act also addresses collective bargaining and unfair labor practices by employers and employees. For example, an employer may not initiate, create, dominate or interfere with the formation or administration of any labor organization and may not encourage or discourage union membership. C.R.S. § 8-3-108. Employees may exercise their rights by peaceful picketing or other means of exercising their First Amendment rights to free speech. C.R.S. § 8-3-109(2).

The act is administered by the Director of the Department of Labor, and the department is responsible for promulgating regulations for the implementation of the Colorado statute. Penalties for violations of the act range from \$50-\$100 for a first offense and up to \$500 for second and subsequent offenses. C.R.S. § 8-3-122. The parties to a labor dispute may agree to engage the Director of the Department of Labor as an arbitrator. The Colorado Industrial Claims Commission may hear disputes in cases involving employers who have eight or more employees. The Colorado Supreme Court ruled that while the act is not applicable to a charitable private hospital, it may be applicable to some nonprofit organizations. See *Industrial Claims Commission v. Wallace Village for Children,* 437 P.2d 62 (Colo. 1968). Colorado courts may also order injunctive remedies requiring either employers or unions to cease specified activities. In some cases, the Wagner Act may preempt the state act, requiring the court to apply the federal act when ruling on labor disputes. *Building Construction Trades Council v. American Builders, Inc.,* 337 P.2d 953 (Colo. 1959).

> ***TIP:*** Employees may not engage in union activities during the time they are to be working, but may do so during their lunch hour. It is deemed discrimination or an unfair employment practice for an employer to terminate an employee due to the employee's participation in a lawful activity, including unionizing, off the premises of the employer during non-working hours. C.R.S. § 24-34-402.5.

RESOURCES: National Labor Relations Act of 1935, 29 U.S.C.A. §§ 151 through 169.

National Labor Relations Board for Region 27,
600 17th Street, 17th Floor, North Tower, Denver, 80202,
(303) 844-3551.

National Labor Relations Board Frequently Asked Question Topics, http://www.nlrb.gov/nlrb/shared_files/faqs/default.asp?useShared.

Labor Peace Act, C.R.S. §§ 8-3-101 through 129.

Colorado Department of Labor and Employment; http://www.coworkforce.com/LAB/ .

3.25

LEGAL SUBJECT: Polygraph Testing

STATEMENT OF ISSUE: Federal law establishes guidelines and restrictions for polygraph (lie detector) testing of job applicants and employees.

CONCERNS/RISKS/ EXPOSURE: The Employee Polygraph Protection Act of 1988 (EPPA) applies to commercial businesses and non-profit corporations, but not governmental agencies or political subdivisions such as public schools. A job applicant cannot be required to take a pre-employment polygraph test. A current employee can be requested to submit to a polygraph examination only under certain specified conditions, *i.e.*, the conditions of (1) an actual loss or injury, (2) access to the property, site or other critical aspect of the investigation, and (3) reasonable suspicion in the context of an ongoing investigation. Employers may not claim "reasonable suspicion" based on employee access alone, without any other specific suspicion. The term "reasonable suspicion" is defined in 29 C.F.R. § 801.12(f)(1) as "an observable, articulable basis in fact which indicates that a particular employee was involved in, or responsible for, an economic loss." This section also provides that "access in the sense of possible or potential opportunity, standing alone, does not constitute a basis for reasonable suspicion." Absent such conditions, an employer may not require a current employee to take an examination and may not discipline or terminate an employee for refusal to submit. Civil penalties include fines up to $10,000 for each violation and private civil actions in state or federal court. Although polygraph test results are admissible in court, currently, both parties must agree that the results will be admissible *prior* to the administration of the test. This generally does not occur, so polygraph results are rarely submitted as evidence.

> ***TIP:*** Courts have considered that the term "employee" under the Fair Labor Standards Act (FLSA) extends to a former employee because the word "derives meaning from the context of that statute, which 'must be read in the light of the mischief to be corrected and the end to be attained.'" *Dunlop v. Carriage Carpet Co.,* 548 F.2d 139, 144 (6th Cir. 1977) (quoting *South Chicago Coal & Dock Co. v. Bassett,* 309 U.S. 251, 259 (1940)). Another court has analogized Carriage Carpet so that a former employee was protected by anti-retaliatory provisions of Title VII of the Civil Rights Act of 1964. R*utherford v. American Bank of Commerce,* 565 F. 2d 1162, 1166 (10th Cir. 1977).

RESOURCES: Employee Polygraph Protection Act of 1988, 29 U.S.C. §§ 2001 through 2009.

Department of Labor Regulations implementing the Employee Polygraph Protection Act of 1988, 29 C.F.R. § 801.

The Employee Polygraph Protection Act of 1988, The Polygraph Place; http://www.polygraphplace.com/docs/information2.htm.

Employee Polygraph Protection Act of 1988, Fact Sheet No. 36, U.S. Department of Labor; http://www.dol.gov/esa/regs/compliance/whd/whdfs36.htm.

3.26

LEGAL SUBJECT: Performance Reviews for Employees and Volunteers

STATEMENT OF ISSUE: Failure to conduct and document regular employee performance appraisals may negatively affect the outcome of employment litigation. Volunteers should similarly be evaluated periodically.

CONCERNS/RISKS/ EXPOSURE: A performance appraisal may also be called a performance review, performance evaluation, personnel rating, merit rating, employee appraisal or employee evaluation. It is defined as any personnel decision that affects the status of an employee regarding the employee's retention, termination, promotion, transfer, salary increase or decrease, or admission into a training program. Performance appraisals play an important role in the evaluation of an employee and the encouragement of an employee to utilize skills, knowledge and interests to the mutual benefit of both employer and employee. It is also an opportunity for the employee to establish personal and organizational goals. When an employee repeatedly fails to perform up to job requirements and has been provided written notice of the need for improvement, termination may be the only recourse. Similarly, if an employee is denied a promotion on the basis of poor performance, written documentation to that effect can be important evidence in the event that litigation follows. There are many good books and articles about designing and implementing performance appraisal systems. An essential element of every system is two-way communication between the employer and the employee. The content of the appraisal should be shared with the employee and documented in a manner that will sustain a challenge that notice of the need for improvement was not provided to the employee.

All of the above applies to performance appraisal of volunteers as well. Volunteers are critical to carrying out the mission of many nonprofits. For example, the Court Appointed Special Advocate Program could not exist without the hundreds of trained volunteers who are assigned to advocate for abused and neglected children in out-of-home placement. Many special events also require numerous volunteers to be successful. A nonprofit that utilizes the skills and support of volunteers should formulate a process for training volunteers and evaluating their performance on a regular basis. *See also* generally, Chapter 8, Volunteers and Volunteer Management, Section 8.03, Hiring and Firing Volunteers, and Section 8.06, Volunteer Policy and Procedures Manual.

> ***TIP:*** After sharing the contents of the appraisal with an employee and obtaining the employee's input and feedback, it is essential to the documentation process that the employee sign the appraisal to acknowledge that the information was shared with the employee on a given date. Employee signature does not signify agreement with the appraisal, only that the information was shared on a given date. If an employee refuses to sign, document that the employee was given the opportunity to review and sign, note the date(s) such opportunity was provided, and note that the employee refused to sign. Avoid, at all costs, awarding merit increases for poor performance.

RESOURCES: D. Arthur, MANAGING HUMAN RESOURCES IN SMALL AND MID SIZED COMPANIES (1995) New York, NY: American Management Association, pp. 170-192.

Evaluation Activities in Organizations; http://www.mapnp.org/library/evaluatn/evaluatn.htm

Nonprofit Employment Law Issues in Texas, "Section Six: Discipline and Performance Management"; http://www.texascbar.org/content/legal_library/pubs/downloads/employmentlaw_sec6.pdf.

3.27

LEGAL SUBJECT: Family and Medical Leave Act

STATEMENT OF ISSUE: Under specified circumstances, the federal Family and Medical Leave Act (FMLA) provides employees up to 12 workweeks of job-protected leave per year, and requires the employer to maintain group health benefits during the exercise of this leave.

CONCERNS/RISKS/ EXPOSURE: The FMLA applies to employers with 50 or more employees. Smaller employers may elect to comply with the Act. To be eligible, an employee must have worked for the employer at least 12 consecutive months and at least 1,250 hours within a 12-month period before the leave begins. The FMLA covers care for a seriously ill family member, an employee's own illness or injury, pregnancy-related leave, leave to care for a newborn or adopted child and a few other circumstances. It also permits an intermittent or reduced work schedule in some instances involving a serious medical condition. Eligible employers must have a written FMLA policy. The employer has the discretion as to whether leave, or a portion thereof, shall be with or without pay. Medical certification may be required within 15 days of the employer's request for such certification. With proper written notice, an employer may require that the employee first take accrued sick, personal and vacation leave prior to FMLA leave. Proper written notice may be in the form of a written personnel policy or a letter of notification to the employee upon receipt of a request for family medical leave under the Act. The employer may also require an employee who is on workers' compensation leave to go on FMLA leave concurrent with workers' compensation. In the event the employee is unable to return to work by the expiration of the 12-week period, the employer can fill the position at the end of 12 weeks.

Upon returning from FMLA leave, the employee must be returned to the original or an equivalent position, which means no loss of pay, benefits or other terms and conditions of employment. An employee whose position has been eliminated is not entitled to return to a different position, but may be permitted to do so by the employer. The employer is not, however, required to return the employee to other than the original or equivalent position. An employer may be liable for unemployment compensation for an employee who cannot be restored to the original or an equivalent position. "Key" employees, *e.g.*, highly compensated or high level individuals, denied job restoration, must be provided written notice of such status and the reason for denial, and must be provided a reasonable opportunity to return to work after being so notified. The employee may be required to provide 30 days' advance notice when foreseeable or as soon as practicable when the need is not foreseeable. This is generally interpreted to mean verbal notice within one to two days of learning of the need to take FMLA leave. An employer who interferes with, denies an employee's right to exercise the FMLA, discriminates against an employee, or discharges the employee for exercising this right may be subjected to investigation by the Wage and Hour Division of the U.S. Department of Labor's Employment Standards Administration (ESA), to litigation by the ESA to compel compliance, and to a private civil action by the employee for violation of the FMLA.

> ***TIP:*** Pregnancy leave as a separate category of leave, which some courts have found to constitute reverse gender discrimination, may not be added to FMLA leave. The Act defines the term "serious health conditions" to include any periods of incapacity or treatment due to pregnancy, including prenatal care. 29 USC § 2611(11)(B). Employers with FMLA policies should ensure that leave is confined to a 12-week period during any consecutive 12-month period. This will prevent the presumption that FMLA eligibility renews each January 1st.

RESOURCES: Family and Medical Leave Act of 1993, §§ 2601 through 2654; compliance guide, found at: 29 C.F.R. Part 825; http://www.dol.gov/dol/allcfr/ESA/Title_29/Part_825/toc.htm.

Employment Standards Administration Wage and Hour Division *FMLA Compliance Guide;* http://www.dol.gov/esa/regs/compliance/whd/1421.htm.

U.S. Department of Labor, 1801 California Street, Suite 935, Denver, CO 80202, (303) 844-4405; http://www.dol.gov/.

3.28

LEGAL SUBJECT: Immigration Reform and Control Act and Form I-9

STATEMENT OF ISSUE: All employers are required to verify that new employees are authorized to work in the United States.

CONCERNS/RISKS/ EXPOSURE: Either prior to or within three business days of commencing employment, the new employee and the employer must both complete Form I-9. This form requests identifying information and the employee's sworn statement that the employee is a United States citizen, has been granted either permanent or temporary resident status by the Immigration and Naturalization Service (INS), or is an alien otherwise eligible to work in the U.S. Other foreign workers may be permitted to seek temporary or permanent work if they meet specified criteria, *e.g.*, if qualified Americans are not available to do the work and the employment of foreign workers does not adversely affect the wages and working conditions of American workers. The employer must check the necessary employee documents and complete the employer portion of the I-9. This form must be completed for all employees, whether part-time, seasonal, or temporary. A foreign worker who cannot produce documents evidencing eligibility to be employed lawfully is called an "undocumented alien." An employer who hires ineligible foreign workers may be fined $2,000 for the first offense, $5,000 for a second offense, and up to $10,000 for any subsequent offense. An employer's failure to comply with other requirements under the IRCA may subject the employer to fines ranging from $100 to $10,000, depending on the nature of the offense.

> ***TIP:*** The IRCA also prohibits discrimination against authorized aliens in expansion of the anti-discrimination provisions regarding national origin under Title VII of the Civil Rights Act of 1964. 42 U.S.C. § 1981.

RESOURCES: Division of Labor Certification, U.S. Employment Service, 200 Constitution Ave., NW, Washington, D.C. 20210.

U.S. Citizenship and Immigration Services (formerly the Immigration and Naturalization Service), Denver District Office, 4730 Paris Street, Denver, CO 80239, (303) 371-3841; http://uscis.gov/graphics/fieldoffices/denver/aboutus.htm or http://uscis.gov/graphics/index.htm. For forms and general immigration information, call USCIS at (800) 375-5283.

Immigration Reform and Control Act, 8 U.S.C. § 1324a-b.

U.S. Department of Justice, Civil Rights Division, employer information line: (800) 255-8155; http://www.usdoj.gov/.

3.29

LEGAL SUBJECT: Leave for Victims of Violence

STATEMENT OF ISSUE: An employee who has been the victim of stalking, domestic abuse or sexual assault may request up to three days of time off or leave to attend to matters related to the act.

CONCERNS/RISKS/ EXPOSURE: An employer must offer either paid or unpaid leave for an employee who is a victim of stalking (as defined in C.R.S. § 18-9-111(4)), domestic abuse (as defined in C.R.S. § 13-14-101(2)), sexual assault (as defined in § 18-3-402) or other crime. The leave may be either paid or unpaid, but the employer should specify in writing beforehand the terms of leave for such cause. The employee must give advance notice to the extent practicable of the time requested and may be required to provide documentation of the need, at the employer's discretion. Whether the leave is paid or unpaid is also at the discretion of the employer. Information regarding the reasons for the leave must be kept confidential, and documentation should be kept separate from the personnel file in a locked location.

> ***TIP:*** Employee victims may be required to apply any available annual leave, personal leave or sick leave before taking unpaid leave. C.R.S. § 24-34-402.7(2)(b).

RESOURCES: C.R.S. § 24-34-402.7.

3.30

LEGAL SUBJECT: Alcohol and Drug Testing

STATEMENT OF ISSUE: Drug use and alcohol misuse can negatively impact job performance and judgment. Employers need to be aware of employer and employee rights when subjecting employees to alcohol and drug testing.

CONCERNS/RISKS/ EXPOSURE: Employers may conduct post-offer, pre-employment drug testing either of all employees or all employees in a certain job class. Testing of current employees is not as straightforward. Alcohol testing may be required if the employer has reasonable grounds to suspect that an employee is under the influence of alcohol during employment and has a policy prohibiting such in the personnel manual. The employer should have a written drug and alcohol policy that clearly prohibits on-the-job possession, prohibits on-the-job manifestation, prohibits on-the-job odors indicating alcohol or drug usage, and prohibits on-the-job distribution of drugs or alcohol. If an employer is not otherwise required by law to have a drug and alcohol testing policy but chooses to implement one, the employer should nevertheless contract with an independent drug and alcohol testing service. Employer supervisors should receive appropriate training in order to make a suspicion-based determination as to whether an employee is impaired in the workplace. Be aware that some Colorado cities and counties have drug and alcohol testing ordinances that may restrict or expand drug and alcohol testing.

Under federal Department of Transportation regulations, anyone who employs drivers for the purpose of operating commercial motor vehicles in commerce in any state must have specific written drug and alcohol testing policies and procedures in place covering those employees. 49 C.F.R. §§ 40.1-40.413. Specifically, commercial driver's license (CDL) employees, including commercial van drivers, must undergo pre-employment, post-accident, random, return-to-duty, and follow-up drug and alcohol testing. The testing should be handled by an independent professional testing agency, under the guidance and direction of a certified medical review officer who is experienced in implementing and enforcing the federal CDL drug and alcohol testing requirements. And employers must certify that supervisors are trained in specific aspects of detecting controlled substance use and alcohol misuse, as well as the effects of such use and misuse. Because federal law in this area is extensive and very detailed, employers with CDL employees should consult with legal counsel to ensure that their policies, procedures, and practices conform to the federal requirements.

Nonprofits that receive federal government goods, services or grant funds valued at $25,000 or more must comply with the Drug-Free Workplace Act. This act requires the employer to (1) publish a statement to employees notifying them that controlled substances are prohibited in the workplace and stating what actions will be taken for violations of this prohibition, (2) establish a drug-free awareness program to educate employees about drug abuse, (3) notify the federal government of any criminal drug conviction arising from drug use in the workplace, (4) impose discipline or require rehabilitation of employees who abuse drugs in the workplace, and (5) make good faith efforts to maintain a drug-free workplace.

> ***TIP:*** Urinalysis, blood and blood-alcohol test records are medical records and thus are considered protected health information subject to the privacy requirements of the Health Insurance Portability and Accountability Act (HIPAA). As such, they must be maintained separately from an employee's personnel records in a locked location. 45 C.F.R. §§ 164.500, 164.501, and 164.514. *See also* Section 3.21, COBRA and HIPAA Provisions.

RESOURCES: J.W. Hunt & P.K. Strongin, THE LAW OF THE WORKPLACE: RIGHTS OF EMPLOYERS AND EMPLOYEES (3rd ed. 1994), Washington, D.C., Bureau of National Affairs.

S. Rosenweig and A. Cohen, *Is Your Substance Abuse Testing Program Litigation Proof?;* http://www.phillyshrm.org/newslet/april03.pdf.

D. Arthur, *Managing Human Resources in Small and Mid-Sized Companies* (1995), New York, NY: American Management Association.

Drug-Free Workplace Act, 41 U.S.C. §§ 701-707.

Federal controlled substances and alcohol use and testing regulations, 49 C.F.R. Part 382.

See Federal government-wide debarment and suspension (non-procurement) regulations under the Drug-Free Workplace Act, 40 C.F.R. Part 32.

3.31

LEGAL SUBJECT: Employee References

STATEMENT OF ISSUE: Employers are frequently asked to provide references for employees at or after separation from employment. Care should be taken as to how the reference is provided to protect the employer from liability.

CONCERNS/RISKS/ EXPOSURE: An employer may be hesitant to provide a reference for a separating or former employee for fear of litigation. An employer, however, may be liable for failing to disclose a known risky employee to an inquiring prospective employer. A Colorado employer may disclose information regarding an employee's or former employee's job performance, which is defined as the employee's work-related skills, suitability for re-employment, skills and abilities as they relate to future employment, and the reason for an employee's separation. An employer that provides information to a prospective employer about an employee's job history or performance is not liable for civil damages for such disclosure or any consequences of the disclosure unless the information provided was false and the employer knew or reasonably should have known that the information was false. It is good practice to have the employee sign a written waiver of employer liability prior to releasing job performance information to a prospective employer. In the absence of a written release, best practice suggests that an employer provide only the dates of employment and the position(s) held. When information is requested about a commercial driver's license (CDL) employee, a written release specifying what information may be disclosed must be obtained prior to releasing information to a potential employer.

> ***TIP:*** An employer that provides written information to a prospective employer about a current or former employee must send a copy of the information provided to the last-known address of the employee, if the employee who is the subject of the information has so requested. The employee may also obtain a copy by appearing at the employer's place of business during normal business hours. C.R.S. § 8-2-114.

RESOURCES: C.R.S. § 8-2-114.

3.32

LEGAL SUBJECT: Employment Terminated by Employer

STATEMENT OF ISSUE: Termination of an employee presents several issues for an employer. Compliance with the Wage Claim Act and common sense in these circumstances may prevent employee actions that are adverse to the employer and potentially dangerous. Similar care should be taken when terminating a volunteer.

CONCERNS/RISKS/ EXPOSURE: An employer should conduct adequate preparations prior to terminating an employee, whether for reasons of reduction in force, poor job performance, or other reasons. An employer conducting a discharge should ensure that written documentation is accurate, have a supervisor-witness present as an observer, and provide the discharged employee with an opportunity to make a statement in defense of the employee's actions, where appropriate. When separation at the behest of the employer occurs, wages or compensation for labor or service earned, vested, determinable and unpaid at the time of discharge are immediately due and payable to the employee. Prompt payment of the employee's final wages at the time of discharge is required by law and may eliminate any cause for a disgruntled employee to return to the workplace.

TIP: If the accounting or other unit responsible for payroll checks is not operational at the time of discharge, the wages are due and payable no later than 6 hours after the start of the accounting or payroll department's next regular business day, unless the unit is located off the work site. In such cases, the employer has 24 hours from the start of the next regular workday to make the check available. C.R.S. § 8-4-109(1) (a). If payment is not made, the employer faces penalties and attorney fees unless the employer has a good faith reason for believing that no wages are due.

RESOURCES: Colorado Wage Claim Act, C.R.S.§§ 8-4-101 through 109.

W. Frank, *25 Ways to Prevent Workplace Violence During Terminations;* available on http://www.all-biz.com/ under the Business Zones: Human Resources link.

3.33

LEGAL SUBJECT: Non-Compete Clauses

STATEMENT OF ISSUE: Colorado law prohibits employers from restricting an employee's subsequent choice of employer through a covenant not to compete, with several exceptions.

CONCERNS/RISKS/ EXPOSURE: Colorado law states that it is unlawful to use any "means of intimidation to prevent any person from engaging in any lawful occupation at any place he sees fit." Employers sometimes attempt to require an employee to sign an agreement that the employee will not accept compensation for performance of similar work for another employer within a specified time of leaving his or her current position. Generally, such covenants are void, *i.e.*, unenforceable, under Colorado law. *See* C.R.S. § 8-2-113 (1) & (2). The statute contains a special section declaring covenants restricting the right of physicians to practice medicine to be similarly void. Exceptions to this rule include: (1) contracts for the protection of trade secrets; (2) contracts for the recovery of educating and training an employee who has served the employer for less than two years; (3) non-compete clauses for executive and management personnel and officers and employees who constitute professional staff to executive and management personnel; and (4) contracts for the purchase and sale of a business or the assets of a business. Although no penalties are assessed for violation of this statute, the clause or contract will be deemed void by the court unless it falls under one of the stated exceptions.

TIP: Even in cases covering the exceptions above, if the covenant or clause is improperly drafted or overly restrictive, it may still be deemed unenforceable by the court because it is not reasonable as to duration or geographic scope. *Electrical Distributors, Inc. vs. SFR, Inc.,* 166 F.3d 1074 (10th Cir. 1999). Some restrictive covenants contain what is called a "savings" clause, which states that even if a portion of the contractual agreement is void and unenforceable, the remainder of the contract will still be enforceable. This practice is known as "bluelining." Such a clause allows a court to modify the contract agreement from an overly broad geographic area to a narrower one. For example, a non-compete agreement that restricts an employee from competing in any geographic location in which the company is located is probably too broad, especially if the company is located throughout the United States. Similarly, non-compete clauses prohibiting employment in a specific industry for more than 2 years have been held unenforceable. If the court concludes that the covenant is overly broad, it may modify the agreement to restrict an employee from competing in the geographic location in which the employee worked while employed with the company. Sample language for such a clause might read: "We agree that, if the court determines that any of the provisions of this agreement are unreasonable or unenforceable, the court may revise the specific terms of this agreement to make it reasonable and enforceable." Another important clause to include is a "survival" clause, which might read: "The non-compete provision in this contract shall survive the termination of the employment relationship."

RESOURCES: C.R.S. § 8-2-113.

Seek the advice of experienced legal counsel for drafting assistance when contemplating the use of a covenant not to compete or a noncompetition clause in an employment contract.

Katz, M.J., *Drafting a Noncompetition Clause for the Colorado Contract*, 20 Colo. Law. 703 (April 1991).

3.34

LEGAL SUBJECT: Safety in the Workplace

STATEMENT OF ISSUE: Employers are required to maintain a safe workplace for employees, which may mean adoption of policies and implementation of practices that promote safety.

CONCERNS/RISKS/ EXPOSURE: The Occupational Safety and Health Act of 1970 (OSHA) applies to employers and their employees in all 50 states, the District of Columbia, Puerto Rico, and all U.S. territories under federal government jurisdiction, as long as the employer is engaged in a business that is "affecting commerce." Coverage is provided either directly through the federal Occupational Safety and Health Administration or through an OSHA-approved state program.

The OSHA standards may require employers to adopt specified practices, means, methods or processes that can reasonably be expected to protect workers in the workplace. These may include such policies as blood-borne pathogens and ergonomics. The standards may require employees to comply with all regulations governing safety in the workplace as well as the employer's policies. The federal Region Eight OSHA office is located in Denver, as is the Denver area OSHA office. *See* below for their addresses and contact information.

Although a number of states have OSHA-approved safety and health plans, Colorado does not. OSHA strongly recommends that employees attempt to resolve safety and health issues with their supervisors or managers before filing a complaint. An employee may file a complaint or written request for an onsite inspection with the Denver area office, or with the Englewood office, depending upon the employer's geographic location. Workers who file a complaint may have their names withheld from their employers. At least one of the following criteria must be met for OSHA to conduct an onsite inspection:

1. A written, signed complaint by a current employee or employee representative with enough detail to enable OSHA to determine that a violation or danger likely exists that threatens physical harm or that an imminent danger exists;
2. An allegation that physical harm has occurred as a result of the hazard and that it still exists;
3. A report of an imminent danger;
4. A complaint about a company in an industry covered by one of OSHA's local or national emphasis programs or a hazard targeted by one of these programs;
5. Inadequate response from an employer who has received information on the hazard through a phone/fax investigation;
6. A complaint against an employer with a past history of egregious, willful or failure-to-abate OSHA citations within the past three years;
7. Referral from a whistle blower investigator; or
8. Complaint at a facility scheduled for or already undergoing an OSHA inspection.

Before beginning an inspection, OSHA staff must be able to determine from the complaint that there are reasonable grounds to believe that a violation of an OSHA standard or a safety or health hazard exists. If OSHA has information indicating the employer is aware of the hazard and is correcting it, the agency may not conduct an inspection after obtaining the necessary documentation from the employer.

If an emergency or hazard occurs and is life-threatening, the local OSHA office should be contacted immediately.

> ***TIP:*** The OSHA Training Institute makes grants to nonprofit organizations that wish to conduct training and education in the workplace. Information about the targeted areas for nonprofit grant applications may be obtained by visiting the following website: http://www.dol.gov/dol/audience/aud-nonprofit.htm. In addition, OSHA offers compliance assistance and a confidential onsite inspection process without penalties to assist with compliance. Many insurance companies will also provide complimentary ergonomic evaluations to their insureds.

RESOURCES: The Occupational Safety and Health Act of 1970, 29 U.S.C. §§ 651 through 678; regulations at 29 C.F.R. §§ 1900 – 2400.

OSHA definition of "imminent danger": http://www.osha.gov/as/opa/worker/danger.html.

OSHA standards protecting "whistle blowers": http://www.osha.gov/as/opa/worker/whistle.html.

Federal Region Eight office: 1999 Broadway, Suite 1690, Denver, CO 80201-6550, (303) 844-1600.

Denver Area OSHA office: 1391 Speer Blvd., Suite 210, Denver, CO 80204-2552, (303) 844-5285; Englewood office: 7935 E. Prentice Avenue, Suite 209, Englewood, CO 80111-2714, (303) 843-4500.

For more information about the complaint process, see: http://www.osha.gov/as/opa/worker/handling.html

For a laminated federal, Colorado and OSHA combined poster, see: http://www.laborposter.com/posters/index.asp (cost is approximately $29.95).

3.35

LEGAL SUBJECT: Employer Searches and Employee Privacy Rights

STATEMENT OF ISSUE: Under certain circumstances an employer may wish to, and may be able to, conduct a search of an employee's personal property on the employer's premises.

CONCERNS/RISKS/ EXPOSURE: The Fourth Amendment to the United States Constitution protects citizens from unreasonable searches and seizures by the government. It is, however, silent with respect to searches by private business. Nongovernmental employers are generally permitted an exemption to this doctrine under certain circumstances. Nevertheless, employers must balance an employee's Fourth Amendment privacy right to be free from unreasonable search and seizure of their person and property with an employer's right to maintain a safe workplace and protect its own interests. The law generally permits searches if the employer has a reasonable basis for suspecting the employee of wrongdoing and the search is confined to non-personal areas of the employee's office or workspace. The office itself, business documents, including telephone logs, and the employee's computer are considered the property of the employer and may be subject to search at any time for any reason.

Courts have found that employees do have reasonable expectations of privacy in their desk (*O'Connor v. Ortega,* 480 U.S. 709 (1987)), their office (*U.S. v. Leary,* 846 F.2d 592 (10th Cir. 1988)), and mail addressed to them and received at their workplace. Opening an employee's mail is a violation of federal law and carries a penalty of up to five years in prison.

18 U.S.C. § 1702. Third-party eavesdropping on employee conversations, absent any warning to the employee that "telephone calls may monitored for quality assurance purposes," other ordinary business purposes, or other exempt purposes under 18 U.S.C. § 2511(2)(a)(i), may constitute a violation of federal wiretapping law. 18 U.S.C § 2511(1)(a); C.R.S. § 18-9-303-304.

Factors determining the reasonableness of a search include: (1) whether the employee was given advance notice; (2) whether the search was justified under the factual circumstances; (3) whether the search was reasonably conducted; and (4) whether the search was conducted in areas that were clearly employer-owned. An employer must have reasonable grounds for believing that the search will produce evidence of work-related misconduct, theft or suspected alcohol or drug use on the employer's property or that the search is necessary for some work-related purpose, *e.g.*, to obtain needed records or other business documents or objects. The search must also be reasonable in scope in light of the objectives of the search so as not to be excessively or unnecessarily intrusive. *Doe v. High-Tech Institute. Inc.*, 972 P.2d 1060 (Colo. App. 1998) (college that tested students for HIV after telling them blood test was for rubella only was held liable for intrusion).

Colorado's stolen property statute, C.R.S. § 18-4-405, allows the owner of stolen property to obtain triple damages as well as attorney fees when bringing an action to recover the property. *Itin v. Ungar*, 17 P.3d 129 (Colo. 2000). Additionally, an employer may deduct from an employee's final paycheck the value of any of the employer's property that has not been returned to the employer. C.R.S. § 8-4-101(c).

An employer may establish and post policies that reduce employees' privacy expectations. This can be done by posting signs to remind employees that personal property is subject to search; that surveillance measures are in place on a regular basis; or by including in the personnel policy that personal property kept in an employer-provided space, such as a locker, is subject to search at any time. An employer may require all employees to sign a waiver that notifies employees that lockers or other employer-provided spaces are subject to random and unannounced searches and that failure to cooperate or consent to a random search may be grounds for immediate discipline or termination. Employer actions may be further restricted by the Employee Polygraph Protection Act, discussed in Section 3.25. The employer also risks the potential commission of the tort of invasion of privacy for intentional, unreasonably intrusive actions that would be highly offensive to an ordinary person and would foreseeably result in extreme mental anguish, humiliation or mental suffering.

> ***TIP:*** An employer must conduct searches of all employees to avoid claims of discrimination on the basis of race, color, religion, national origin, age, sex or disability. Employers may not violate constitutional rights or commit a tort (assault, battery, defamation) by subjecting employees to unannounced body or strip searches or using offensive language or physical actions when conducting a search. Consent may be a defense to an invasion of privacy claim as long as the consent is voluntary and not coerced. *People v. Reddersen,* 992 P.2d 1176 (Colo. 2000).

RESOURCES: *Small Business Searches,* Business Week Online, http://businessweek.findlaw.com/employmentbook/HFCHP5_f.html.

American Civil Liberties Union Briefing Paper #12, *"The Rights of Employees,"* http://www.lectlaw.com/files/emp08.htm.

Wetanson, B., *"Big Brother" in the Workplace,* WorkingWorld.com; http://www.workingworld.com/magazine/viewarticle.asp?articleno=69.

Rich, L., *Right to Privacy in the Workplace in the Information Age,"* http://publaw.com/privacy.html.

Electronic Communication Privacy Act, 19 U.S.C. §§ 2510 through 2520 and §§ 2701 through 2711.

CHAPTER 4: FUNDRAISING AND CHARITABLE SOLICITATION

4.01

LEGAL SUBJECT: Colorado Charitable Solicitations Act/Colorado Registration

STATEMENT OF ISSUE: This act is designed to reduce fraud upon the public by individuals or entities in the soliciting of charitable contributions; increase the confidence of contributors; and help the public to make informed choices about the charities they choose to support.

CONCERNS/RISKS/ EXPOSURE: Effective May 9, 2002, the law requires charities, paid solicitors, and professional fundraising consultants to register and provide basic financial information to the State of Colorado. Registration with the Colorado Secretary of State is accomplished online at http://www.sos.state.co.us/. Charitable organizations must file: (i) a Registration Statement; (ii) an annual financial report or an electronic copy of federal Form 990; and (iii) an Annual Registration Renewal. If the charity has contracted with an external paid solicitor, it must also file a Solicitation Notice and a Solicitation Campaign Notice Registration. The Charities Registration Program is an Internet-only system. Paper forms are not accepted. The application fee for charities is \$10.00, for paid solicitors and for professional fundraising consultants, \$175.00. Fee information for amendments and renewals is provided on the Colorado Secretary of State website.

Organizations that are exempt from the filing requirements are: (1) religious organizations that are exempt from filing a Form 990; (2) political parties, candidates for federal or state office, or Political Action Committees (PACs) that are already required to file financial information with federal or state election committees; and (3) charities that do not receive more than $25,000 in gross revenue per year (excluding government grants or contributions from other § 501(c)(3) organizations), or do not receive contributions from more than ten people in a fiscal year.

The law pertains to solicitations made in the State of Colorado. Accordingly, out-of-state charities, paid solicitors, and professional fundraising consultants who are not based in Colorado must also comply with all applicable registration requirements. Violations of the statute may constitute charitable fraud, with charges ranging from a misdemeanor to a felony, and deceptive trade practices under the Colorado Consumer Protection Act, subjecting the violator(s) to civil remedies, or criminal penalties, or both.

> ***TIP:*** Each chapter, branch, or affiliate of a charitable organization that is required to register must file a separate registration statement. In the alternative, they may report the necessary information to their parent charitable organization that can then file a consolidated registration statement.

RESOURCES: Colorado Charitable Solicitations Act, C.R.S. §§ 6-16-101 through 6-16-113.

Colorado Consumer Protection Act, C.R.S. §§ 6-1-101 through 6-1-511.

Secretary of State, Licensing Section, 1560 Broadway, Suite 200, Denver, CO 80202; (303) 894-2680; online at http://www.sos.state.co.us/.

Colorado Requirements and Laws For Charitable Solicitations, IKNOW: Interactive Knowledge for Nonprofit Organizations Worldwide; http://www.iknow.org.

4.02

LEGAL SUBJECT: Out-of-State Registration Requirements

STATEMENT OF ISSUE: Solicitations, however made, in states other than Colorado are subject to out-of-state registration requirements.

CONCERNS/RISKS/ EXPOSURE: The need to register in the approximately 40 states that require registration prior to charitable solicitation is not only time consuming but, in filing fees alone, can become very costly. In an attempt to streamline the process, a number of groups and nonprofit leaders, including the National Association of State Charities Officials (NASCO) and the National Association of Attorneys General (NAAG) developed a Unified Registration Statement (URS) for Charitable Organizations. The form is now accepted by over 30 states in lieu of their own state registration form. This standardized registration form is useful for organizations that solicit funds in multiple states. Multi-state registration is much more complex when a charitable organization partners with a paid solicitation service or professional fundraiser to conduct an interstate campaign. In these circumstances, the advice of experienced legal counsel is strongly recommended.

> ***TIP:*** Registration using the URS does not necessarily satisfy any given state's annual financial reporting requirements. The secretary of state or office of the attorney general of each state can assist an organization with specific reporting requirements.

RESOURCES: For information regarding the Unified Registration Statement, see: http://www.multistatefiling.org/.

Current Controversies: *Out of State Solicitation;* an on-line compendium of federal and state regulations for U.S. Nonprofit Organizations; http://www.muridae.com/nporegulation/foreign_solicitation.html.

National Association of Secretaries of State; http://www.nass.org/sos/sos.html.

State Attorneys General, National Fraud Information Center; http://www.fraud.org/welcome.htm.

Colorado Secretary of State; http://www.sos.state.co.us/.

4.03

LEGAL SUBJECT: Online Charitable Solicitation/The Charleston Principles

STATEMENT OF ISSUE: Nonprofits' online fundraising activities may constitute "foreign" solicitation, subjecting the organization to the solicitation registration requirements, regulations and statutes of all 50 states.

CONCERNS/RISKS/ EXPOSURE: The Internet has allowed nonprofits to launch e-mail solicitation campaigns without incurring printing or postage costs and with little investment of human capital. Approximately 40 states and several cities regulate charitable solicitations. Most require the submission of fees, some ongoing, and paperwork for the privilege of soliciting residents of the state or municipality. These costs are added to those of the campaign itself. In the current absence of a federal charitable solicitation law, if a nonprofit chooses online solicitation, it must register as a charitable organization in each of the 50 states. However, Internet solicitations are so new that it is not clear whether the registration requirements for doing business in a particular state apply equally when the only activity carried on by the charitable organization is solicitation through a website. It is fairly certain that a charity that uses an interactive website to accept online donations should register in every state. Three federal court cases decided as of this writing have upheld a state's right to require registration of the charity in order to conduct interstate solicitations.

In 1999, the attendees of a meeting of the National Association of State Charities Officials (NASCO) in Charleston, South Carolina began a discussion regarding the use of the Internet in charitable solicitations. The result of those discussions is a set of advisory guidelines regarding Internet solicitation known as the Charleston Principles. These principles identify organizations that should register in order to avoid enforcement action when they use the Internet to solicit donations.

> ***TIP:*** The need to register with many states due to Internet solicitation includes not only the solicitation of funds via an organization's own website but also via one of the growing number of commercial "donation" sites such as igive.com or givetocharity.com.

RESOURCES: E. Mercer, *How Can We Use the Internet for Fundraising?* (1998); http://www.nonprofit-info.org/misc/981027em.html.

Tread Cautiously When Fundraising Online, The Nonprofit Center: Helping Organizations build a better New Jersey; http://www.njnonprofits.org/online_fr.html.

What You Need to Know About Colorado's New Charitable Solicitations Law; http://www.canpo.org/charitable_solicitations.cfm.

Charities are Doing the Charleston (In Principle Style); on WebNP: The Internet for Nonprofits (formerly MyNoodle.org); http://webnp.nt5.us/articles2/060402_charleston.htm.

Charleston Principles, click on link on the home page of the National Association of State Charities Officials; http://www.nasconet.org/.

4.04

LEGAL SUBJECT: Telephone Solicitations and Marketing (Do Not Call and Do Not Fax Lists)

STATEMENT OF ISSUE: Even when all appropriate registrations are made, contacting individuals or companies via telephone or fax for either fundraising or marketing has become increasingly controversial in legal and ethical terms, and questionable as a best practice in the context of public relations.

CONCERNS/RISKS/ EXPOSURE: Use of the telephone for fundraising purposes is one of the more controversial methods of charitable solicitation, since paid telemarketers who solicit charitable donations are frequently paid a percentage of the funds raised which, while not illegal, is regarded as an unethical practice by the National Association of Fundraising Executives. Abuses where telephone solicitors charge organizations upwards of 80 to 90 percent of funds raised are increasingly being reported and scrutinized in the media. In addition, the Colorado do-not-call law is touted as the most popular consumer protection measure ever passed by the state legislature and the 10th Circuit Court of Appeals recently upheld the constitutionality of a federal do-not-call list. *Mainstream Marketing Services, Inc. v. FTC,* No. 03-1429, 358 F.3d 1228 (10th Cir. 2004).

In May of 2003, the Federal Trade Commission announced "Operation Phoney Philanthropy." In cooperation with state charities regulators, Operation Phoney Philanthropy targets fraudulent fundraising appeals (often made via telephone) through enforcement and education. Specifically targeted are organizations that create sham nonprofit organizations that purport to benefit a community protection organization such as police or firefighters and organizations that represent that all or substantially all of a donation will go to a charity, when in fact the solicitor is receiving a substantial percentage of each donated dollar.

The Federal Communications Commission (FCC) has recently crafted regulations that govern unsolicited fax solicitations pursuant to amendments to the Telephone Consumer Protection Act of 1991, which would require all organizations, including nonprofits, to obtain written consent from a recipient prior to sending a fax that is commercial in nature. There is no exclusion for faxes to individuals or corporations with whom an organization has a prior established relationship. As of this writing, the effective date of these regulations has been stayed until January 1, 2005.

In October of 2003, the Direct Marketing Association (DMA), a trade association for direct marketers, revised its telemarketing guidelines to include among its other Guidelines for Ethical Business Practice (adherence is required for membership in the DMA) the adoption of a block on cell phone telephone numbers, the use of national and state do-not-call registries, as well as fax guidelines that essentially track the FCC regulations regarding faxes, even though the FCC regulations do not go into effect until January of 2005.

TIP: With the public both wary of and more vocally annoyed by unsolicited telephone calls and other intrusions to their homes, organizations should weigh carefully the potential downside of hiring a telephone solicitor, or randomly faxing information or marketing material. These contacts are essentially SPAM without the Internet and are increasingly viewed with suspicion by a public with fewer charitable dollars to give. In the words of Barbara Shaw, Executive Director of the Colorado Association of Nonprofit Organizations, "[A]ny time there's any kind of questionable activity, then people back off." "Philanthropic pittances: Charitable giving often diluted by paid telemarketers," *The Boulder Daily Camera,* Clint Talbott, August 31, 2003.

RESOURCES: *FTC and States Unite to Fight Fundraising Fraud;* http://www.ftc.gov/opa/2003/05/opp.htm.

The Lure of Contingency Fees; http://webnp.nt5.us/articles2/111902_contingency_fees.htm.

Colorado No-Call List website; http://www.coloradonocall.com/index.cfm.

Colorado Association of Nonprofit Organizations; http://www.canpo.org.

Colorado Springs Chamber Nonprofit Partnership; http://chambernonprofitpartnership.org.

4.05

LEGAL SUBJECT: Acknowledgment of Cash Donations

STATEMENT OF ISSUE: IRS regulations require written acknowledgment of donor gifts above designated amounts. These regulations are designed to prevent donors from deducting more than they contribute to charity.

CONCERNS/RISKS/ EXPOSURE: Written acknowledgment must be provided for gifts of $250 or more. A volunteer who incurs an unreimbursed expenditure of $250 or more in connection with goods or services rendered to the charity is also entitled to a written acknowledgment. The acknowledgment must also include a description of any goods or services provided by the organization as consideration for the contribution, including a good faith estimate of the value of the goods or services. Additionally, the charitable organization must provide a written disclosure statement for each contribution in excess of $75 for which the charity provides goods or services—a "quid pro quo"—gift, unless the goods or services provided are token items of insubstantial value, *e.g.*, key ring, address labels, etc. Failure to provide a written disclosure, or an incomplete disclosure, warrants a $10 penalty for each offense, up to a maximum of $5,000 for each fund raising event or mailing.

> ***TIP:*** It is good practice to acknowledge every donation in writing. *See also* Section 4.07, Non-cash Donations and Fair Market Value.

RESOURCES: 34 C.F.R., Parts 1 and 602, "Deductibility, Substantiation and Disclosure of Certain Charitable Contributions," Bureau of National Affairs; http://www.bna.com.

The Internal Revenue Service; http://www.irs.gov/.

4.06

LEGAL SUBJECT: Restricted Gifts

STATEMENT OF ISSUE: A donor may restrict the manner in which the gift is used by the charitable organization. Can the organization use the funds in a different way?

CONCERNS/RISKS/ EXPOSURE: To be restricted, the donor must execute a writing that conveys the gift (a "gift instrument") and states the restricted purpose(s). Verbal conveyances are insufficient to enforce desired restrictions. Valid gift instruments include a deed, will, grant, agreement, memorandum, or other writing. The document must state that the gift funds may not be entirely spent when received, but rather are subject to the written restrictions of the gift instrument.

> ***TIP:*** In some instances a restriction on a gift can be altered if an organization's circumstances change due to internal or external causes and the funds would better be spent in other ways. There are three possibilities for dealing with such a situation: (1) review the gift instrument accompanying the donation to determine if there was, in fact, a restriction on the funds; (2) if an explicit restriction exists, consider asking the donor for consent (in writing) to remove or alter the restriction; (3) if the donor is unavailable, due to death or incapacity, the organization may file the required pleadings and documents with the appropriate court for judicial release of the restriction. S.P. Englund, *Are Restricted Funds Really Restricted?,* Nonprofit Law, P.C.; http://www.nonprofitlaw.com/quicktipsrfund.shtml.

RESOURCES: Answers to frequently asked questions: "What Risks Are Associated with Nonprofit Fundraising?" by the Alliance for Nonprofit Management; http://www.allianceonline.org/FAQ/risk_management/what_risks_are_associated.faq.

4.07

LEGAL SUBJECT: Non-cash Donations and Fair Market Value

STATEMENT OF ISSUE: IRS rules regarding acknowledgment of donations apply to non-cash items. The donor is responsible for determining the value of the property donated.

CONCERNS/RISKS/ EXPOSURE: Many charitable organizations accept donations of goods or property in addition to cash donations. These may include donation of vehicles (automobiles), clothing, toys, household items, equipment (computers), and items to be sold at silent auctions. The donor is responsible for determining the fair market value of the goods or services donated. If the donor notifies the charity that the anticipated fair market value of the donated property is over $250, the charity must provide a signed, written acknowledgment of donated property. Donations below $250 may be receipted by the charity providing the name of the charity, the date of the donation and a place for the donor to describe the goods or services donated. Because the charity may not know the fair market value of the property donated, it is advisable to provide a receipt for every donation received. IRS publication 561, Determining the Value of Donated Property, may be useful for donors as it sets forth procedures for determining the value of donated property for purposes of taking a tax deduction. Reference to this publication could be made in any solicitation materials distributed by the organization. Generally, the donor may deduct up to the fair market value of the item, or the price the item would sell for according to bluebook value (automobiles), at consignment or thrift store average price, at the appraised cost, at the net value of stock based upon the dates acquired and donated, and so forth. Items valued above $500 require the filing of Form 8283 with the donor's tax return. Items valued at $5,000, or above, including automobiles, require an appraisal, with the exception of publicly traded securities. It is not the responsibility of the donee (charitable organization) to determine value.

> ***TIP:*** Charitable organizations may provide guidance and information regarding how to determine the value of donated property. Providing such information by direct mail (with appropriate registration) can be a useful mechanism for contacting potential donors and "reminding them" of property that they have been meaning to value and donate.

RESOURCES: The Internal Revenue Service; http://www.irs.gov/.

"Noncash Gifts," The Tax Guide; http://taxguide.completetax.com/text/Q08_6210.asp.

4.08

LEGAL SUBJECT: Deductibility of Lottery and Raffle Tickets

STATEMENT OF ISSUE: Purchasing a lottery or raffle ticket does not constitute a charitable contribution and is not tax deductible.

CONCERNS/RISKS/ EXPOSURE: Purchasing a lottery or raffle ticket is merely purchasing a chance to win and is not a charitable contribution. The fair market value of the chance at winning is equal to the price of the ticket purchased. Thus there is no donation and no deduction. Bingo games, lotteries, raffles, and games of chance are regulated by both state and federal laws.

> ***TIP:*** While the price of a lottery ticket is not deductible, much of the proceeds of the Colorado Lottery do go to fund nonprofit organizations such as Great Outdoors Colorado, parks, and recreation providers, and to address health and safety issues in public schools.

Where Do Lottery Proceeds Go?, The Colorado Lottery; http://www.coloradolottery.com/about/proceeds.cfm.

Is the Cost of a Raffle Ticket Deductible?, Internet Nonprofit Center; http://www.nonprofits.org/npofaq/11/06.html.

4.09

LEGAL SUBJECT: Bingo and Raffles

STATEMENT OF ISSUE: Charitable organizations that use gaming activities to raise revenue must comply with Colorado's Bingo and Raffle Law.

CONCERNS/RISKS/ EXPOSURE: The Colorado General Assembly repealed and reenacted the nonprofit gaming law in 1999. The law requires a charitable organization to have been in existence continuously for a period of at least five years (or be a proven successor to an organization that meets this criteria) immediately prior to applying for a bingo-raffle license. A nonprofit organization must pay a licensing fee to the Secretary of State's office to obtain a license to conduct any legal gaming activity. Failure to comply with this and other requirements of Colorado's reenacted law exposes a nonprofit to prosecution for a class two misdemeanor, which is punishable by penalties ranging from 3-12 months, imprisonment or fines of \$250 to \$1,000, or both. C.R.S. §§ 12-9-114 and §§ 18-1-106(1). Law enforcement agencies are responsible for investigation of complaints regarding violations of the gaming activity law and prosecution of violations.

> ***TIP:*** Bingo-raffle volunteers who act in good faith and within the scope of their official function and duty toward a charitable organization are immune from civil actions against them unless the harm caused was due to willful and wanton misconduct, gross negligence, reckless misconduct or flagrant indifference to the rights of others.

RESOURCES: Colorado Bingo and Raffles Law, C.R.S. §§ 12-9-101 through 12-9-114.

Ginny's Kids International, Inc. v. Office of Secretary of State, 29 P.3d 333 (Colo. App. 2000); this case discusses requirements for eligibility to obtain a license as a successor organization.

Colorado Secretary of State (Licensing), Bingo & Raffles; http://www.sos.state.co.us/pubs/bingo_raffles/bingo.htm.

CHAPTER 5: RISK MANAGEMENT ISSUES

5.01

LEGAL SUBJECT: Risk Management Generally

STATEMENT OF ISSUE: Nonprofit organizations practice good risk management to stay out of trouble rather than to get out of trouble.

CONCERNS/RISKS/ EXPOSURE: Risk is an uncertainty about an event that may threaten the nonprofit organization's ability to accomplish its mission. Knowledge and practice of good risk management activities conserves the assets and resources of a nonprofit and protects people from harm. Such practices usually combine business and legal issues. Important questions to ask include:

- What could go wrong?
- What should we do to prevent harm?
- How do we pay for both prevention and the repercussions of something going wrong?
- What risk and safety issues are unique to our organization, and how do we plan for these issues?

While it is impossible to eliminate all risks, prevention of many risks is feasible with a quality risk management plan. Risk management is about more than just purchasing insurance coverage sufficient to pay a claim. Risk management involves proper employment practices; up-to-date employee policies, sufficient training of volunteers including board members;

careful drafting and revision of bylaws; up-to-date operational policies, including conflicts; sound financial management, development of and adherence to appropriate safety protocols; consistent application of all policies and procedures; and compliance with state and federal solicitation and other laws regulating commerce. Another essential element of developing a plan is the conducting of a legal audit. Insurance policies should be evaluated annually to ensure appropriate types of coverage, as well as sufficient coverage amounts. *See* Section 5.04, Checklist for Legal Audit.

> ***TIP:*** Risk management is about more than just purchasing insurance coverage sufficient to pay a claim. While it is important to have adequate insurance in place, a good risk management system will work against the likelihood of ever having to use an insurance policy.

RESOURCES: *Advice,* Nonprofit Risk Management Center; http://nonprofitrisk.org.

Liability, Internet Nonprofit Center; http://www.nonprofits.org/.

Risk Management FAQ's, Alliance for Nonprofit Management; http://www.allianceonline.org/FAQ/risk_management.

Program Risk Management Series, Nonprofit Risk Management Center Publications; http://nonprofitrisk.org/pubs/pubs.htm.

The Top 5 Reasons Associations Get Sued, nonprofitlaw.com; http://www.nonprofitlaw.com/top5.shtml.

Nonprofit Quicktips℠, nonprofitlaw.com; http://www.nonprofitlaw.com/qtindex.shtml.

5.02

LEGAL SUBJECT: Background Checks of Employees and Volunteers

STATEMENT OF ISSUE: Hiring an employee who works with children or other vulnerable groups without conducting a background check increases an organization's risks of criminal sanctions, as well as civil liability.

CONCERNS/RISKS/ EXPOSURE: Pre-employment background checks of potential employees' and volunteers' criminal records, driving records, and other relevant information may reduce liability risks. Organizations that need to conduct frequent background checks, *e.g.*, child care centers, may wish to purchase screening or background check software or subscribe to a service that conducts checks for them. (*See* Chapter 3, Employment, and Chapter 8, Volunteer Management.) Software should be endorsed by reputable organizations such as the National Association of Independent Private Investigators, police organizations, or the Federal Bureau of Investigation.

> ***TIP:*** Unless otherwise required by law, background checks should be used as a screening process once an employee or volunteer has been selected, not as a selection criterion. Take care that a potential employee does not quit any current employment prior to the successful completion of a background check.

RESOURCES: Background Check Guide software (Net Detective); information and instant download available, http://www.background-check-guide.com/.

5.03

LEGAL SUBJECT: Liability Trends for Nonprofits

STATEMENT OF ISSUE: Nonprofit organizations experience many of the same liabilities as for-profit corporations with similar trends in claims.

CONCERNS/RISKS/ EXPOSURE: The single greatest source of liability faced by nonprofits and for-profits alike is employment issues. The Equal Employment Opportunity Commission (EEOC) receives between 80,000 and 85,000 employment claims a year. In 2003, the EEOC statistics show the breakdown on individual charges filed was: race discrimination (35.1%); sexual harassment (30.0%); age (23.5%); and disability (18.9%). (Total exceeds 100 percent because a single complaint may claim multiple types of discrimination.) Some 25 percent of these EEOC claims alleged retaliation in addition to discrimination. The Nonprofit Insurance Alliance of California (NIAC) reports that wrongful termination suits constitute 60 percent of all suits filed against nonprofit boards. The Nonprofit Risk Management Center classifies employment claims as among the most difficult to resolve due to the emotional attachment of most plaintiffs to their jobs and their need to work.

Other sources of liability include donors who sue nonprofits over how the organizations use their funds. In the shadow of nonprofit fraud, there is also the growing risk of Intermediate Sanctions. *See* Section 2.10, Excess Benefit Transactions and Intermediate Sanctions. In addition, great potential for liability risk is associated with the growth of the Internet and its use among nonprofit organizations. Websites expose nonprofits to defamation, copyright and trademark infringement, and invasion of privacy actions. Some of the risks associated with Internet use have not yet been identified.

Although nonprofits have become more savvy about insurance protection, they need to be more aware of and demand coverage for such generally uninsured areas as punitive damages, employment practices, defense expenses that go beyond policy limits, claims by independent contractors and leased employees, claims against the nonprofit for acts or omissions committed by independent contractors or other agents, breach of fiduciary duties, and taxes on "excess benefits" to highly compensated employees. Increased jury verdicts necessitate the need to obtain umbrella or excess coverage. In addition, new court precedent suggests that board members and corporate officers may be held personally liable for certain types of claims. Fraud, theft and misappropriation of funds or property also jeopardize a nonprofit's ability to deliver its mission. Media coverage of such crimes may negatively affect donor gifts and the organization's goodwill.

> ***TIP:*** Nonprofit organizations, as well as for-profits, face exposure to liability for vehicular accidents caused by their employees; and with Colorado's transition from Personal Injury Protection to Tort Liability, there will be an increase in lawsuits involving motor vehicle accidents.

RESOURCES: *Liability Basics for Nonprofit Organizations,* Nonprofit Risk Management Center; http://www.eriskcenter.org/knowledge/normac/liability.html.

Risk Management FAQs, Nonprofit Risk Management Center; http://www.allianceonline.org/FAQ/risk_management.

Protecting Highly Compensated Employees from the Tax on "Excess Benefits," nonprofitlaw.com; http://www.nonprofitlaw.com/quicktipex.shtml.

5.04

LEGAL SUBJECT: Checklist for Legal Audit

STATEMENT OF ISSUE: An essential element of developing a plan for risk management is the Legal Audit.

CONCERNS/RISKS/ EXPOSURE: A nonprofit legal audit should cover everything that a for-profit legal audit would cover, plus issues such as IRS information returns, intermediate sanctions, private inurement, unrelated business income tax and volunteer management. General areas of an audit include: organizational and governance practices; human resources (employment and volunteer policies and manuals, job descriptions, compliance with state and federal laws, etc.); environmental compliance (including OSHA); consumer protection laws; financial practices; intellectual property (website disclaimer, copyright and trademark protection and compliance); contract review (facility and equipment, debt instruments, service providers); membership practices; lobbying activities; fundraising practices (restricted gifts, trust documents, solicitation practices); and insurance issues and coverage (general liability coverage, bonding, D&O policies, unemployment; workers' compensation; event coverage; and umbrella/excess insurance coverage). A thorough review of all of these operational activities gives a current status and allows the organization's directors and managers to identify areas that need attention in order to bolster the risk management plan.

> ***TIP:*** Legislation and court decisions continually affect existing law. Therefore, audits should be conducted with regularity to ensure legal compliance. Website information must be monitored constantly due to ease of access by nonpermitted persons. Employment policies should be reviewed annually to ensure compliance with court precedent and ever-changing state and federal law.

RESOURCES: C. McNamara, Ed., *Checklist for An Assessment of Legal Activities in U.S. Nonprofit Organizations,* Free Management Library; http://www.managementhelp.org/.

Tips for Nonprofit Accountability, PNN Online; http://www.pnnonline.org/article.php?sid=734.

"The Nonprofit Corporation's Checklist," in GUIDEBOOK FOR DIRECTORS OF NONPROFIT CORPORATIONS, (1993), American Bar Association: Chicago, IL, 750 North Lake Shore Dr. Chicago, IL 60611; (800) 285-2221.

The Association Legal At-Risk Test, nonprofitlaw.com; http://www.nonprofitlaw.com/At-risk.shtml.

5.05

LEGAL SUBJECT: Directors' and Officers' Insurance

STATEMENT OF ISSUE: Directors and officers of nonprofit corporations may be personally liable for intentional actions taken, which someone else believes are wrong. This exposure may be a disincentive to serve in a volunteer capacity.

CONCERNS/RISKS/ EXPOSURE: Board members are exposed to two types of risk: (1) liability to third parties for injury or property damage arising from acts or omissions in the performance of their duties on behalf of the organization; and (2) liability to the organization itself for failure to fulfill the required fiduciary duties. Employment related claims constitute a majority of the Directors' and Officers' (D&O) claims filed against nonprofits. D&O insurance coverage is essential to protect board members from legal claims.

Generally, D&O insurance covers "wrongful acts" and claims, *e.g.*, alleged acts, errors and omissions, misleading statements, neglect and breach of duty, but may contain significant exclusions from coverage. The policy may be an "occurrence" policy, which means that any claim filed during the time the policy is in effect will be covered. Or, it may be a "claims-made" policy, which requires that the incident giving rise to the claim occurred during the policy coverage period. It is important to note what D&O insurance does not cover, including: fines and penalties imposed by law, libel and slander, dishonesty, failure to maintain or procure insurance, bodily injury and property damage claims, pollution claims, claims for intentional misconduct and punitive damages, and suits by one board member against another. The larger the organization and the wealthier the board members, the more likely they are to be sued, so the greater the need for D&O coverage. Some policies may be expanded to include other volunteers in addition to board members. Because D&O coverage can be fairly expensive, small organizations may wish to inquire about limited coverage or larger deductibles. A "Duty to Defend" policy may be added to define the insurer's obligation to pay for defense costs as they are incurred rather than reimbursing costs after resolution.

> ***TIP:*** It is always wise to have a proposed policy reviewed by an insurance professional other than the one selling the policy.

RESOURCES: *Directors & Officers: Key Facts About Insurance & Legal Liability,* Nonprofits' Insurance Alliance of California; http://www.niac.org/.

"Some Legal Considerations for Board Members" and "Insurance Against Liability" articles available at Management Assistance Program for Nonprofits; http://www.mapfornonprofits.org/.

Directors Often Fear Risks of Personal Liability, Ready Reference #30, Don Kramer's Nonprofit Issues, Inc.; http://www.nonprofitissues.com/.

Twelve D&O Buying Tips, Alliance for Nonprofit Management; http://www.allianceonline.org/.

5.06

LEGAL SUBJECT: Bonding of Employees

STATEMENT OF ISSUE: Bonding reduces the risk of liability for employees who are entrusted with assets of the organization.

CONCERNS/RISKS/ EXPOSURE: A surety bond may be obtained from an insurance provider to protect the organization against losses incurred due to theft, embezzlement, misappropriation, or other actions that threaten the financial stability and assets of the organization. A surety bond indemnifies the organization and covers actual losses. Colorado law addresses the execution of surety bonds by insurers. The employer may refuse to hire an individual who cannot be bonded due to a prior conviction, but the job description should state that the ability to obtain bonding insurance is a requirement of the position. If the employer wishes to hire an employee with a prior conviction record who is otherwise qualified for the job, but the insurer will not provide a bond, the employee may contact the Job Service Office, a division of the U.S. Employment Service, to apply for a bond through a federally sponsored program for rehabilitated individuals.

> ***TIP:*** Though unpaid, volunteers are staff and should be treated essentially as your employees are treated (*see* Chapter 8, Volunteers and Volunteer Management). Accordingly, an organization should consider bonding any volunteers who have access to money or are otherwise involved in the financial management of the organization. "Manage Volunteers Professionally" Volunteer Center of Sonoma County, Santa Rosa California; http://www.nationalscripcenter.org/pdf/ad_summer_03_28-29.pdf.

RESOURCES: Job Seeker and Employer Services, listed in the blue pages section under State government, lists job services offices by county or region of the state.

Bonds Executed by Qualified Surety Companies, C.R.S. §§ 10-4-301 through 10-4-305.

Nonprofit Security, Nonprofitexpert.com; http://www.nonprofitexpert.com/.

Insurance Questions for Nonprofits, Internet Nonprofit Center; http://www.nonprofits.org/.

5.07

LEGAL SUBJECT: Event Insurance: Temporary and for Small Organizations with a Single Event

STATEMENT OF ISSUE: Organizations that conduct only a single fundraising event should obtain single-event coverage for liability that may arise during the course of the event.

CONCERNS/RISKS/ EXPOSURE: General liability insurance can be costly for a small nonprofit that has only one or two paid employees and relies on volunteers to conduct a single, large fundraising event on an annual basis. Temporary insurance for a single event may be purchased and is a wise investment. Many municipalities require proof of insurance, or event insurance, before issuing events permits for such things as parades; street-closure permits; park permits; facility use; and the like.

> ***TIP:*** It is important to check with liability carriers to determine if coverage extends to events where liquor is served. Many policies exclude coverage for such events.

RESOURCES: Contact the Colorado Association of Nonprofit Organizations (CANPO) for resources and vendors that cover single events. http://www.canpo.org/.

Sound Advice for Functions and Events, Nonprofit Insurance Alliance of California;
http://www.niac.org/NIAC2/ResourceCenter/DownloadableFiles/EventsBook1.pdf
or order booklet with forms for $1.00 from NIAC, (831) 459-0980.

5.08

LEGAL SUBJECT: Training for Loss Prevention

STATEMENT OF ISSUE: The appropriate training of all constituent members of a nonprofit organization including board members, management, staff, volunteers, and clients is essential to good risk management.

CONCERNS/RISKS/ EXPOSURE: Poorly trained individuals put a nonprofit organization at legal risk. Board members need to be aware of their fiduciary duties and other obligations to the nonprofit organization (*see* Section 1.01, The Fiduciary Duties: Care, Loyalty, and Obedience, and Section 1.02, Risk Management Issues for Directors). Employees, be they management or staff, must understand the myriad of employment and other operational issues that pertain to them. Volunteers need to be trained to understand and respect their rights and responsibilities as representatives of the organization. Clients too, need to be "trained" in that they must be clearly apprised of the services they will receive so that their expectations comport with the nature of the service provided by the nonprofit.

Inconsistent, poor, or no training can cause problems well beyond management inefficiencies and poor morale. Physical harm to employees, volunteers or clients that occurs when training can be shown to have prevented the harm, can result in tort claims such as negligent supervision and negligent training. Depending on the severity of the negligence, an organization's insurer may decline coverage. Organizations can also be held liable if an individual appears to be acting as an agent of the organization when some malfeasance or harm occurs.

> ***TIP:*** Training and, in particular, the documentation that training has occurred, can provide a partial defense to unemployment and litigation claims. Accordingly, appropriate records, signed by the trainee, should be maintained to document that training has occurred.

RESOURCES: *Building Effective Nonprofit Boards,* Boardsource; http://www.ncnb.org/.

Free Complete Toolkit for Boards, Management Assistance Program for Nonprofits; http://www.mapnp.org/library/boards/boards.htm.

Links to Nonprofit Resources, The Foundation Center; http://fdncenter.org/research/npr_links/index.html.

CHAPTER 6: TORTS, LIABILITY, AND PROTECTION

6.01

LEGAL SUBJECT: Tort Liability Generally

STATEMENT OF ISSUE: Tort actions involving nonprofits, their directors, officers, volunteers, and staff expose the organization and its directors and managers to fines, damages, and even criminal penalties.

CONCERNS/RISKS/ EXPOSURE: A "tort" is a negligent or intentional act that results in an injury to another person for which he or she can seek damages. It is a personal wrong against an individual or entity, as opposed to a criminal matter, which is a wrong committed against the maintenance of a safe and peaceful society, *e.g.*, robbery or murder. In a tort action based on negligence, the person or entity claiming the injury (*i.e.*, the plaintiff) must show that the defendant owed a legal duty of care to the plaintiff, the defendant breached that duty, the plaintiff suffered injury, and the defendant's breach caused the plaintiff's injury. *Ryder v. Mitchell*, 54 P.3d 885 (Colo. 2002).

In a *strict liability* action, the law imposes liability regardless of whether negligence has occurred. For example, strict liability is applied when an organization fails to comply with statutes mandating reporting of suspected child abuse or if a worker is injured in the performance of work duties (*e.g.*, workers' compensation), or in certain cases when there is an inherently unsafe condition on the organization's premises. *Vicarious liability* holds the employer responsible for the actions of its employees, directors, or volunteers in the commission of a tort. Thus, the organization may be liable to an injured party based on actions of its own employees, directors, or volunteers, even if the organization itself did nothing negligent. Torts may arise from either intentional or unintentional conduct. Sometimes a tort results from the *lack* of action or failure to carry out a duty. *See also* Section 1.01, The Fiduciary Duties: Care, Loyalty and Obedience; Chapter 5, Risk Management Issues; and Chapter 7, Litigation.

> ***TIP:*** Different types of torts may carry different statutes of limitations, *i.e.*, the maximum amount of time permitted between the injury and filing a lawsuit to recover damages for the injury. C.R.S. §§ 13-80-102 and 13-80-103. Precisely when the accident occurred may not always be clear, and is defined at C.R.S. § 13-80-108. In most cases, the statute of limitations "begins to run" when the injured person discovered or reasonably should have discovered the injury and its cause.

RESOURCES: *Volunteer Legal Handbook Section II (B), Legal Short Course Tort Liability;* http://www.ptialaska.net/~jdewitt/vlh/Law/VLHTort Liability.html.

Liability Basics for Nonprofit Organizations, Risk Management Resource Center; http://www.eriskcenter.org/knowledge/normac/liability.html.

C.R.S. §§ 13-80-102 and 103.

6.02

LEGAL SUBJECT: Endorsements and Licensing Liabilities

STATEMENT OF ISSUE: Nonprofit organizations, especially associations that endorse products or services, or "rent" their membership lists to vendors for the promotion and sale of vendor products, may expose the organization to both tax and tort liability.

CONCERNS/RISKS/ EXPOSURE: Endorsements have become a popular means of generating revenue from both members and non-members and may be an important source of marketing for the organization. If a purchaser suffers either a loss or injury caused by the third-party product or service endorsed by the organization, both the vendor and the organization may be named as defendants in a civil action for damages. Although this type of liability is not common, if the organization was significantly involved in the control, assumed responsibility, or was negligent by association, it may be liable for somc portion of the injured party's damages. Negligence by association simply means that the nonprofit that endorses the product may be named as a defendant in a lawsuit against the vendor or maker of the product due to the fact that the nonprofit promoted and associated itself with a defective or harmful product. The negligence of the vendor or maker is imputed to the nonprofit as well.

Ways to minimize this risk include: (1) exercise diligence in selecting vendors and agreeing to endorsements; (2) make use of disclaimers to explain the organization's limited role with respect to endorsed products or services; (3) maintain liability insurance sufficient to cover defense costs and some level of damages; (4) refrain from control of or involvement in the endorsed product or service; and (5) always insist on a written contract with the vendor and include language that limits the liability of the organization. The Federal Trade Commission Act (FTCA) prohibits false or misleading advertising and its regulations contain guidelines that must be followed when associations endorse products. The rules require that an association's endorsement "be reached by a process sufficient to ensure that [it] fairly reflects the collective judgment of the organization." Additionally, the FTCA establishes standards for what constitutes unfair competition and for investigating business activities that might lead to monopolization of a market or restraint of trade. Thus, nonprofit associations that endorse or license products or services may also face charges of antitrust violations under federal law. Providing misleading information to the public, or to a person intended to receive or benefit from your service, may also result in statutory penalties under Colorado's Consumer Protection Act. C.R.S. § 6-1-105. *See* Section 2.11, Unrelated Business Income Tax (UBIT), Section 2.12, Sponsorship Payments and UBIT; and Section 6.06, Antitrust and Unfair Trade Practices.

> ***TIP:*** To avoid liability under the FTCA, an endorsement must be supportable by the association, preferably through a study or analysis of identical products, the application of objective standards to those products, and a conclusion as to why the endorsement of a particular product makes the most business sense (to both the association and its members). Furthermore, depending upon the circumstances, there may be a continuing obligation to verify that the endorsed product is still living up to the claims made about it. 15 U.S.C. §§ 41 through 59 and C.R.S. § 6-1-105.

RESOURCES: J.S. Tennebaum, *Endorsements & Licensing,* Florida Society of Association Executives; http://www.fsae.org/index.cfm?pageID=65.

Federal Trade Commission Act, 15 U.S.C. §§ 41 through 59.

6.03

LEGAL SUBJECT: Liability for Donated Food

STATEMENT OF ISSUE: Charitable organizations that distribute donated food may risk liability for harm caused by the food.

CONCERNS/RISKS/ EXPOSURE: Donation of food for distribution to those in need is a charitable action that is to be encouraged. The Bill Emerson Good Samaritan Food Donation Act promotes food recovery by limiting the liability of donors except in instances of gross negligence or intentional misconduct. It protects charitable organizations from some types of liability for food collected and distributed to others. The Act was named in honor of the late Congressman who was a champion of efforts to expand food donations to the poor and to protect those who make donations. Nonprofit organizations are not subject to civil or criminal liability arising from the nature, age, packaging or condition of apparently wholesome food, or an apparently fit grocery product that the organization received in good faith from a person or gleaner for ultimate distribution to needy individuals. The Act does not apply to an injury or death of an ultimate user or recipient of the food or grocery product that results from an act or omission of the person, gleaner, or nonprofit organization, as applicable, where such act or omission constitutes gross negligence or intentional misconduct.

Colorado statutes also protect nonprofits from civil and criminal liability for transferring gleaned or donated foods to another nonprofit, as long as there is no evidence of willful, wanton or reckless actions that result in injury to the recipients of the food. The statute *does not* protect a nonprofit from liability for the provision of donated food that results in injury or death of an ultimate consumer or recipient that results from an act of omission and that constitutes gross negligence or intentional misconduct.

> ***TIP:*** Neither the Good Samaritan Act nor the Colorado statute supersede any applicable state or local health regulations; therefore, nonprofits need to be aware of Colorado Department of Public Health and Environment regulations and any municipal health code requirements covering food distribution. C.R.S. § 13-21-113(4).

RESOURCES: Bill Emerson Good Samaritan Food Donation Act, 42 U.S.C. § 1791; http://www4.law.cornell.edu/uscode/42/1791.html.

C.R.S. § 13-21-113.

6.04

LEGAL SUBJECT: Libel, Slander, and Defamation of Character

STATEMENT OF ISSUE: Successful actions for defamation of character expose a nonprofit organization to substantial attorney fees and damages as well as criminal penalties.

CONCERNS/RISKS/ EXPOSURE: Defamation is the publication of untrue statements about a living person or persons or an organization that injures the victim's character or reputation. Slander is defamation by spoken word, radio or television. Libel is defamation by published written word or picture. Although truth is generally considered a defense, there is often a fine distinction between fact and opinion. Even if one states the truth, if damage can be proven, the speaker may not be able to sustain a successful defense. The motive must not be improper, *i.e.*, it must not be malicious. The successful defense of a defamation suit can still cost many thousands of dollars in attorney fees, and the claim will likely be excluded from the organization's insurance coverage. A prevailing plaintiff may be entitled to punitive damages and compensatory damages. Nonprofit organizations should be particularly vigilant about information provided in media interviews, postings on websites and newsletter articles.

> ***TIP:*** Risk may be significantly minimized if communications that are critical of individuals or organizations are clearly identified and presented as opinions, not facts. *New York Times Co. v. Sullivan,* 376 U.S. 254 (1964). Publication of true information involving protected health information of a client, while not defamatory, may violate the new privacy regulations under the Health Insurance Portability and Accountability Act (HIPAA), which may include significant penalties.

RESOURCES: B.W. Sanford, SYNOPSIS OF THE LAW OF LIBEL AND THE RIGHT OF PRIVACY, New York; Scripps-Howard Newspapers (1977). Contains a checklist of words to avoid and people to be avoided.

Libel, Slander and Defamation of Character Quick Tips; http://www.dancingwithlawyers.com/freeinfo/libel.shtml.

G. Barry, *Libel, Slander, Defamation Online: What's the Difference?* http://www.spawn.org/marketing/slander.htm.

6.05

LEGAL SUBJECT: Board Member and Volunteer Immunity When Assisting Youth Organizations

STATEMENT OF ISSUE: Colorado protects board members and volunteers of direct service from liability under certain circumstances.

CONCERNS/RISKS/ EXPOSURE: To encourage voluntary assistance to nonprofit organizations serving youth, Colorado law protects board members and volunteers from liability for "actions taken or omissions made in the performance of ... duties ... except for willful and wanton acts." C.R.S. § 13-21-116(2)(b)(I). This statute also states that one who volunteers to serve a nonprofit organization for young people and acts in good faith, "shall not be deemed to have assumed a duty of care where none otherwise existed" when performing the voluntary service or an act of assistance for the benefit of another person or to protect the person's health or safety. C.R.S. § 13-21-116(2)(a). This immunity extends only to volunteers who are specifically assisting with youth programs and sporting activities and does not apply to claims by third parties. *Jones v. Westernaires, Inc.* 876 P.2d 50 (Colo. App. 1993). *See also* Section 1.01, The Fiduciary Duties: Care, Loyalty, and Obedience.

> ***TIP:*** Volunteer immunity from liability has been held not to apply if the nonprofit organization serving youth receives compensation for its services. *Gilmore v. Concerned Parents of Pueblo, Colorado* 28 P.3d 963 (Colo. App. 2000).

RESOURCES: C.R.S. § 13-21-116.

6.06

LEGAL SUBJECT: Antitrust and Unfair Trade Practices

STATEMENT OF ISSUE: State and federal laws prohibit a variety of trade practices and enforce the provisions through civil as well as criminal penalties.

CONCERNS/RISKS/ EXPOSURE: Competition in the marketplace is valued and protected under two Colorado laws—the Colorado Antitrust Act of 1992 and the Unfair Trade Practices Act, both of which are enforced by the attorney general's office. Violations may bring civil penalties in the form of injunctions, fines and actual or treble damages. Additionally, a court may, in its discretion, award the prevailing party its expert fees, costs of the action and reasonable attorney fees. Health care coverage cooperatives have limited exemptions from requirements of the Colorado Antitrust Act. Under Colorado's Unfair Trade Practices Act, which only provides for civil penalties, violations may include price fixing, false advertising, or sales below cost. This Act also extends prosecution to directors, officers, or agents, who assist, either directly or indirectly, in the violation, and holds them personally responsible. C.R.S. § 6-2-104.

In addition to the state laws, nonprofits may face prosecution for federal antitrust violations and unfair trade practices. The Federal Trade Commission Act and Sherman Antitrust Act have been interpreted to apply to nonprofits as well as for-profit businesses. Nonprofit associations, for example, are, by their very nature, entities with common business interests and are especially likely to come under the scrutiny of antitrust laws. Associations may be subject to antitrust liability if: (1) a product or service endorsed by the association is construed as a boycott or concerted refusal to deal with a competing vendor or vendors; or (2) the association unreasonably denies nonmembers access to the endorsed product or service. In determining the reasonableness of the eligibility requirements, a court would look at the market power of the association and the intent and effect of the exclusion.

General federal antitrust actions may include concerted action, standard setting, certification, and other anti-competitive activities. Violation of the Sherman Act is a felony and carries a penalty of up to $350,000 for an individual and up to $10,000,000 for corporations. The Federal Trade Commission (FTC) may bring a civil action against an alleged violator and may issue a cease and desist order. If the violator does not comply with the order, the FTC may grant relief that includes, but is not limited to, rescission or reformation of contracts, the refund of money or return of property, the payment of damages, and public notification respecting the rule violation or the unfair or deceptive act or practice, as the case may be. The act does not, however, authorize the imposition of any exemplary or punitive damages. *See also* Section 9.05, Antitrust Violations.

> ***TIP:*** Nonprofit associations whose activities provide substantial financial benefits for their members need to be careful about potential antitrust violations. The U.S. Supreme Court clarified the circumstances under which an abbreviated competitive effects test would be applied to determine anticompetitive activity. *California Dental Ass'n v. Federal Trade Comm'n,* 526 U.S. 756 (1999) (If anticompetitive effects of given restraints are far from obvious, the rule of reason demands more than an abbreviated analysis of the facts; see also *National Collegiate Athletic Association v. Board of Regents of University of Oklahoma,* 468 U.S. 85 (1984) (An abbreviated, or "quick-look" analysis is appropriate for determining antitrust violations only when an observer with

even a rudimentary understanding of economics could conclude that the arrangements in question have an anticompetitive effect on customers and markets.)

RESOURCES: Colorado Antitrust Act of 1992, C.R.S. §§ 6-4-101 through 121.

Unfair Trade Practices Act, C.R.S. §§ 6-2-101 through 117.

Sherman Antitrust Act, 15 U.S.C. §§ 1 through 7.

Federal Trade Commission Act, 15 U.S.C. §§ 41 through 59.

6.07

LEGAL SUBJECT: Volunteer Immunity Generally

STATEMENT OF ISSUE: Volunteers may be reluctant to offer their services if doing so puts them at risk of tort actions and damages resulting from their activities as volunteers.

CONCERNS/RISKS/ EXPOSURE: It is important to balance the rights of injured persons with the ability of a person to volunteer service to a nonprofit without the fear of personal liability. Colorado's Volunteer Service Act was adopted to protect volunteers performing service for nonprofits. This statute does not protect the nonprofit organization itself from civil liability.

An individual volunteer is immune from civil liability on the basis of any act or omission that results in injury or damage as long as: (1) the volunteer was acting in good faith within the scope of the volunteer's official functions and duties for the nonprofit; and (2) the damage or injury was not caused by the volunteer's willful and wanton conduct. The federal Volunteer Protection Act of 1997 provides similar protection to volunteers, including most nonprofit board members. *See also* Chapter 8, Volunteers and Volunteer Management, Section 8.04, Liability for Volunteers' Actions.

> ***TIP:*** An injured person may, however, bring a civil suit against a volunteer based on a negligent act or omission involving the operation of a motor vehicle during an activity, within the limits of applicable insurance coverage maintained by or on behalf of the volunteer with respect to the negligent operation of a motor vehicle in such circumstances. C.R.S. § 13-21-115.5(4) & (5).

RESOURCES: Volunteer Service Act, C.R.S. § 13-21-115.5.

Volunteer Protection Act of 1997, 42 U.S.C. §§ 14501 through 14505.

6.08

LEGAL SUBJECT: Liability for Actions of Employees and Volunteers

STATEMENT OF ISSUE: Employers may be liable to third parties for the actions or omissions of their employees and volunteers.

CONCERNS/RISKS/ EXPOSURE: An employer may be responsible for torts committed by an employee who is acting within the course and scope of his or her employment. This is known as the doctrine of *respondeat superior,* or literally, "let the master respond." It is sometimes referred to as vicarious liability, as well. The concept is grounded in the historical relationship of masters and their apprentices. It implies a duty on the employer's part to provide adequate training and supervision to the employee, while anticipating that the employee will perform within the scope of the employer's instruction and training, as well as the employee's prescribed duties. An employee is acting within the scope of employment if the employee is engaged in the work that has been assigned by the employer, or if the employee is doing what is necessarily incidental to the work which has been assigned, or which is customary within the business in which the employee is engaged. *Russell v. First American Mortgage Co.,* 565 P.2d 972 (Colo. App. 1977). Nonprofit employers may be similarly liable for the actions or omissions of volunteers serving the organization.

Three requirements must be met in order to impose liability on the employer: (1) there must be an injury caused by the negligence or will of the servant (the employee or volunteer); (2) there must be a master-servant (employer) relationship; and (3) the servant (employee or volunteer) must have been acting within the scope of employment. Thus, an employer that has policies regarding use of the Internet, but fails to monitor use, and fails to discipline those who violate the policy, may be liable for illegal employee actions on the Internet. For example, an employer may be liable for computer crimes committed by an employee during work hours using employer-provided equipment, if the employer knew or should have known of the illegal activity. Furthermore, an employer may be held liable for the actions of a volunteer under certain circumstances, *i.e.*, when a volunteer is acting with the authority of the nonprofit and in doing so causes injury to another. *American Society of Mechanical Engineers, Inc. v. Hydrolevel Corp.*, 456 U.S. 556 (1982) (under rules of agency law, principals are liable when their agents act with apparent authority and commit torts). Commonly, when an employee or volunteer injures another while performing work for the employer, the employer will be sued on the basis of respondeat superior. Additional claims such as negligent entrustment, negligent hiring, and negligent supervision, are generally included. *See also* Section 8.04, Liability for Volunteers' Actions.

> ***TIP:*** When the employer has not taken the care that an ordinarily prudent person would take in selecting the person for the business in hand and properly supervising the person, liability may be incurred. What precautions must be taken depend upon the situation. One can normally assume that a person who offers to perform simple work is competent. If, however, the work is highly complex or is likely to subject third persons to serious risk of great harm, there is a special duty of investigation. *Destefano v. Grabrian,* 763 P.2d 275 (Colo. 1988). Merely checking to see only that an applicant for a driving position has a valid driver's license may not be sufficient to protect the employer. The prudent employer would run a motor vehicle division check on the applicant's driving record and may need to run a criminal background check as well to determine if any driving violations resulted in criminal conviction.

RESOURCES: J. Oshinsky and G. Dias, *Liability of Not for Profit Organizations and Insurance Coverage for Related Liability;* http://www.icnl.org/journal/vol4iss23/oshinsky1.htm.

M. Ishman, *Computer Crimes and the Respondeat Superior Doctrine: Employer Beware!;* http://www.ishmanlaw.com/resources/Respondeat_Superior.pdf.

Russell v. First Am. Mortgage Co., 565 P.2d 972 (Colo. App. 1977).

Destefano v. Grabrian, 763 P.2d 275 (Colo. 1988).

6.09

LEGAL SUBJECT: Liability for Intentional Torts

STATEMENT OF ISSUE: Employers may be liable for intentional injuries to employees and third parties under a variety of negligence theories.

CONCERNS/RISKS/ EXPOSURE: Employers may be liable to employee and third-party victims of intentional torts under a variety of tort theories. The most commonly alleged theories are negligent hiring, negligent supervision, and negligent retention. In each case, there must be a demonstrable duty that the employer owes to its employees, customers, suppliers, and others who come in contact with its employees. A non-employee victim generally must show that the employer breached the duty it owed to the victim and that the employer's breach of that duty was the direct cause of the victim's injury. Workplace violence is becoming increasingly more common. A person injured during an act of workplace violence may allege that an employer is guilty of negligent hiring or retention of the individual who committed the violence. Negligent hiring may mean a poorly conducted background check or no background check at all. An employee intentionally injured by another employee, *e.g.*, rape or other act of violence, has recourse against the employer only under Colorado's workers' compensation laws. *In re Questions Submitted by the United States Court of Appeals for the Tenth Circuit*, 759 P.2d 17 (Colo. 1988). *See also* Section 9.06, Background Checks of Employees and Volunteers.

> ***TIP:*** The Colorado Supreme Court has established that negligent hiring is a theory upon which an injured individual may recover from the employer for damages caused by an employee. *Connes v. Molalla Transportation System, Inc.*, 831 P.2d 1316 (Colo. 1992).

RESOURCES: OSHA, *Guidelines for Preventing Workplace Violence for Health Care and Social Service Workers* (1996); OSHA, *Recommendations for Workplace Violence Prevention Programs in Late-Night Retail Establishments* (1998).

The General Duty Clause, § 5(a)(1) of the OSHA Act, provides: "Each employer shall furnish to each of his employees employment and a place of employment which are free from recognized hazards that are causing or likely to cause death or serious physical harm to his employees." 29 U.S.C. § 654(a)(1).

OSHA, OSHA *Policy Regarding Violent Employee Behavior* (Dec. 10, 1992). *See also* OSHA, *Criminal Violence in the Workplace* (May 13, 1992).

See U.S. Office of Personnel Management, *Dealing with Workplace Violence, a Guide for Agency Planners* (1998).

Taco Bell v. Lannon, 744 P.2d 43 (Colo. 1987) (in negligence action against fast food restaurant for injuries sustained by patron during armed robbery, court determined restaurant had legal duty to take reasonable measures to protect patrons from consequences of criminal acts on part of unknown third persons).

RESOURCES: *Moses v. Diocese of Colorado,* 863 P.2d 310 (Colo. 1993), *cert. denied,* 511 U.S. 1137 (1994) (Episcopal priest was not acting within scope and course of employment while engaged in sexual relations with parishioner; therefore diocese and bishop were not vicariously liable for his tortious conduct).

6.10

LEGAL SUBJECT: Wrongful Discharge

STATEMENT OF ISSUE: An employer cannot rely on the at-will employment doctrine in Colorado as protection from a claim of wrongful discharge under certain circumstances.

CONCERNS/RISKS/ EXPOSURE: Historically, Colorado has followed the "at-will" legal doctrine that an employee may be terminated at any time for any reason, or for no reason at all, as long as termination was not the result of prohibited discrimination, the employee's exercise of a legal right or obligation, *e.g.*, jury duty, or for being a whistle blower, *i.e.*, reporting the employer's illegal acts. Employee termination for any of these reasons exposes an employer to a suit for wrongful discharge, as well as claims under other applicable laws, even when the employment is considered at-will.

Wrongful discharge claims may also arise because court cases in recent years have begun to limit the meaning of "at-will." For example, if an employer fails to follow discipline or grievance procedures described in an employee handbook, the employee may be able to assert a successful claim for breach of contract against the employer. In another example, the court concluded that an employee was wrongfully terminated when firing was the employer's reaction to an employee's complaints about unpaid overtime. *Hoyt v. Target Stores*, 981 P.2d 188 (Colo. App. 1998). On the other hand, the Colorado Supreme Court has taken the position that lying on a résumé or other misconduct evidence acquired could constitute a defense to an employee's claim for wrongful discharge. *Crawford*

Rehabilitation Services, Inc. v. Weissman, 938 P.2d 540 (Colo. 1997). This is an expansion of the U.S. Supreme Court opinion that allowed after-acquired evidence to be a partial defense. *McKennon v. Nashville Banner Publishing Co.*, 513 U.S. 352 (1995). *See also* Section 3.01, Employee Handbook or Personnel Manual, and Section 3.02, Employment at Will.

> ***TIP:*** Defense of a wrongful discharge claim requires analysis of many factors. One strategy that might reduce the risk of a successful claim for breach of contract based on the employee handbook is to include a mandatory internal grievance process that the employee must follow before resorting to a lawsuit. An employee's failure to fully comply with the internal grievance procedure may be an effective defense. *McGuire v. Continental Airlines, Inc.* 210 F.3d 1141 (10th Cir. 2000). Be aware, however, that the employer's failure to follow the procedure may be sufficient to overcome the presumption of at-will employment.

RESOURCES: N. Davidovich, *Employers: Can You Reduce the Risk of Lawsuits for Wrongful Termination by Inclusion of Internal Grievance Procedures in Employee Handbooks?;* http://www.talk-law.com/grievance.shtml.

N. Davidovich, *Public Policy and Employment at Will in Colorado;* http://www.talk-law.com/pubpol.shtml.

J. Louden, *Wrongful Termination of Employees;* http://www.frascona.com/resource/jhl494wt.htm.

Colorado Court Establishes Absolute After Acquired Evidence Defense for Employers; www.kutakrock.com/Index/Memoranda/body_colorado_court_establishes_abs.html.

6.11

LEGAL SUBJECT: Violation of Client Civil Rights

STATEMENT OF ISSUE: Discrimination against clients in programs and services of a nonprofit may be prohibited by one or more of the civil rights acts.

CONCERNS/RISKS/ EXPOSURE: It is illegal to discriminate in the provision of programs or services on the basis of race, color, religion, sex, national origin or disability under the various civil rights laws. For example, Title VIII of the Civil Rights Act of 1964 as amended by the Fair Housing Act of 1968, prohibits discrimination in the sale, rental, and financing of dwellings, and in other housing-related transactions on the basis of race, color, national origin, religion, sex, family status, or disability. Section 504 of the Rehabilitation Act of 1973 prohibits discrimination on the basis of disability by entities that receive any federal funding. The Americans with Disabilities Act prohibits discrimination by businesses on the basis of disability in accessibility to programs or the provision of services. Title IX of the Civil Rights Act of 1964 prohibits federally assisted programs from discriminating on the basis of sex.

These and other forms of discrimination in the provision of programs or services to clients may expose a nonprofit to civil suits, including damages. Training of employees in nondiscriminatory practices is imperative. Posting of nondiscrimination statements where clients will see them, printing such statements on organization literature, in policies, in annual reports, and in marketing materials is a good reminder to clients and employees of the organization's nondiscrimination policies. *See generally* Chapter 3, Employment Issues, for a discussion of each of the anti-discrimination laws, and especially Section 3.10, Discrimination on the Basis of Race, Color, Religion, National Origin, or Sex; Section 3.11, Age Discrimination in Employment Act; Section 3.13, Section 504 of the Rehabilitation Act of 1973; and Section 3.14, Americans with Disabilities Act.

TIP: Colorado law prohibits discrimination on the basis of disability, race, creed, color, sex, marital status, national origin or ancestry in any public accommodation, goods, services, privileges, facilities, or advantages. C.R.S. § 24-34-601. Many foundations request a copy of the nonprofit grant applicant's anti-discrimination policy and may penalize the applicant for failure to have a policy that prohibits all forms of discrimination in hiring, firing, programs or services, including discrimination based upon sexual orientation.

RESOURCES: C.R.S. § 24-34-601.

CHAPTER 7: LITIGATION

7.01

LEGAL SUBJECT: Lawsuit Basics

STATEMENT OF ISSUE: Knowing the basic elements of a lawsuit can take some of the fear and mystery out of being served with a complaint and summons regarding a lawsuit.

CONCERNS/RISKS/ EXPOSURE: Nonprofits may sue and be sued under a number of state and federal statutes and common law principles. There are statutes that limit the amount of time within which a plaintiff has to file a lawsuit to protect his or her rights or claims. This is referred to as the *statute of limitations* with respect to a particular action. The length of time depends on the type of action and damages sought. Generally, the length of time ranges from one to three years, but may be more or less, depending on the claim. In some discrimination scenarios, a claim may go back several years if there is an allegation called a "continuing violation," meaning that the alleged illegal conduct has occurred continuously both before and after the running of the statute of limitations. A suit may be filed with one of several trial courts depending on the statute, regulation or other alleged violation or right to be protected. Some claims may also be filed with an administrative agency such as the Equal Employment Opportunity Commission (EEOC) or with a quasi-judicial body such as the Division of Administrative Hearings. For some claims, filing with the administrative agency is required prior to filing a lawsuit. In some situations, the statute of limitations is "stayed" while the administrative body investigates the claim. In Colorado, a plaintiff may file in small claims court, county court, state district court, or federal district court, usually in the *jurisdiction* where the event or action leading to the lawsuit occurred and depending on which court has jurisdiction over the *subject matter* of the complaint.

A plaintiff commences a lawsuit by filing a complaint, which alleges the facts and the areas of law applicable to the legal issue. The organization's registered agent must be "served" by a process server with the *Complaint and Summons, i.e.*, a process server delivers the complaint to the agent along with a notice to appear in court on the complaint. It is important not to avoid service nor to panic upon receipt of service. The agent or director should contact the general liability insurance provider for the organization and deliver a *copy* of the served documents as quickly as possible. Most policies require notice of a lawsuit or an anticipated lawsuit within a specified time period. A copy should also be immediately sent to legal counsel for the organization. A defendant has a limited amount of time in which to file an *Answer* to the complaint, usually 20 to 30 days, depending on the court. Thus, prompt communication with the insurer and the organization's attorney is essential. The Answer contains a statement of the facts and responds to the allegations in the Complaint. The insurer will advise whether the policy covers the subject matter of the lawsuit, whether the insurer will defend the suit with counsel of the insurer's or insured's choosing, depending on the policy coverage, whether the organization will be advanced legal costs or be reimbursed, or if the subject matter is not covered under the policy. If the policy provides for advancement or reimbursement of legal costs, the organization must retain an attorney to provide representation as quickly as possible. This is one reason why it is extremely beneficial for the organization to have developed a relationship with one or more attorneys. The attorney retained by the organization or provided by the insurer will then meet with the executive director and any designated legal committee members or board members to discuss the next steps.

> ***TIP:*** A nonprofit corporation's registered agent is the nonprofit corporation's agent for service of process in a lawsuit. C.R.S. § 7-125-104. The Secretary of State's office requires all corporations, including nonprofits, to report any change of address for the registered agent. This can be done by downloading the proper form from the Business Section of the Colorado Secretary of State's web page at: http://www.sos.state.co.us/. There is a small filing fee.

RESOURCES: *What Nonprofit Managers Need to Know About Lawsuits,* available from Nonprofit Insurance Alliance of California (NIAC), http://www.niac.org/ResourceCenter/ResourceDisplay.cfm then click on the "Publications" link to select the item and download a test version (25 pages) or order a 25-page booklet with forms and glossary from NIAC for $1.00.

The Best Defense: 10 Steps to Surviving a Lawsuit (1998), available from the Nonprofit Risk Management Center, 1001 Connecticut Avenue, NW, Washington, D.C. 20036; (202) 785-3891; approximately $12.00, http://www.nonprofitrisk.org/pubs/best.htm.

7.02

LEGAL SUBJECT: Terminology of Lawsuits

STATEMENT OF ISSUE: Understanding basic lawsuit (litigation) terminology can assist with communication between the directors/managers of a nonprofit corporation and legal counsel provided by the insurer or retained by the organization.

CONCERNS/RISKS/ EXPOSURE: It is important that communication between the organization and its legal counsel be clearly understood by both. There are several legal dictionaries that provide in-depth definitions of terms, but may not give the contextual information to assist a lay person with the practical meaning of a legal term. Whenever a legal term is used, it is important that the CEO/executive director fully understands the term and any action that may be required. The organization should never hesitate to ask its legal counsel for clarification.

The person or entity commencing the lawsuit and filing the complaint is usually called the *Plaintiff*, *Petitioner*, or *Complainant*. If the claim is subject to mandatory arbitration, the person initiating the litigation is called the *Claimant*. The person or entity against which the lawsuit is brought is usually called the *Defendant* or *Respondent*. The Plaintiff and Defendant are each a *Party* to the lawsuit. *See* Section 7.01, Lawsuit Basics, for information regarding how a lawsuit is commenced, who is served and how a nonprofit should respond to being served with a Summons and Complaint.

Motions of various kinds and responses to them are common in most lawsuits. Motions may be filed by either party. A motion is a written request of the court to act in a certain manner or make a decision about an aspect of the case. Some common motions request the court to dismiss the complaint, to require the other party to produce evidence, to prevent evidence from being admitted, to allow for an extension of time to respond, or to decide the case based on the Complaint, the Answer, and certain documentary evidence, which is called a motion for summary judgment. Motions are often accompanied by written *briefs* that analyze the applicable law established by earlier cases. *See* the Introduction for a discussion of case law and precedent. The attorney representing the nonprofit should provide a brief explanation of each motion filed and the reason for filing the motion.

Depositions, i.e., testimony under oath, usually recorded by a court reporter, of employees or others who may have information relevant to the lawsuit may also take place. The nonprofit may also be served with, or may serve on the opposing party, written *Interrogatories, Requests for Production of Documents,* and *Requests for Admissions,* known collectively as *Written Discovery.* Depositions and written interrogatories are forms of *discovery* or ways both sides obtain information about what the other side knows. The purpose of discovery is to learn as much about the case as possible prior to trial, which, theoretically, avoids surprise and encourages settlement. Prior to trial there is often a *settlement* conference or attempt at mediation. Some courts and administrative agencies require the parties to engage in good faith settlement negotiations prior to trial or hearing. If an insurer's policy provides both a defense and indemnity to the claim, the insurer will generally be in control of settlement and settlement terms, and the organization may be obligated under the terms of the insurance policy to cooperate with insurance defense counsel on all aspects of the litigation, including settlement. It generally takes much longer for a case to go to trial than most people think, especially if the case is filed in federal court. Even if a case has been scheduled for trial, that trial date is often changed because courts often schedule multiple cases for trial simultaneously to avoid a hole in the trial schedule if a case settles, and because criminal cases that arise must take precedence over civil cases. If a trial court decision is appealed, it may take several years before the appeal is heard and decided. *See also* Section 7.01, Lawsuit Basics.

> ***TIP:*** Directors and officers of nonprofit organizations can reduce exposure to personal and organizational liability by reviewing the original IRS application to know the legal form of the organization and its structure; by obtaining a copy of the articles of incorporation and bylaws and reading them; by comparing the structure and procedures followed by the organization to the governing documents; and by reviewing the minutes of each board meeting attended. *Guidebook for Directors of Nonprofit Corporations,* American Bar Association; *Starting and Managing a Nonprofit Organization: A Legal Guide,* pp. 268-279.

RESOURCES: *What Nonprofit Managers Need to Know About Lawsuits,* available from Nonprofit Insurance Alliance of California (NIAC), http://www.niac.org/ResourceCenter/ResourceDisplay.cfm then click on the "Publications" link to select the item and download a test version (25 pages) or order a 25-page booklet with forms and glossary from NIAC for $1.00.

B. Hopkins, *Starting and Managing a Nonprofit Organization: A Legal Guide* (3rd Ed. 2001). New York: John Wiley and Sons.

Guidebook for Directors of Nonprofit Corporations (1993), Chicago, IL: American Bar Association. To order, call (800) 285-2221.

The Best Defense: 10 Steps to Surviving a Lawsuit (1998), available from the Nonprofit Risk Management Center, 1001 Connecticut Avenue, NW, Washington, D.C. 20036; (202) 785-3891; approximately $12.00, http://www.nonprofitrisk.org/pubs/best.htm.

7.03

LEGAL SUBJECT: Public Relations Concerns

STATEMENT OF ISSUE: News about a lawsuit filed against a nonprofit organization can wreak havoc on the nonprofit.

CONCERNS/RISKS/ EXPOSURE: The naming of a nonprofit as a defendant in a lawsuit may impact donors, board members, employees, volunteers, recipients of services, and the organization's image in the community. Negative impressions and damage to the organization's image can last for a long time. A reasonable response to a media question is far better than saying "No comment." It may be extremely helpful for the organization to work with a public relations firm or consultant to develop a media plan that can be communicated to all employees and volunteers. It is also advisable to have a "crisis media plan" developed prior to such an event so that it can be activated with little preparation once negative information is publicized by the print or television media. In addition, the organization's legal counsel should be consulted prior to a media response to determine the impact any media response may have on the pending litigation.

> ***TIP:*** Every nonprofit should have a basic media communication plan that identifies the spokesperson(s) for the organization, directs employees and volunteers to defer to the spokesperson when contacted by the media, and contains the method of communicating an imminent matter to all, whether through a phone tree, e-mail or some other device.
>
> *What Nonprofit Managers Need to Know About Lawsuits, Nonprofit Insurance Alliance of California.*

RESOURCES: *What Nonprofit Managers Need to Know About Lawsuits,* available from Nonprofit Insurance Alliance of California (NIAC), http://www.niac.org/ResourceCenter/ResourceDisplay.cfm then click on the "Publications" link to select the item and download a test version (25 pages) or order a 25-page booklet with forms and glossary from NIAC for $1.00.

K. Bonk, H. Griggs, & E. Tynes, THE JOSSEY-BASS GUIDE TO STRATEGIC COMMUNICATIONS FOR NONPROFITS: A STEP BY STEP GUIDE TO WORKING WITH THE MEDIA TO GENERATE PUBLICITY, ENHANCE FUNDRAISING, BUILD MEMBERSHIP, CHANGE PUBLIC POLICY, HANDLE CRISES AND MORE.

J. Radtke, STRATEGIC COMMUNICATIONS FOR NONPROFIT ORGANIZATIONS: SEVEN STEPS TO CREATING A SUCCESSFUL PLAN (Nonprofit Law, Finance, and Management Series), available through Amazon.com. This is a hands-on guide targeted to helping nonprofit organizations get their message across in an age of information overload.

S. Clawson-Freeo, *Crisis Communication Plan: A PR Blue Print,* Northern Illinois University; http://www3.niu.edu/newsplace/crisis.html.

7.04

LEGAL SUBJECT: Civil Actions Against Nonprofits

STATEMENT OF ISSUE: Any civil action permitted under Colorado law may be brought against a nonprofit organization unless nonprofit organizations are specifically exempt.

CONCERNS/RISKS/ EXPOSURE: Some nonprofit boards and managers believe that the organization's nonprofit status means that it cannot be sued. However, Colorado law permits any civil action that may be brought within the state to be brought against a nonprofit corporation. For this reason it is essential that nonprofits carry both directors' and officers' insurance and general liability insurance in sufficient amounts to cover claims. *See also* generally, Chapter 5, Risk Management Issues; Chapter 6, Torts, Liability, and Protection; and Chapter 9, Criminal Issues. It is important to note that a board member may also be named individually in the lawsuit where there is an allegation that the board member breached a fiduciary duty owed to the organization.

> ***TIP:*** The assets of the nonprofit corporation, which would otherwise be immune from levy and execution on a judgment under certain provisions in C.R.S. §§ 7-121-101 through 7-137-301 of the Colorado Revised Nonprofit Corporation Act, are subject to levy and execution to the extent that the nonprofit would be reimbursed by proceeds of applicable liability insurance policies. C.R.S. § 7-123-105. The directors, officers, employees, and members of a nonprofit are generally not personally liable for the acts, debts, liabilities, or obligations of the nonprofit corporation. C.R.S. § 7-126-103. They may, however, be liable for pre-incorporation transactions. C.R.S. § 7-122-104. And they may be personally liable when there has been commission of certain unlawful transactions, or a breach of fiduciary duties. C.R.S. §§ 7-128-401 – 403 and 501.

RESOURCES: Colorado Revised Nonprofit Corporation Act, C.R.S. §§ 7-121-101 through 7-137-301, and specifically, §§ 7-123-105, 7-126-103.

7.05

LEGAL SUBJECT: Preventive Law

STATEMENT OF ISSUE: Litigation is not entirely avoidable; however, practicing preventive law can help an organization greatly reduce the risk of involvement in litigation.

CONCERNS/RISKS/ EXPOSURE: Even if the nonprofit believes that it is wholly innocent of the allegations made, it must still defend against any lawsuits brought against it, which takes considerable time, resources, and energy away from the organization. It is far better to be proactive to reduce the risk of litigation whenever possible.

Preventive law is simply following the old adage that "An ounce of prevention is worth a pound of cure." Many nonprofits relish the freedom from bureaucracy that they enjoy in the delivery of their missions and in their overall operations. The lack of formality and the high level of trust that often accompanies the work of nonprofits may be detrimental to the organization in the long run if the result is a somewhat *laissez-faire* approach to prevention. When rules, boundaries, or responsibilities are clearly set, there is less likelihood that misunderstanding or miscommunication will occur. The most common sources of litigation are employment practices, disputes between the organization and vendors or landlords, and intellectual property issues, including use of the Internet. Properly drafted contracts and agreements, legal employment practices fairly and consistently applied, clear job descriptions, and well-kept financial and personnel records are imperative. Despite best practices, people may become disgruntled or suffer injury, entities may seek redress for real or perceived wrongs, and seemingly innocent actions may constitute violations of the Internal Revenue Code. Some organizations establish an internal team to address potential or actual legal, accounting and personnel issues. The organization may seek to develop relationships with professionals who have experience in these areas and have an interest in the organization, not as board members, but as committee members or professionals-on-call. Investment in professional advice before taking action is rarely money wasted. Conducting a legal audit and performing other risk management activities, as described in Chapters 5 and 6, can also assist in preventing litigation. *See also* Section 5.01, Risk Management Generally.

> ***TIP:*** Demonstrating compliance with Generally Accepted Accounting Principles (GAAP), FASB, or other published standards may mitigate a nonprofit's position regarding fiscal challenges. Douglas Sauter, "Remodeling the House of GAAP," *Journal of Accountancy,* July 1991, pp. 30-37; Adrian P. Fitzsimons, Marc H. Levine, "A Roadmap Through GAAP," *The Practical Accountant,* May 1993, pp. 47-52. Good risk management includes periodically updating insurance policies, employee policies, board policies, and general policies to ensure that everything is up to date, and complies with current law.

RESOURCES: *The Best Defense: 10 Steps to Surviving a Lawsuit* (1998), available from the Nonprofit Risk Management Center, 1001 Connecticut Avenue, NW, Washington, D.C. 20036; (202) 785-3891; approximately $12.00, http://www.nonprofitrisk.org/pubs/best.htm.

P. Delaney, B. Epstein, R. Nach, & S. Weiss Budak, GAAP 2004: INTERPRETATION AND APPLICATION OF GENERALLY ACCEPTED ACCOUNTING PRINCIPLES (2003), available in paperback from Wiley Publishing; http://www.wiley.com/.

7.06

LEGAL SUBJECT: Communicating During a Lawsuit

STATEMENT OF ISSUE: A lawsuit against the nonprofit may affect many aspects of the organization, including fundraising, public relations, and important relationships within the community. Communication during a pending lawsuit must be conducted with great care.

CONCERNS/RISKS/ EXPOSURE: Frequently, the plaintiff in a lawsuit against a nonprofit is a disgruntled employee, volunteer, or donor. The organization should not take any adverse action against a person or entity because of the pending lawsuit. Communication with the news media may be even more problematic, especially if the plaintiff is using the media to harm, or undermine the organization. It is wise to consult with legal counsel before communicating with the media or simply to refer all media requests to the attorney representing the organization. *See also* Section 7.03, Public Relations Concerns. It is important to notify the staff about the lawsuit and keep employees informed of the status without discussing sensitive, privileged, or confidential information. Specific facts of the case should not be discussed with staff, volunteers, donors or other constituencies. Attorney *work product*, such as research, a memorandum of law, charts, or other documents prepared by the attorney in anticipation of or in preparation for litigation should not be shared with staff. To do so may constitute a waiver of the attorney-client privilege. Staff may be informed of general progress in a case, or the lack thereof, as often happens with court cases, especially federal court cases, which can move extremely slowly. Employees should be asked not to discuss the lawsuit and should be informed that the organization has selected a single spokesperson for both internal and external communications. Employees should direct all inquiries to the single spokesperson. Board members and other volunteers should be kept informed as well, with board members receiving the information necessary to make decisions on behalf of the organization if required to do so. Similarly, volunteers and board members should be asked not to speak about the lawsuit outside the organization and to refer all questions to the identified spokesperson. Members, donors, and supporters should be informed about the lawsuit, especially if media involvement is anticipated. Consult with the organization's attorney prior to submitting any press release. Avoid admitting any liability, but express commitment to safety and continuing commitment to the organization's mission.

> ***TIP:*** If the lawsuit is filed by an employee or recently terminated employee, it is very important that the employer not take any adverse or retaliatory action against the employee, including a negative reference to an already-separated employee. To do so could place the employer at risk of a claim for retaliation, wrongful discharge or discrimination. *Sauers v. Salt Lake County,* 1 F.3d 1122 (10th Cir. 1993) (retaliation claim against employer was viable even where employee failed to establish actionable harassment claim). When discussing the status of the case with anyone below top management, it is important to discuss only matters that are part of the court public record. Discussing any sensitive issues with staff who are not part of top management may constitute waiver of the attorney-client privilege, and could also give rise to a claim for breach of confidentiality.

RESOURCES: *Tell Me About It: Communicating with Key Constituencies During a Lawsuit,* Nonprofit Risk Management Center, http://www94311.temp.w1.com/nwsltr/archive/nl998_3.htm.

S. Gallagher & E. Aro, *Avoiding Employment Related Liability: Ten Tips from the Frontline,* http://www.ncsl.org/programs/legman/aslcs/gall.pdf.

Legal Threats Shift the Balance of Power in the Workplace, DENVER BUSINESS JOURNAL; http://denver.bizjournals.com/denver/stories/2003/04/07/smallb2.html.

The Best Defense: 10 Steps to Surviving a Lawsuit (1998), available from the Nonprofit Risk Management Center, 1001 Connecticut Avenue, NW, Washington, D.C. 20036; (202) 785-3891; $12.00.

7.07

LEGAL SUBJECT: Attorney-Client Privilege and Work Product

STATEMENT OF ISSUE: Parties to a lawsuit must comply with each other's discovery requests unless the request is for information protected by attorney-client privilege or the work product rule.

CONCERNS/RISKS/ EXPOSURE: Clients are encouraged to tell their attorneys everything necessary to prepare their cases, just as patients serve themselves best when they share all necessary information with their physicians. To encourage this type of communication, the law protects all communication between an attorney and client during the course of representation. C.R.S. § 13-90-107(1)(b). Because this privilege exists for the personal benefit and protection of the client, only the client can give consent to waive this *privileged communication.* Rule 1.6 of the Colorado Rules of Professional Conduct specifically prohibits an attorney from disclosing information related to representation of a client unless the client consents.

The *Work Product Rule* arises out of this privilege and applies to documents and tangible items prepared in anticipation of or related to trial. It protects these items from discovery by the opposing party and opposing counsel. A party may object to the production of any document or other tangible item on the basis that it is work product related to representation in a court proceeding. Colorado Rules of Civil Procedure (C.R.C.P.) Rule 26. The court will then rule as to whether the discovery requested is privileged.

Neither the attorney-client privilege nor the work product rule is absolute. In some cases the court may find that the privilege conflicts with prevailing social public policies and must give way. *People v. Salazar*, 835 P.2d 592 (Colo. App. 1992).

> ***TIP:*** A client may be deemed to have waived the privilege by testifying about the privileged documents or using them to refresh the client's memory. *Hill v. Hill,* 107 P.2d 597 (Colo. 1940). Sharing privileged materials or communication with others may also constitute a waiver of the privilege.

RESOURCES: C.R.S. § 13-90-107(1)(b).

Colorado Rules of Professional Conduct, Volume 12, Colorado Revised Statutes.

CHAPTER 8: VOLUNTEERS AND VOLUNTEER MANAGEMENT

8.01

LEGAL SUBJECT: Volunteer Risk Management

STATEMENT OF ISSUE: An organization's risk of liability for the actions of its volunteers is as great as for compensated employees. Risk management can reduce the chances of both nonprofit corporate liability and individual liability, although risk management cannot completely eliminate the risk of liability.

CONCERNS/RISKS/ EXPOSURE: Volunteers are workers who serve without compensation. They often have as great or even greater contact with the public than employees. Liability for a nonprofit organization typically arises from ignorance on the part of its volunteers, not malicious conduct. But liability may also arise from negligence, recklessness, or even criminal acts by volunteers. For this reason, careful screening of volunteers, careful placement, job descriptions, quality orientation programs, training, education, specific skill development, periodic reviews and evaluations of performance, and most importantly, appropriate supervision, all constitute important strategies for managing the risk of liability.

The federal Volunteer Protection Act of 1997 (42 U.S.C. §§ 14501 through 14505) protects volunteers from personal liability when they are acting within the scope of responsibility and authority granted by the nonprofit and the harm that occurs has not been caused by intentional misconduct or criminal misconduct, gross negligence, recklessness, or indifference to the rights or safety of the person harmed. Colorado also provides some protection from civil liability for volunteers assisting organizations that provide assistance or services to youth. C.R.S. § 13-21-116. The Colorado Volunteer Service Act, C.R.S. § 13-21-115.5, however, exempts from immunity injuries sustained as a result of the operation of a motor vehicle. Thus, volunteers remain potentially liable for injuries, damages, or losses sustained as a result of motor vehicle operations.

> ***TIP:*** A good self-test for an organization regarding potential liability in the context of volunteers is "The Volunteer Legal At-Risk Test" by Sandra K. Pfau Englund at WebNP, The Web for Nonprofits; http://webnp.nt5.us/articles3/050603_volunteer_risk.htm.

RESOURCES: *Managing Volunteers: Balancing Risk and Reward,* booklet available for download from Nonprofits' Insurance Alliance of California; http://www.niac.org/NIAC2/ResourceCenter/DownloadableFiles/VolunteersBook1.pdf.

Myths About Nonprofit Liability and Risk Management, Risk Management Resource Center; http://www.eriskcenter.org/knowledge/normac/myths.html.

J.D. Dewitt, Guess & Rudd, P.C., THE VOLUNTEER LEGAL HANDBOOK (6th ed.); http://www.ptialaska.net/~jdewitt/vlh/Law/VLHLawIntro.html (although this publication focuses on the law of Alaska, it contains valuable general information as well).

8.02

LEGAL SUBJECT: Volunteer Protection Act of 1997 and Colorado Volunteer Service Act

STATEMENT OF ISSUE: A volunteer serving a nonprofit organization puts personal assets at risk in the event a tort action seeking damages arises from the volunteer activity. State and federal laws protect volunteers from this type of personal liability under certain circumstances. However, these laws do not protect the organization from civil liability arising out of a volunteer's acts or omissions.

CONCERNS/RISKS/ EXPOSURE: The contributions of volunteers are essential to the success and impact of the nonprofit sector. In order to encourage volunteerism, Congress passed the Volunteer Protection Act of 1997, (42 U.S.C. §§ 14501 through 14505) which sets a minimum federal standard for immunity of volunteers to civil lawsuits. It defines volunteers as individuals who perform services for a nonprofit entity without receiving compensation or anything of value in lieu of compensation in excess of $500 per year. Volunteers include directors, officers, trustees, and other direct service volunteers. State laws that provide protections in excess of those under the federal act remain in force. Colorado has also adopted the Volunteer Service Act. C.R.S. § 13-21-115.5. Both the state and federal law protect individual volunteers from liability under the following circumstances:

- The volunteer is acting within the scope of the volunteer's responsibilities in the organization.
- The volunteer possessed any credentials or licensing required for the activity.

- The harm was not caused by willful criminal misconduct, gross negligence, reckless misconduct, or flagrant indifference to the rights or safety of others.
- The harm was not caused by operation of a motor vehicle, vessel, aircraft or other vehicle which requires the operator to be licensed by the state.
- The harm was not caused by a crime of violence, hate crime, or sexual offense for which the volunteer has been convicted, nor for violation of any state or federal civil rights law; or for conduct while under the influence of alcohol or drugs.

Under Colorado law, a board member is also protected from liability for "actions taken or omissions made in the performance of the board member's duties as a board member except for wanton and willful acts or omissions." C.R.S. § 13-21-116. Neither state nor federal law protects the nonprofit organization itself from civil liability for harm caused by a volunteer who is acting within the above parameters. Nor do these laws protect volunteers from civil suits brought against them by the nonprofit for which they volunteer. Related laws protect specific categories of professions or services from liability as well. These include school crossing guards, volunteers for organizations that serve youth under the age of 18, mental health care providers, developmental disability service providers, and those conducting equine or llama activities. It is important to communicate these protections to volunteers and prospective volunteers as the purpose of these protections is to encourage and increase volunteerism.

> ***TIP:*** The volunteer protection statutes protect the volunteer from liability as stated above but do not protect the organization itself nor do they protect the volunteer from suits brought by the organization. Accordingly, an organization still needs both general liability and Directors' and Officers' liability coverage. For only a few hundred dollars a year, some personal umbrella policies can protect the volunteer from actions brought by the nonprofit organization. All insurance policies should be read carefully for exclusions from coverage.

RESOURCES:

Federal Law Protects Nonprofit Volunteers, available for download from Don Kramer's Nonprofit Issues on the Ready Reference page; http://www.nonprofitissues.com/public/indices/byfeature/ready.html.

L.A. Runquist & J.F. Zybach, *The Volunteer Protection Act of 1997: An Imperfect Solution;* http://runquist.com/article_vol_protect.htm.

R.O. Dawson, *The Volunteer Protection Act of 1997,* University of Texas School of Law; http://tarlton.law.utexas.edu/dawson/horselaw/volunter.htm.

K. Lankford, *Opening an Umbrella Policy,* Kiplinger.com; http://www.kiplinger.com/columns/ask/archive/2003/q0912.htm.

8.03

LEGAL SUBJECT: Hiring and Firing Volunteers

STATEMENT OF ISSUE: Although volunteers do not receive compensation, their hiring and termination may still expose the non-profit organization to liability.

CONCERNS/RISKS/ EXPOSURE: Some organizations, such as CASA (Court Appointed Special Advocates), rely almost entirely on volunteers to implement their mission. Other organizations may rely on volunteers only during special events. Volunteers are entitled to the same protections under the anti-discrimination laws as employees. *See* Chapter 3, Employment Issues. Effective management of volunteers can help a nonprofit avoid potential litigation related to their hiring and firing. The reasons for hiring or firing a volunteer are generally the same as for an employee. It is important that the volunteer have a clear understanding of the duties, expectations, and policies under which the volunteer is required to perform assigned volunteer duties. *See* Section 8.06, Volunteer Policy and Procedures Manual, for development of pre-hiring/hiring materials and their use. Firing a volunteer is much less stressful and less likely to result in litigation if clear expectations are provided before hiring. These include a job description, written acknowledgment of volunteer policies, and criteria for evaluation of performance. Once hired, a volunteer should be supervised, trained, coached, and evaluated as any employee would be. If these procedures are in place and followed, the nonprofit manager should be able to document performance, notices regarding improvement, actions taken to assist with improvement, and other mitigating measures taken by the organization prior to termination of the volunteer. Termination should generally be an action of last resort, particularly since termination usually means that the volunteer management system failed in some way.

> ***TIP:*** Volunteer board members are treated differently from direct service volunteers. Their service and termination of service are usually covered by the organization's bylaws. Hiring and termination decisions are made by the board as a whole based upon the procedures articulated in the bylaws.

RESOURCES: S. McCurley, *How to Fire a Volunteer and Live to Tell About It,* available on CASAnet website at; http://www.casanet.org/program-management/volunteer-manage/fire.htm.

See generally, http://nonprofit.about.com/ for links and information relevant to nonprofits and volunteer management.

8.04

LEGAL SUBJECT: Liability for Volunteers' Actions

STATEMENT OF ISSUE: Nonprofit organizations may be legally liable for actions of their volunteers.

CONCERNS/RISKS/ EXPOSURE: Nonprofits that utilize volunteer services risk exposure to civil and criminal liability for the actions of their volunteers. Conduct by a volunteer may be considered conduct of the organization itself, whether the act is an act of commission or omission. A nonprofit may have one or more defenses to a court action, *e.g.*, if the volunteer acted outside of the scope of the assigned responsibilities, acted with gross negligence or willful misconduct or failed to meet other criteria for immunity under the Volunteer Protection Act of 1997 and Colorado's Volunteer Services Act. Total elimination of risk is impossible, but such risk can be minimized. It is far better to rely upon preventive measures than corrective ones. Appropriate screening of volunteers prior to accepting them for a volunteer position and education of volunteers regarding the laws with which they must comply during their service to the organization is imperative. For more specific information regarding preventive actions, *see* Section 3.08, Pre-Employment Background Checks of Employees and Volunteers; Section 8.01, Volunteer Risk Management; Section 8.06, Volunteer Policy and Procedures Manual; Section 9.06, Background Checks of Employees and Volunteers; Chapter 5, Risk Management Issues; and Chapter 6, Torts, Liability, and Protection, for specific areas of liability risk.

> ***TIP:*** Written substantiation of an organization's volunteer screening guidelines can be helpful proof that appropriate screening efforts were taken prior to accepting a volunteer. Establish in advance what characteristics a volunteer must have for a specific position, such as "ability to lift heavy items" for a volunteer who will be picking up and moving boxes of books, and what criteria will be used to disqualify an applicant, such as traffic violations for positions that require driving.

RESOURCES: J.D. Dewitt, Guess & Rudd, P.C., THE VOLUNTEER LEGAL HANDBOOK (6th ed.); http://www.ptialaska.net/~jdewitt/vlh/Law/VLHLawIntro.html (although this publication focuses on the law of Alaska, it contains valuable general information as well).

Society for Nonprofit Organizations, Nonprofit Links/Volunteer Resources; http://www.snpo.org/resources/volunteers.php.

Does Liability for Negligent Hiring Apply to Volunteers?, Energize, Inc.; http://www.energizeinc.com/art/asta.html.

Myths About Nonprofit Liability and Risk Management, Risk Management Resource Center; http://www.eriskcenter.org/knowledge/normac/myths.html.

8.05

LEGAL SUBJECT: Liability to Volunteers

STATEMENT OF ISSUE: Nonprofit organizations may be legally liable for injuries that occur to volunteers.

CONCERNS/RISKS/ EXPOSURE: An organization can be liable for injuries to volunteers if the injury occurs at or while traveling to the place of volunteer service. The organization is required to provide a safe work environment for its volunteers just as it is for its employees, and can be held responsible if it was negligent regarding safety issues. Volunteers, including uncompensated board members, officers and directors, and uncompensated interns, are not covered by workers' compensation insurance.

> ***TIP:*** While preventive risk management is preferable, various insurance policies are available to protect organizations from liability for injury to volunteers including general commercial liability coverage, special event coverage, volunteer accident and injury coverage, and automobile liability coverage.

RESOURCES: *Managing Volunteers: Balancing Risk and Reward,* booklet available for download from Nonprofits' Insurance Alliance of California; http://www.niac.org/NIAC2/ResourceCenter/DownloadableFiles/VolunteersBook1.pdf.

J.D. Dewitt, Guess & Rudd, P.C., THE VOLUNTEER LEGAL HANDBOOK (6th ed.); http://www.ptialaska.net/~jdewitt/vlh/Law/VLHLawIntro.html (although this publication focuses on the law of Alaska, it contains valuable general information as well).

Arrive Safe and Sound: Tips to Help With Your Nonprofit's Vehicle Safety Program, booklet available for download from Nonprofits' Insurance Alliance of California; http://www.niac.org/NIAC2/ResourceCenter/DownloadableFiles/AutoBook.pdf.

Non Profit Insurance Center; http://www.nonprofitinsurancecenter.com/.

Volunteers Insurance Service; http://www.cimaworld.com/htdocs/volunteers.cfm.

8.06

LEGAL SUBJECT: Volunteer Policy and Procedures Manual

STATEMENT OF ISSUE: Development of a policy and procedures manual for volunteers may reduce the risk of liability for the organization.

CONCERNS/RISKS/ EXPOSURE: Volunteers are vital to most nonprofit organizations. They fulfill roles in client services, clerical and administrative support, community relations and governance. Recruitment, training, management, evaluation, and termination of volunteers should be conducted in the same manner as paid staff in order to maximize the benefits of volunteers to the organization and to reduce the likelihood that claims might be filed against the nonprofit by volunteers. Policies establish criteria for compliance, address problems or crises, as well as routine matters, clarify responsibilities, define lines of communication and authority, and bring structure to the operation of the organization. They also ensure continuity over time, evidence beliefs and values of the organization, and may protect the organization and its assets. Accordingly, a volunteer policies and procedures manual should be an integral part of effective volunteer management.

A typical manual should include a definition of the role of volunteers, job descriptions and qualifications for various volunteer activities, the volunteer application and interview process, screening of volunteers, training and supervision, evaluation, corrective actions, termination, laws of the workplace, expected conduct while serving the organization, and risk management issues. It should also include policies and procedures for sexual harassment, discrimination, and the like. However, the existence of a policies and procedures manual is only as good as its implementation. The mere fact that an organization has a manual does no good if the policies and procedures are not followed, or are not consistently followed.

> ***TIP:*** Some organizations may also wish to use a volunteer contract and/or a confidentiality agreement to be signed upon commencement of volunteer activities.

RESOURCES: L. Graff, "Benefits of Policies," from BY DEFINITION: POLICIES FOR VOLUNTEER PROGRAMS, (1997); Graff and Associates, http://www.energizeinc.com/art/abyd.html.

Volunteer Contract Can Define Commitments, available for download from Don Kramer's Nonprofit Issues on the Ready Reference page; http://www.nonprofitissues.com/public/indices/byfeature/ready.html.

Checklist of Human Resources Management Indicators for Nonprofit Organizations: Volunteer HR Management, Management Assistance Program for Nonprofits; http://www.mapnp.org/library/org_eval/uw_hr.htm.

8.07

LEGAL SUBJECT: Special Issues When Clients Are Vulnerable

STATEMENT OF ISSUE: An organization must pay special attention to the qualifications and background of volunteers who work directly with vulnerable populations.

CONCERNS/RISKS/ EXPOSURE: Organizations will be held to a higher standard of scrutiny regarding volunteer screening and management when its clients are members of a vulnerable class of people. Accordingly, criminal history and licensure screening checks are of special importance when the clients an organization serves are elderly, abused, infirmed, youth or children. Some background checks are required by state law and regulations *e.g.*, child care.

As with employees, background checks should be used as a screening process once a volunteer has been selected, not as selection criteria for a volunteer. A volunteer has the same privacy rights and protections during and after the interview process as an employee. Prospective volunteers should be notified in advance that a comprehensive background check will be conducted as part of the hiring process. This provides notice to the prospective volunteer, and often, acts as a prescreening process; those with problems in their backgrounds sometimes withdraw themselves from consideration if they know that a background check will be performed. Planned Parenthood of the Rocky Mountains has an excellent form for use with volunteers. *See* below for the website.

If it is too onerous for an organization to conduct background checks in all 50 states, it would be prudent to, at a minimum, check each state in which a volunteer who will work directly with vulnerable clients has resided since the age of 18. In addition, all references should be contacted and claims to licensure verified as in good standing. An FBI check can also be conducted.

In Colorado, criminal histories can be obtained from:

Colorado Bureau of Investigation
690 Kipling St.
Denver, CO 80215
(303) 239-4300
https://www.cbirecordscheck.com/Index.asp

The Colorado State Sex Offender Registry can be obtained from:

Colorado Bureau of Investigation
690 Kipling St.
Denver, CO 80215
(303) 239-4222
http://sor.state.co.us/default.asp

The Colorado Child Abuse Registry was abolished in 2003 in favor of an automated system maintained by the Colorado Department of Human Services.

> ***TIP:*** Good volunteers are hard to find. Accordingly, an organization should consider the nature and circumstance of a crime if one is disclosed during the interview process before rejecting an applicant. A petty crime many years ago that is unrelated to the role the volunteer will play at an organization should not be an automatic disqualifier.

RESOURCES: Planned Parenthood of the Rocky Mountains Volunteer Application (rev. 01/03), which includes permission for background check, confidentiality agreement and verification of health insurance coverage; http://www.pprm.org/pprm/volunteer.html#Application.

Nonprofit Safety Guide, WebNP, The Internet for Nonprofits; includes sources for criminal background and sex offender registry checks in all 50 states; http://webnp.nt5.us/safety/.

Checking Criminal Histories: Considerations Before You Begin, Risk Management Resource Center; http://www.eriskcenter.org/knowledge/normac/criminal.html.

Must We Do Criminal Background Checks on our Volunteers?, Internet Nonprofit Center; http://www.nonprofit-info.org/npofaq/04/25.html.

Barriers to Preventing Abuse, Energize, Inc.; http://www.energizeinc.com/art/achila.html.

CHAPTER 9: CRIMINAL ISSUES

9.01

LEGAL SUBJECT: Criminal Liability of Corporations

STATEMENT OF ISSUE: The Colorado Criminal Code imposes criminal liability on corporate entities for a variety of offenses.

CONCERNS/RISKS/ EXPOSURE: A charitable organization may be criminally liable for offenses committed by employees, directors, officers, managers and volunteers. Although the individual may face prosecution, the charitable organization may also face fines.

An offense committed by a corporate entity, if a felony when committed by an individual, subjects the corporation to a fine within the presumptive ranges authorized by statute. Practicing good risk management and conducting a legal audit on a regular basis can help identify and rectify any criminal conduct within the organization. *See* Chapter 5, Risk Management. Some insurers provide Volunteer/Employee Dishonesty or "fidelity" coverage for events that take place as a result of an employee or volunteer action that is criminal or negligent.

> ***TIP:*** The conduct constituting the offense must be engaged in, authorized, solicited, requested, commanded or knowingly tolerated by the board of directors or by a highly managerial agent acting within the scope of employment or in behalf of the organization. C.R.S. § 18-1-606(1)(b).

RESOURCES: C.R.S. §§ 18-1-606 (criminal liability) and 18-1-105(1)(a)(III), presumptive ranges for fines.

Volunteers Insurance Service; http://www.cimaworld.com/htdocs/volunteers.cfm.

Nonprofits' Insurance Alliance of California; http://niac.org.

9.02

LEGAL SUBJECT: Criminal Liability of an Individual for Corporate Actions

STATEMENT OF ISSUE: An individual may be personally, criminally liable for the conduct of the organization under certain circumstances.

CONCERNS/RISKS/ EXPOSURE: Colorado's Criminal Code holds an individual person criminally liable for conduct that constitutes an offense if the person commits the offense in the name of, or causes the offense to occur in the name of, or on behalf of, the corporate entity. The offender will be subject to criminal conviction and sentencing to the same extent as if the offender committed the offense in the offender's own name. For example, an officer or director of a nonprofit corporation may be criminally liable for embezzlement or theft of property of a third person through a corporate act when the act is performed by the director, is performed at the director's direction or is performed with the director's permission. The director need not even participate personally in the transaction in order to be criminally liable. Liability for criminal actions cannot be shifted to an independent third party insurer under a directors' and officers' policy.

> ***TIP:*** The risk of criminal activity in a financial context can be minimized by putting good financial controls in place such as requiring two signatures on checks over $1000.00 and having a thorough external audit of the organization's financial statements on an annual basis.

RESOURCES: C.R.S. § 18-1-607

B.R. Hopkins, STARTING AND MANAGING A NONPROFIT CORPORATION, 3rd ed. (2001), New York; John Wiley & Sons, Inc.; http://www.wiley.com/WileyCDA/.

GUIDEBOOK FOR DIRECTORS OF NONPROFIT CORPORATIONS (1993), Chicago; American Bar Association; http://www.abanet.org/abapubs/home.html.

9.03

LEGAL SUBJECT: Copyright Infringement and Fair Use

STATEMENT OF ISSUE: Copyright infringement subjects a nonprofit organization to both civil and criminal penalties.

CONCERNS/RISKS/ EXPOSURE: A copyright is a type of protection provided to "original works of authorship" under federal and international laws. Protected works include those of a literary, dramatic, musical, or artistic nature and some other intellectual works. Copyrights give the owner the exclusive use of the item or work and afford the owner the sole right to give permission for the use of the item or work by others. In the case of works "made for hire," *i.e.*, by an employee, the employer, not the employee, is considered to be the owner/author, absent an express written agreement to the contrary. The 1976 Copyright Act (17 U.S.C. §§ 101 through 1332) permits actual or statutory damages, up to $150,000, plus attorney fees and costs to the holder of an infringed copyright. Criminal penalties are imposed for conviction of willful infringement of a copyright. Willful infringement includes fraudulent removal of a copyright notice, issuance of a fraudulent copyright notice, as well as reproduction and distribution by electronic means, which includes installation of licensed software in excess of the number of licenses purchased, *i.e.*, one copy on multiple computers.

Although the 1976 Copyright Act makes it illegal to violate any of the rights granted owners, there are some specific exemptions from copyright liability. The exemption most applicable to nonprofit entities is the fair use exception. Fair use typically applies to the use of copyrighted material for teaching, research, and similar activities, but use for educational purposes alone does not constitute fair use. Factors considered in the fair use analysis include: 1) the purpose and character of the use (commercial or nonprofit educational); 2) the nature of the copyrighted work; 3) the amount and substantiality of the portion used in relation to the work as a whole; and 4) the effect of the use on the potential market for or value of the work. So, for example, quoting all three lines of a haiku poem in a television commercial typically would not fall under the fair use exception, even though quoting several hundred words from a Steven King novel in a master's thesis on popular fiction probably would qualify as fair use.

The Digital Millennium Copyright Act of 1998 (DMCA) amended the 1976 Act to conform with two World Intellectual Property Organization copyright treaties that updated and reinforced international copyright standards for the digital environment and global marketplace. The DMCA makes it illegal to manufacture, import, distribute, or provide products or services that are primarily designed for the purpose of circumventing controlled access to, or otherwise protect the rights of copyright owners in, copyrighted works. It also covers acts of circumvention, such as breaking through encryption measures in order to gain unauthorized access to copyrighted materials. Those who violate these prohibitions are subject to both civil and criminal liability, including statutory damages up to $25,000, criminal fines up to $500,000, and imprisonment up to five years for the first offense, and fines up to $1 million and imprisonment up to ten years for any subsequent offense.

As with the 1976 Act, certain exceptions are permitted. Nonprofit educational institutions are totally exempt from criminal liability and can avoid civil damages for innocent violations when they can demonstrate that they were not aware of the violation or did not believe their acts constituted a violation. Colleges, universities and other educational institutions that function as "service providers" (*i.e.*, provide on-line access to copyrighted materials) may qualify for limitations on liability. Those institutions of higher education involved in online distance education are likely to be most affected by the DMCA. Often, copyright holders will allow, either free or at a nominal cost, limited use of copyrighted material if credit is given. A simple written note or letter—signed by the copyright holder and granting permission to reprint the material in question, under whatever terms are specified (*e.g.*, a one-time license to reprint an article in a particular magazine)—is all that is required.

Nonprofits may also register their own intellectual property with the U.S. Copyright Office, http://www.copyright.gov/. Registration does not create the copyright in a given work; copyright attaches automatically when the work is created. But registering the copyright establishes a public record of the copyright claim and allows the copyright owner to file a lawsuit in court against anyone who infringes on the copyright. One should note, however, that while "original works of authorship" are copyrightable, works consisting entirely of information that is common property and containing no original authorship are not. Standard calendars and lists taken from public documents are two examples of non-copyrightable works. Moreover, according to the U.S. Copyright Office website, "Copyright does not protect ideas, concepts, systems, or methods of doing something. You may express your ideas in writing or drawings and claim copyright in your description, but be aware that copyright will not protect the idea itself as revealed in your written or artistic work." http://www.copyright.gov/help/faq/faq-protect.html.

> ***TIP:*** The ownership of intellectual property such as a copyright is established with its creation. While useful, there is no need to register or identify the owner with a © for ownership to attach. Registration does shift the presumption of ownership to the registrant in the event of an infringement. Registration and identification as a copyrighted work also puts others on notice that the copyright owner may challenge a violation of his/her copyright ownership.

RESOURCES: *Copyright Basics,* United States Library of Congress, Copyright Office; http://www.copyright.gov/circs/circ1.html.

Slapped Hard for Softlifting: The True Story of a Business Charged with Software Pirating, a booklet available for $12.95, plus tax, from: BHG, Inc., P.O. Box 309, Garrison, ND 58540-0309, or call (800) 229-5028.

Getting Permission [for using copyrighted material], University of Texas; http://www.utsystem.edu/OGC/IntellectualProperty/permissn.htm.

Fair Use Overview and Meaning for Higher Education, Consortium for Educational Technology in University Systems; http://www.cetus.org/fair5.html.

Fair Use Online, Harvard Law School; http://cyber.law.harvard.edu/fairuse/.

How Colleges and Universities Can Comply with the Digital Millennium Copyright Act of 1998, NACS, Inc; http://www.nacs.org/public/copyright/act.asp.

The Digital Millennium Copyright Act (an overview with links to the full text), UCLA Online Institute for Cyberspace Law and Policy; http://www.gseis.ucla.edu/iclp/dmca1.htm.

9.04

LEGAL SUBJECT: Trademark/Servicemark Infringement

STATEMENT OF ISSUE: Trademark or Servicemark infringement subjects a nonprofit organization to both civil and criminal penalties.

CONCERNS/RISKS/ EXPOSURE: Trademarks and servicemarks are distinctive symbols, pictures or words that sellers affix to distinguish and identify the origin of their products or services, *e.g.*, the Nike "swoosh." Even color combinations have been mark protected. Like copyrights, trademarks and servicemarks give the owner the exclusive use of the item and afford the owner the sole right to give permission for the use of the symbol, picture, words, or colors. The federal Lanham Act allows a trademark or servicemark to be registered with the Patent and Trademark office and provides protections to the holder. Additionally, trademarks (which include servicemarks) are registered and protected under Colorado law. C.R.S. §§ 7-70-101 through 7-73-109. Colorado law permits civil penalties for trademark infringement, including damages, attorney fees, and costs. Misuse, trafficking in articles or supplies, or removal of trademarks subjects a person or entity to misdemeanor charges and fines up to $50, or imprisonment for 30 to 60 days for the first offense, and both fines and imprisonment for subsequent offenses. The Colorado Consumer Protection Act also protects the public from deceptive trade practices and unfair competition practices. Violations bring civil penalties up to $10,000 for each violation in addition to other penalties or remedies available under the act, as well as remedies under the common law, *e.g.*, court-ordered damages. *See also* Section 9.03, Copyright Infringement and Fair Use.

> ***TIP:*** A mark is established by use, not by registration. An "intent to use" can be filed with the Patent and Trademark office; but in general, unless the trademark is used in trade or commerce, an organization cannot claim ownership.

RESOURCES: Colorado Consumer Protection Act, C.R.S. §§ 6-1-101 through 6-1-511.

Colorado Trademark laws, C.R.S. §§ 7-70-101 through 7-73-109.

Trademark Law: An Overview, Legal Information Institute, Cornell University; http://www.law.cornell.edu/topics/trademark.html.

The Lanham Act, 15 U.C.S. §§ 1051 through 1129.

9.05

LEGAL SUBJECT: Antitrust Violations

STATEMENT OF ISSUE: Nonprofit organizations are held to the same antitrust restrictions as for-profit corporations and may be exposed to criminal penalties.

CONCERNS/RISKS/ EXPOSURE: The U.S. Supreme Court has ruled that antitrust laws are applicable to nonprofit organizations. *See National Collegiate Athletic Ass'n v. Board of Regents of Univ. Of Oklahoma*, 486 U.S. 85 (1984). In addition to existing federal antitrust laws (Sherman Antitrust Act), the Colorado Antitrust Act of 1992 also covers antitrust violations. Fines up to $1 million may be imposed for violations that constitute a Colorado class five felony. These include illegal restraint of trade or commerce through conspiracy or other action (such as price-fixing), creation of a monopoly, and bid-rigging. Most of the antitrust cases in the nonprofit field have involved health care nonprofits, *e.g.*, hospital mergers, and physicians organized into nonprofit trade associations. However, member organizations should also be aware of activities that could be deemed collusion in restraint of trade.

> ***TIP:*** Even with the best of intentions, organizations should take care not to confer with others in a manner that might be construed as an unreasonable restraint of trade. Some communications that constitute price-fixing or otherwise unduly influence the marketplace are *per se* illegal. Actions that actually serve to improve competition or are in the public interest such as conducting surveys or permissible lobbying efforts are evaluated under a "rule of reason." Some nonprofit attorneys advocate that an organization adopt a written antitrust policy in order to avoid innocently straying into activity that constitutes an unreasonable restraint of trade.

RESOURCES: Colorado Antitrust Act of 1992, C.R.S. §§ 6-4-101 through 122.

Unfair Trade Practices Act, C.R.S. §§ 6-2-101 through 117.

Sherman Antitrust Act, 15 U.S.C. §§ 1 through 7.

Antitrust [Law]: An Overview (with links to additional resources), Legal Information Institute; http://www.law.cornell.edu/topics/antitrust.html.

Antitrust Audits: Do you Need One? How to Get Started, WebNP, The Internet for Nonprofits; http://webnp.nt5.us/articles2/101502_antitrust_audits.htm.

NonprofitLaw.com, The Internet Site for Nonprofit Organizations, Sandra Pfau Englund, Nonprofit Law P.C; http://www.nonprofitlaw.com/.

9.06

LEGAL SUBJECT: Background Checks of Employees and Volunteers

STATEMENT OF ISSUE: Hiring an employee who works with children or other vulnerable groups without conducting a background check increases an organization's risks of criminal sanctions, as well as civil liability.

CONCERNS/RISKS/ EXPOSURE: Pre-employment background checks of potential employees' and volunteers' criminal records, driving records and other relevant information may reduce liability risks. Organizations that need to conduct frequent background checks, *e.g.* child care centers and hospice care facilities, may wish to purchase screening or background check software or subscribe to a service that conducts checks for them. Software should be endorsed by reputable organizations such as the National Association of Independent Private Investigators, police organizations, or the Federal Bureau of Investigation. The Colorado Child abuse registry was abolished in 2003 and replaced by an automated data system maintained by the Colorado Department of Human Services.

> ***TIP:*** Planned Parenthood of the Rocky Mountains has an excellent form for use with volunteers. *See* below for the website. Also provided below are links to the Colorado Bureau of Investigation to obtain criminal record histories and sex offender registries.

RESOURCES: Background Check Guide software (Net Detective); information and instant download available; http://www.background-check-guide.com/.

Planned Parenthood of the Rocky Mountains Volunteer Application (rev. 01/03), which includes permission for background check, confidentiality agreement and verification of health insurance coverage; http://www.pprm.org/pprm/volunteer.html#Application.

In Colorado, criminal histories can be obtained from:

Colorado Bureau of Investigation
690 Kipling St.
Denver, CO 80215
(303) 239-4300
https://www.cbirecordscheck.com/Index.asp

The Colorado State Sex Offender Registry can be obtained from:

Colorado Bureau of Investigation
690 Kipling St.
Denver, CO 80215
(303) 239-4222
http://sor.state.co.us/default.asp

9.07

LEGAL SUBJECT: Charitable Fraud

STATEMENT OF ISSUE: Charitable fraud can be a felony or a misdemeanor under the Colorado Charitable Solicitations Act, and deceptive trade practices violate the Colorado Consumer Protection Act.

CONCERNS/RISKS/ EXPOSURE: Fraud is the intentional deception of a person with the intent of depriving them of property or otherwise causing injury. In Colorado, a fraudulent representation includes any assertion by words or conduct, and can include a failure to disclose a material fact. Fraudulent practices may include spending restricted funds on other uses or misrepresenting fundraising activities. It is also unlawful to represent that a contribution to a charitable organization will be used for a purpose other than the purpose for which the charitable organization actually intends to use such contribution, or that a greater amount of the contribution will go to a charitable organization than the actual portion that will go to such organization. C.R.S. § 6-16-111.

Courts can assess penalties as well as fines, and may even order jail time for charitable fraud. The court may also order that the organization cease operation until the fraudulent practices are eliminated and assurances of compliance are provided, if the organization is found guilty of misrepresentation. One charity conducted a mail campaign to raise funds purportedly to purchase medical equipment for sick children. The organization's Form 990, however, stated that the organization's major activity was public education, not health, and that only two percent of its revenue was spent on medical expenditures. The organization was censured by the court for fraudulent solicitation.

> ***TIP:*** The Colorado Attorney General has been particularly active in the past two years enhancing consumer protections especially in the realm of charitable solicitations. *See* Consumer Protection; Colorado Attorney Generals office http://www.ago.state.co.us/CONSPROT.stm.

RESOURCES: Colorado Charitable Solicitations Act, C.R.S. §§ 6-16-101 through 6-16-113.

Colorado Consumer Protection Act, C.R.S. §§ 6-1-101 through 6-1-511.

Secretary of State, Licensing Section, 1560 Broadway, Suite 200, Denver, CO 80202; (303) 894-2680.

Charitable Solicitations: The Unified Registration Statement; http://www.multistatefiling.org/.

G. Kastel, *First Amendment Does Not Shield Charities That Mislead Donors,* Faegre & Benson; http://www.faegre.com/articles/article_951.aspx.

CHAPTER 10: LOBBYING, POLITICAL ACTIVITY, AND ADVOCACY

10.01

LEGAL SUBJECT: Lobbying Generally

STATEMENT OF ISSUE: Nonprofits are permitted to lobby and need to understand how lobbying is defined.

CONCERNS/RISKS/ EXPOSURE: Nonprofits have rights to free speech just like individuals do, but those rights are tempered by public policy that limits the use of tax-deductible dollars to subsidize nonprofit influence. Consequently, if any part of the activities of a nonprofit involves attempting to influence elections, or if a substantial part of the activities of a nonprofit involves attempting to influence legislation, the nonprofit will not qualify for tax-exempt status under § 501(c)(3) and contributions to the nonprofit will not be deductible. *See* Section 10.02, Political Activities of § 501(c)(3) Organizations, for a discussion of election-related activities that may be conducted by § 501(c)(3) organizations, and *see* Section 10.04, Lobbying Activities: Election Under § 501(h) and the Expenditures Test, for a discussion of the amount of lobbying by § 501(c)(3) organizations that is permitted.

A nonprofit that is exempt from tax under § 501(c), except those exempt under § 501(c)(3), may attempt to influence elections, but may be subject to tax under § 527(f). *See* Section 10.06, Political Action Committees. The lobbying activities of a nonprofit that is exempt under § 501(c), other than § 501(c)(3), are not limited, provided that the lobbying activities are consistent with the exempt purposes of the organization.

Ordinarily, dues paid to a membership organization, such as a § 501(c)(6) business league, are deductible business expenses. However, expenses that are directly or indirectly attributable to lobbying or political expenditures are not deductible. IRC § 162(e), Treas. Reg. §§ 1.162-20(c)(3), 1.162-20(d). If a membership organization engages in lobbying, it must notify its members of the portion of dues paid that is allocable to the lobbying expenditures of the organization. IRC § 6033(e)(1)(A)(ii). The members may not deduct the portion of dues attributable to lobbying activities.

Generally speaking, nonprofits should lobby. The U.S. Treasury Department recognized that lack of lobbying by organizations with substantial expertise deprives legislatures of this expertise. Lobbying promotes a balance in the presentation of viewpoints and information. Lobbying is a must for most nonprofits today because government impacts every human being in the United States as well as every institution. Nonprofit history demonstrates the ability of the sector to shape American policy on a wide variety of subjects and at a variety of levels.

The IRS rules do not prohibit foundations from awarding grants to tax-exempt organizations that lobby. However, foundations may choose not award to grants specifically for the purpose of lobbying. *See also* Section 10.03, Lobbying Activities: 1976 Lobby Law and the Internal Revenue Code, Section 10.04, Lobbying Activities: Election Under § 501(h) and the Expenditures Test, and Section 10.08, Lobbying Disclosure Act of 1995.

> ***TIP:*** Use of federal funds to lobby or promote changes in public policy may be prohibited. The U.S. Supreme Court held that should government subsidize one protected right (family planning), it does not follow that government must subsidize analogous counterpart rights (abortion services). *Rust v. Sullivan,* 500 U.S. 173 (1991). *See also* OMB (Office of Management and Budget) Circular A-122.

RESOURCES: "Ten Reasons to Lobby for Your Cause," Independent Sector; http://www.independentsector.org/Nonprofit_Information_Center/TenREasonstoLobby.pdf.

"Can Your Nonprofit Organization Lobby?" Coalition on Homelessness and Housing in Ohio; http://www.cohhio.org/resources/nonprofitlobbying.html.

"Why Lobby? Ten Reasons to Lobby for Your Cause," Minnesota Council of Nonprofits; http://www.mncn.org/lobbywhy.htm.

Colorado Sunshine Law, C.R.S. §§ 24-6-301 through 309.

Colorado Secretary of State Office; http://www.sos.state.co.us/.

Cost Principles for Non-Profit Organizations, OMB Circular A-122; http://www.whitehouse.gov/omb/circulars/a122/a122.html.

The Alliance for Justice; http://www.allianceforjustice.org/.

WORRY FREE LOBBYING FOR NONPROFITS: HOW TO USE THE 501(H) ELECTION TO MAXIMIZE EFFECTIVENESS, A Handbook for Funders and Grantees Published by the Alliance for Justice; http://www.allianceforjustice.org/images/collection_images/Worry-Free%20Lobbying%202003.pdf.

Publication 557, "Tax-Exempt Status for Your Organization," Internal Revenue Service; http://www.irs.gov/pub/irs-pdf/p557.pdf.

RESOURCES: Rev. Rul. 78-113

Rev. Rul. 78-114

Rev. Proc. 98-19

Regan v. Taxation with Representation of Washington, 461 U.S. 540, 103 S.Ct. 1997, (1983).

10.02

LEGAL SUBJECT: Political Activities of § 501(c)(3) Organizations

STATEMENT OF ISSUE: Although it may lobby to influence legislation and may engage in limited political activities, a § 501(c)(3) organization is strictly prohibited from influencing the candidate election process.

CONCERNS/RISKS/ EXPOSURE: To protect its tax-exempt status, a § 501(c)(3) organization must refrain from participating or intervening in any political campaign on behalf of, or in opposition to, any candidate for public office. A *candidate* is someone who is *a contestant, or a potential or proposed contestant*, for an elected office. Elected office is any office filled by a vote of the public, *e.g.*, state, federal and local elected offices, including county commissioner, school board member or party official. Participation in a campaign can take the form of publishing or distributing statements to support or oppose a candidate; formally or informally endorsing a candidate; keeping campaign materials onsite, *e.g.*, yard signs, bumper stickers; distributing campaign literature to staff or clients; using the organization's telephones for a candidate phone bank; making direct financial or in-kind contributions; campaigning on employer time; conducting opposition research; or organizing volunteers to support a candidate.

Permissible political activities must not constitute a substantial part of the § 501(c)(3) organization's activities. Sanctions for excess political activity are imposed by the IRS and may include excise taxes on the organization's political expenditures and on individual directors or managers who approved the political expenditures. Permissible activities include: publishing incumbents' voting records if it is a routine practice, is not done only during campaign periods, and is distributed to members only and not to the general public (exception is broad-focused groups such as the League of Women Voters); preparing and publishing candidate questionnaires; providing issue education; holding public candidate forums where all candidates are invited and given identical questions; conducting educational workshops on the voting process; engaging in get-out-the-vote activities and encouraging voter participation; conducting surveys and polls; and participating in nonpartisan voter registration activities. A nonprofit may contact candidates to inform them of its positions on issues. Officers, individual members, or employees of a nonprofit may engage privately in campaign activities, but must refrain from actions that imply they are spokespersons for the nonprofit organization. They may identify themselves with the organization but must make it clear that they are speaking solely for themselves and not on behalf of the organization. *See also* Section 10.07, Federal Election Campaign Act of 1971 and the Bipartisan Campaign Reform Act.

TIP: A nonprofit may be approached by a political candidate to obtain a copy of the organization's membership list. The Colorado Revised Nonprofit Corporation Act states that the consent of the board of directors is required before the organization's "membership list or any part of it, may be obtained or used by any person for any purpose unrelated to a member's interest as a member." C.R.S. § 7-136-105(1). Similarly, the membership list may not be sold without the consent of the board of directors. C.R.S. § 7-136-105(2)(c). If a nonprofit gives its list to a candidate, it may be treated as making a campaign contribution. To avoid such a charge, something of value would need to be provided in return. A nonprofit that sells its membership list to a candidate, or anyone else for that matter, may also be subject to unrelated business income tax. *See* Section 2.11, Unrelated Business Income Tax (UBIT). The safest practice may be a policy that the membership list is not provided to anyone, but if this information is publicly available, the person inquiring may be directed to a web page or other location where members are publicly posted.

RESOURCES: *Update on Permissible Activities of 501(c)(3) Organizations During a Political Campaign;* http://www.ombwatch.org/article/articleview/402/1/51/.

Tax Information for Charities & Other Non-Profits; http://www.irs.gov/charities/.

Independent Sector, publications and ordering information; http://www.independentsector.org/pubs_cart.htm.

Internal Revenue Code § 4911

Internal Revenue Code § 4912

Internal Revenue Code § 4955

Rev. Rul. 67-71

Rev. Rul. 74-574

Rev. Rul. 76-456

Rev. Rul. 78-248, 1978-1 C.B. 154 (1978).

Rev. Rul. 80-282, 1980-2 C.B. 178 (1980).

Publication 557, "Tax-Exempt Status for Your Organization," Internal Revenue Service; http://www.irs.gov/pub/irs-pdf/p557.pdf.

10.03

LEGAL SUBJECT: Lobbying Activities: 1976 Lobby Law and the Internal Revenue Code

STATEMENT OF ISSUE: The 1976 Lobbying Law applies to both state and federal lobbying activities and supports lobbying by nonprofits within certain restrictions.

CONCERNS/RISKS/ EXPOSURE: Most tax-exempt organizations may lobby under IRS rules as long as the lobbying activities are consistent with the exempt purposes of the organizations. However, § 501(c)(3) organizations have IRS-imposed restrictions on how much and what kind of lobbying they may do. Prior to 1976, the IRS could only apply an ambiguous and subjective "no-substantial-part" test to determine whether a § 501(c)(3) organization's lobbying activities exceeded the permissible level. Courts and nonprofits both struggled to define what "no substantial part" meant. There was no clear definition as to what activities constituted lobbying and how to factor in volunteer time, resources, etc. Some courts found that activities in excess of five percent of an organization's resources could be deemed substantial. The 1976 Lobbying Law and the treasury regulations promulgated under it clarified what constitutes lobbying and how § 501(c)(3) organizations may engage in lobbying within the restrictions without jeopardizing their tax-exempt status. *See* Section 10.04, Lobbying Activities: Election Under § 501(h) and the Expenditures Test.

The Internal Revenue Service defines lobbying as any attempt to *influence legislation* in one of two ways: direct lobbying or grassroots lobbying. *Direct lobbying* means an attempt to influence legislation by communicating with a member of a legislative body or other government official, *e.g.*, a governor, who participates in the formulation or passage of legislation. The legislative body may be a legislature, board of county commissioners, city council or other elected body. Direct lobbying includes urging the public to vote for or against a ballot initiative or referendum because, in such cases, the public is the legislative body. Direct lobbying has three elements: (1) the communication involves a specific piece of legislation; (2) the principal purpose is to influence the adoption, repeal, veto, passage or defeat of the legislation; and (3) the entity doing the communicating expresses a specific viewpoint. Direct lobbying does *not* include contacts with executive branch employees for purposes of influencing regulations. *But see* Section 10.08, Lobbying Disclosure Act of 1995. In addition, the following legislation-related activities are *not* considered lobbying by the IRS:

- Lobbying by volunteers, unless the organization reimburses volunteers for their lobbying-related expenses;
- Communicating by the organization to its members regarding legisla tion, as long as the organization doesn't directly encourage its members to lobby;
- Providing responses to written requests from a legislative body for technical advice;
- Taking action in self-defense on matters that affect the organization's own existence, powers, tax exempt status and the like;
- Publishing results of nonpartisan analyses, studies or research on legislative issues, presenting pertinent facts to assist the audience in formulating an independent opinion; and
- Presenting for discussion broad social or economic policies, the resolution of which would require legislation, even if specific legislation on the issue(s) is pending, as long as the presentation does not address specific merits of the current legislation.

Grassroots lobbying means an attempt to influence legislation by encouraging individual members of the general public to lobby a specific piece of legislation. The organization may provide information to the public about how to contact legislators or other decision makers. Mass media is often employed to effect grassroots lobbying.

> ***TIP:*** An organization that spends substantial resources on influencing legislation is considered an "action organization" and, as such, will not qualify for exemption from tax under § 501(c)(3). Treas. Reg. § 1.501(h)-1(a)(4).

RESOURCES: "Can I Lobby?" Donors Forum of Chicago; http://www.donorsforum.org/policy/np_lobby.html.

"IRS Rules Define How to Measure Lobbying Activities to Stay Within the Legal Limits," Internet Nonprofit Center; http://www.nonprofits.org/npofaq/11/08.html.

WORRY FREE LOBBYING FOR NONPROFITS: HOW TO USE THE 501(H) ELECTION TO MAXIMIZE EFFECTIVENESS, A Handbook for Funders and Grantees Published by the Alliance for Justice; http://www.allianceforjustice.org/images/collection_images/Worry-Free%20Lobbying%202003.pdf.

Rev. Rul. 67-368

Rev. Rul. 61-177

Internal Revenue Code § 4911(d)

J.E. Kindell and J.F. Reilly, "Lobbying Issues," Internal Revenue Service; http://www.irs.gov/pub/irs-tege/topic-p.pdf.

10.04

LEGAL SUBJECT: Lobbying Activities: Election Under § 501(h) and the Expenditures Test

STATEMENT OF ISSUE: Substantial engagement in lobbying activities by a § 501(c)(3) nonprofit organization may result in loss of nonprofit status and loss of tax-deductibility for contributions. Section 501(c)(3) organizations may choose to track their lobbying expenditures under the § 501(h) expenditures test, which gives greater assurance of IRS compliance, but which may subject the organization to tax on excess lobbying expenditures.

CONCERNS/RISKS/ EXPOSURE: The annual Form 990, Return of Organization Exempt from Income Tax, requires nonprofits to report their lobbying expenditures. Passage of the Tax Reform Act of 1976 (The 1976 Lobby Law) and the treasury regulations promulgated pursuant to the Act give § 501(c)(3) charitable organizations an alternative to the no-substantial-part test and offer clearer guidance regarding lobbying activities and restrictions. The addition of § 501(h) to the Internal Revenue Code permits public charities, except for churches, to "elect" an expenditure test in lieu of the no-substantial-part test. The expenditure test is a simple, generous formula, easily applied. If an organization elects to report its lobbying activities under § 501(h), it may spend 30 percent of the first $500,000, or up to $150,000, of its annual expenditures on lobbying, 22.5 percent of the next $500,000 on lobbying, and so forth, up to $1.5 million per year. The organization may not spend more than 37.5 percent of its total annual lobbying expenditures on grassroots lobbying.

If an election under § 501(h) is in effect, the organization will be subject to a 25 percent tax on the amount of excess lobbying expenditures per year. The amount of excess equals the amount of lobbying expenditures that exceed 20 percent of the first $500,000 of its annual expenditures on lobbying, 15 percent of the next $500,000 on lobbying, and so forth. The amount of excess also includes the amount of expenditures on grassroots lobbying exceeding 25 percent of its total annual lobbying expenditures. A charitable organization that conducts primarily grassroots lobbying should *not* elect § 501(h), as its lobbying activities would be severely limited. Other reasons not to elect are too little lobbying activity, too much lobbying activity but a very large budget, or aggregation of affiliates, which is covered in Section 10.05, Treatment of Affiliated Organizations Choosing Election Under § 501(h).

The charitable organization must formally choose or "elect" to report its lobbying expenditures under I.R.C. § 501(h) by filing the one-page IRS Form 5768, "Election/Revocation of Election By an Eligible Section 501(c)(3) Organization to Make Expenditures To Influence Legislation," http://www.irs.gov/pub/irs-pdf/f5768.pdf. Election may be made any time during the organization's tax year and is effective that tax year and every succeeding tax year unless revoked by filing the same form and checking the revocation box. Upon revocation, the organization reverts to the no-substantial-part test.

> ***TIP:*** The expenditure test considers expenditures on lobbying averaged over a four-year period. Thus, an organization may spend 15 percent one year and 35 percent another year, allowing for situations in which state legislatures meet less frequently than annually. However, if the average of the four years is more than 50 percent of the expenditure limits, the organization may lose its tax-exempt status. I.R.C. §§ 501(h) and 4911.

RESOURCES: "IRS Rules Define How to Measure Lobbying Activities to Stay Within the Legal Limits," Internet Nonprofit Center; http://www.nonprofits.org/npofaq/11/08.html.

WORRY FREE LOBBYING FOR NONPROFITS: HOW TO USE THE 501 (H) ELECTION TO MAXIMIZE EFFECTIVENESS, A Handbook for Funders and Grantees, published by the Alliance for Justice; http://www.allianceforjustice.org/images/collection_images/Worry-Free%20Lobbying%202003.pdf.

J.F. Kindell and J.F. Reilly, *Lobbying Issues,* Internal Revenue Service; www.irs.gov/pub/irs-tege/topic-p.pdf.

Internal Revenue Code § 501(h)

Internal Revenue Code § 4911

Internal Revenue Codc § 4912

10.05

LEGAL SUBJECT: Treatment of Affiliated Organizations Choosing Election Under § 501(h)

STATEMENT OF ISSUE: When two or more § 501(c)(3) organizations are affiliated, there may be additional limitations and reporting requirements for lobbying activities under § 501(h).

CONCERNS/RISKS/ EXPOSURE: When two or more nonprofits are members of an affiliated group and one of the members has elected the § 501(h) expenditures test, the calculations of lobbying and tax-exempt purpose expenditures must be made by taking into account the expenditures of the entire group. Two organizations are deemed to be affiliated if one organization is bound by the decisions of the other on lobbying and legislative issues under its bylaws or the governing board of one organization includes enough representatives of the other, known as an interlocking governing board, to cause or prevent action on legislative issues by the first organization. Even if a number of nonprofits are affiliated only in a chain fashion, they may all be treated as a single group of affiliated nonprofits. In the case where several autonomous nonprofits control a single organization, but no one nonprofit alone controls the single organization, the autonomous nonprofits will not be considered an affiliated group by application of the interlocking governing board rule. *See also* Section 10.04, Lobbying Activities: Election Under § 501(h) and the Expenditures Test.

> ***TIP:*** If the affiliated group's aggregate lobbying expenditures exceed the permitted limits, each of the electing members must pay a proportionate share of the excise tax imposed for the excess. The non-electing members will be subject to the "no substantial part" test. I.R.C. § 4911(f)(1)(B). *See also* I.R.C. § 4911 generally.

RESOURCES: B. Hopkins, The Law of Tax Exempt Organizations, 8th ed., John Wiley & Sons (2003); http://www.wiley.com/WileyCDA/WileyTitle/productCd-0471268208.html.

"IRS Rules Define How to Measure Lobbying Activities to Stay Within the Legal Limits," Independent Sector, http://www.nonprofits.org/npofaq/11/08.html.

Worry-Free Lobbying for Nonprofits: How to Use the 501(h) Election to Maximize Effectiveness, A Handbook for Funders and Grantees, published by the Alliance for Justice, http://www.allianceforjustice.org/images/collection_images/Worry-Free%20Lobbying%202003.pdf.

J.F. Kindell and J.F. Reilly, "Lobbying Issues," Internal Revenue Service; http://www.irs.gov/pub/irs-tege/topic-p.pdf.

Internal Revenue Code § 501(h)

Internal Revenue Code § 4911

Internal Revenue Code § 4912

10.06

LEGAL SUBJECT: Political Action Committees

STATEMENT OF ISSUE: Establishment of a political action committee (PAC) is an option for nonprofits that wish to impact federal campaigns.

CONCERNS/RISKS/ EXPOSURE: Both tax law and federal election law prohibit tax-exempt organizations from making *direct* contributions to political campaigns, but the Internal Revenue Code permits tax-exempt organizations, other than § 501(c)(3) organizations, to establish, solicit and administer separate segregated funds for political action purposes. These separate funds are frequently referred to as PACs, although § 527 of the Code uses the term "political organization." A PAC, whether incorporated or not, is organized and operated primarily for the purpose of directly or indirectly accepting contributions or making expenditures for an exempt function, which is defined as the activity of influencing or attempting to influence the selection, nomination, election or appointment of a person to any state, federal or local public office. Tax-exempt organizations most likely to employ PACs include § 501(c)(6) trade, business and professional associations as well as § 501(c)(4) social welfare organizations, both of which generally have members.

The Federal Election Commission has issued an advisory opinion in which it stated that a § 501(c)(3) college could not establish a separate segregated fund, but that the IRS does not prohibit groups of individuals from establishing a non-connected PAC. AO No. 1984-12. So, while a § 501(c)(3) organization itself may not establish a PAC, individuals associated with the § 501(c)(3) may establish an "unconnected" PAC. As long as there is no direct or indirect support from the § 501(c)(3) to the PAC, the organization's tax-exempt status is protected. Criteria that indicate that a PAC is not connected include the following:

- The PAC is formed by members of the governing board of the § 501(c)(3) organization in their individual capacity;
- The PAC operates and is governed independently of the § 501(c)(3);
- The PAC derives no financial support from the § 501(c)(3);
- The PAC reimburses the organization for expenses incurred on behalf of the PAC;
- The PAC pays fair market value for rent or facilities;
- The § 501(c)(3) avoids any conduct that might even suggest favoring the solicitation activity of the PAC; and
- Neither the organization nor the PAC assert proprietary interest or control over the use of the name of the PAC.

Section 527(f) imposes a tax related to the exempt function expenditures of a PAC at the highest corporate rate. Expenditures for political activities that are made between elections may also be subject to § 527(f) taxation if they are related to the selection, nomination or election of an individual in the next election cycle. Treas. Reg. § 1.527-(2)(c)(1). Section 527 enables a PAC fund to be treated as a tax-exempt political organization if complex segregation requirements are met. If tax-exempt treatment is desired with respect to the segregated exempt function expenditures, a PAC must notify the IRS of its intent to be treated as exempt under § 527 within 24 hours of formation. An organization that engages solely in lobbying activities, as opposed to election-related activities, cannot qualify as a § 527 political organization. Private Letter Ruling 9244003. *See also* Section 10.07, Federal Election Campaign Finance Act of 1971 and the Bipartisan Campaign Reform Act.

TIP: The Federal Election Campaign Act's prohibition on direct corporate political donations was challenged by a § 501(c)(4) nonprofit as a violation of its First Amendment rights. The U.S. Supreme Court held that the ban on direct corporate political contributions was intended, in part, to prevent the amassing of "political war chests" and applied equally to nonprofit advocacy organizations. *Federal Election Commission v. Beaumont,* 539 U.S. 146 (2003). *See also* 2 U.S.C. § 441 and 11 C.F.R. §§ 114.2(b), 114.10 (2003).

In PLR 200103084, the IRS considered a situation in which a § 501(c)(3) organization controlled a § 501(c)(6) business league through an identical board of directors. The business league wished to organize a political committee, retaining the power to appoint the board of directors of the PAC. The IRS determined that, under the facts presented, the creation of the political committee would not jeopardize the tax-exempt status of the § 501(c)(3) organization or the § 501(c)(6) organization, and that neither the § 501(c)(3) organization nor the § 501(c)(6) organization would be subject to tax under § 527(f).

RESOURCES: B. Hopkins, STARTING AND MANAGING A NONPROFIT ORGANIZATION: A LEGAL GUIDE, 3rd. ed., pp. 210-222, John Wiley & Sons (2001); http://www.wiley.com/WileyCDA/WileyTitle/productCd-047139727X.html.

B. Hopkins, THE LAW OF TAX EXEMPT ORGANIZATIONS, 8th ed., pp. 411-425, Wiley & Sons (2003); http://www.wiley.com/WileyCDA/WileyTitle/productCd-0471268208.html.

Federal Election Commission v. Beaumont, 539 U.S. 146 (2003); http://www.supremecourtus.gov/opinions/02pdf/02-403.pdf.

Branch Ministries v. Rossotti, 211 F.2d 137 (D.C. Circuit 2000).

Federal Campaign Finance Act, 2 U.S.C. § 401 through 441.

Rev. Rul. 81-95

Internal Revenue Code § 527

10.07

LEGAL SUBJECT: Federal Election Campaign Act of 1971 and the Bipartisan Campaign Reform Act

STATEMENT OF ISSUE: The Federal Election Campaign Act and the Bipartisan Campaign Reform Act of 2002 prohibit nonprofit organizations from engaging in electioneering communications regarding candidates for federal office.

CONCERNS/RISKS/ EXPOSURE: The Federal Election Campaign Act of 1971 (FECA) was amended by the Bipartisan Campaign Reform Act of 2002 (BCRA), also known as the McCain-Feingold Law after its sponsors. Together, these Acts establish limits on federal campaign activities. Neither the statutes nor their regulations are fully aligned with the Internal Revenue Code requirements concerning nonprofits and political activities. The BCRA prohibits unions and corporations (including most nonprofits) from referring to federal candidates in television or radio broadcast communications made within 30 days of a primary or 60 days of a general federal election. Such ads are deemed to be prohibited *electioneering communications.* The ban applies regardless of whether the groups funded the costs of the communication directly or indirectly. As a result, it covers a range of broadcast communications, including paid advertisements and public service announcements.

In *McConnell v. Federal Election Commission*, the U.S. Supreme Court, by a slim 5-4 margin, upheld key provisions of the BCRA. The appeal included challenges to the definition of issue advertising as well as allegations that various provisions of the BCRA infringe on freedom of speech rights. Specifically, the

Supreme Court upheld the BCRA's prohibition on electioneering communications if the ads feature or name an incumbent or political candidate and are funded through corporate or labor union money, sometimes termed "soft money." Such funds are so named because they are not direct contributions to a candidate, but are made to national political committees or other groups that promote access to candidates. Only advertisements purchased by a federally registered political action committee (PAC) are permissible. *See also* Section 10.10, Amendment 27 and Colorado Campaign Finance Reform, and 10.06, Political Action Committees.

The BCRA also requires the Federal Election Commission to create regulations defining "coordination." Coordinated activities, involving independent interest groups that share goals and donors with a candidate for federal office, are illegal for corporations and labor unions under the FECA. Coordinated activities are considered in-kind contributions because of the involvement of the candidate in some kind of activity by the organization that influences the election. The new regulations dramatically increase the types of activities and contacts that combine to create the appearance of coordination. Many nonprofits face a difficult decision, whether to give up their legitimate lobbying activities or face accusations of coordination under the new law's broad definition. Under the new regulations a three-part test is used to determine if coordination occurred. In brief, the test examines who paid for the communication, the content of the communication, and the conduct involved.

> ***TIP:*** Nonprofits must take great care to exclude the name of any candidate for federal office from any broadcast information or public service announcement within the 30- and 60-day time frames specified in the statute. They must also be careful about affiliating with other corporations, either nonprofit or for-profit, to express support for issues associated with a candidate. *McConnell v. FEC,* 540 U.S. ___ (December 10, 2003).

RESOURCES: *Nonprofit Organizations and Lobbying, Political Activity and Voter Education;* National Association for the Education of Young Children; http://www.naeyc.org/affiliates/acb/chapter7.pdf.

Nonprofit Advocacy and Public Policy: Campaign Finance, Alliance for Justice; http://www.allianceforjustice.org/nonprofit/public_policy/Campaign_Finance.html.

McConnell v. FEC, 540 U.S. ___ (December 10, 2003); http://www.supremecourtus.gov/opinions/03pdf/02-1674.pdf.

10.08

LEGAL SUBJECT: Lobbying Disclosure Act of 1995

STATEMENT OF ISSUE: The Lobbying Disclosure Act applies only to federal lobbying activities and requires registration and reporting by lobbyists. Contacts with the federal government's executive branch that were previously not considered lobbying are now classified as lobbying under this law.

CONCERNS/RISKS/ EXPOSURE: The Lobbying Disclosure Act of 1995 became effective January 1, 1996, and repealed the Federal Regulation of Lobbying Act of 1946. It significantly expanded the registration and reporting requirements for organizations seeking to impact policy and implementation of federal government programs. The Act defines lobbying more broadly than the IRS's definition of lobbying and allows the imposition of substantial fines for knowing noncompliance. Routine or occasional interactions with the senior executive branch officials or senior congressional staff are probably not "lobbying contacts." However, repeated contacts with legislators or executive officials, or employment of an in-house or contract lobbyist to make such contacts on behalf of the organization for the purpose of effecting policies and programs, could subject the organization to the registration and reporting requirements under this law. Lobbying activities, for reporting purposes of the Lobbying Disclosure Act, include the planning, research and other background preparation as well as the oral, written or electronic communications.

A lobbyist is subject to registration and reporting requirements if the individual: (1) is paid to make multiple lobbying contacts; (2) spends 20 percent or more of the individual's *compensated time for a particular client*; (3) over a six-month period; and (4) for the purpose of influencing federal legislation, program implementation or policy-making on behalf of the particular client. If a trade association or lobbying coalition retains a lobbyist or firm to engage in lobbying activities, it is the association or coalition, not the individual members, that is the lobbyist's client. The amount of compensated time is computed based on the activities of all employees of the potential registrant, not simply on the lobbying activities of those individuals identified as "lobbyists."

The Act specifies 19 types of exempt communication. Technical Amendments to the Act in 1998 have further clarified these exemptions as well as the definition of a covered executive branch official. The registration form and reporting form were also revised, making previously submitted documents obsolete.

> ***TIP:*** The definition of federal "lobbying" in this Act differs significantly from the Internal Revenue Code definition. In addition to attempting to influence elected officials, the definition for registration and reporting purposes includes lobbying contacts with senior executive officials or congressional staff to influence the regulations, policies or programs developed by federal administrative agencies or the executive branch. This is important because § 501(c)(4) nonprofits that lobby Congress or federal agencies within this definition are precluded from receiving federal grants or contracts. Lobbying Disclosure Act of 1995, 2 U.S.C. § 1611.

RESOURCES: Lobbying Disclosure Act of 1995, 2 U.S.C. §§ 1601 through 1612.

The Lobbying Disclosure Act of 1995: "What Me Lobby?"; http://www.ffhsj.com/cmemos/0071719.htm.

U.S. Senate "Lobbying Disclosure Act Guidance"; http://www.senate.gov/legislative/common/briefing/lobby_disc_briefing.htm.

Congressional lobbying forms LD-1 and LD-2 and electronic filing center; http://www.senate.gov/legislative/common/generic/lobbying_registration.htm.

10.09

LEGAL SUBJECT: State and Local Lobbying

STATEMENT OF ISSUE: State and local laws and regulations may impose restrictions on lobbying and registration requirements in addition to those required at the federal level.

CONCERNS/RISKS/ EXPOSURE: The State of Colorado defines lobbying as any direct or indirect communication with a covered official, or by any covered official, to influence any bill, resolution, amendment, nomination, appointment, or report, or any other matter, pending or proposed "for consideration by either house of the general assembly or committee thereof, whether or not the general assembly is in session." Lobbying also includes influencing the "drafting, consideration, amendment, adoption or defeat of any rule, standard or rate of any state agency having rule-making authority."

Participation in any lobbying activity in Colorado for pay requires registration with the Secretary of State's office and filing monthly disclosure reports with the office, whether one is a professional lobbyist or only lobbies occasionally for one's organization. The annual registration fee is between $25 and $50, depending upon whether the registration is filed electronically or manually, although the fee may be waived for professional lobbyists for nonprofit organizations. 8 CCR 1505-8, Rule 4. Disclosure reports may also be filed electronically.

It is important to check with local government to determine if there are any local lobbying requirements. For example, the City and County of Denver has its own extensive rules for those who lobby the City Council and other elected officials.

> ***TIP:*** Failure to register with the Secretary of State's office or to file disclosure statements is a misdemeanor punishable by a fine of up to $5,000 and/or imprisonment for up to 12 months. C.R.S. § 24-6-309.

RESOURCES: Colorado Secretary of State; http://www.sos.state.co.us/.

Colorado statutes on regulation of lobbyists, C.R.S. §§ 24-6-301 through 309

10.10

LEGAL SUBJECT: Amendment 27 and Colorado Campaign Finance Reform

STATEMENT OF ISSUE: Nonprofits in Colorado need to be aware of activities that might unintentionally bring them within Article XXVIII of the Colorado Constitution (Amendment 27).

CONCERNS/RISKS/ EXPOSURE: In November 2002, Colorado voters, by a 2-to-1 margin, passed Amendment 27 and its comprehensive campaign finance reform for state-level campaigns. Conduct regulated by the amendment includes political contributions, independent expenditures and electioneering communications. It lowers the limits on contributions to political action committees (PACs) from $25,000 annually to $500 per two-year cycle and limits PAC contributions to political candidates. *See also* Section 10.06, Political Action Committees. Candidates must disclose donors who contribute $100 or more, including the donor's name, occupation and employer.

While Amendment 27 regulations affect most of a Colorado nonprofit's political activities, nonprofits need to be particularly concerned about electioneering communications, defined under Colorado law as any communication that:

1. unambiguously refers to any candidate;
2. is broadcasted, printed, mailed, delivered, or distributed within 30 days before a primary election or 60 days before a general election; and
3. is broadcasted to, printed in a newspaper distributed to, mailed to, delivered by hand to, or

otherwise distributed to an audience that includes members of the electorate for such public office.

The simple inclusion of a candidate's name or photo in any broadcast, published or distributed communication, even if the reference has absolutely nothing to do with the current campaign, may be construed as electioneering communication. Excluded from the definition, however, are news articles, editorial endorsements, opinion or commentary, and letters to the editor printed in a newspaper, magazine or other periodical or broadcast by a facility not owned or controlled by a candidate or political party; communication referring to the candidate only as part of a popular name of a bill or statute; and communications made in the course and scope of business or by a membership organization solely to its members and their families. An organization that spends $1000 or more on electioneering communications in a calendar year must disclose all of its spending and the name, address, occupation, and employer of individuals who contributed more than $250 to the organization in reports to the Secretary of State. Colo. Const. Art. XXVIII § 6; C.R.S. § 1-45-108(2).

A nonprofit organization that forms an issue committee whose *major purpose* is to support or oppose a ballot referendum or initiative may be subject to Amendment 27. Examples of past issues that a nonprofit may have opposed or promoted are the TABOR Amendment, the Amendment 23 Education Initiative, and the Gallagher Amendment. Issue committees that accept contributions or make expenditures of $200 or more to support their major purpose will be subject to Amendment 27 registration, filing and disclosure requirements. An issue committee must disclose the name, occupation, and employer of any donor contributing $100 or more to the committee. Colo. Const. Art. XXVIII § 7. Filings may be made electronically with the Secretary of State's office on designated reporting forms.

Any nonprofit that violates any provision of Amendment 27 relating to contributions may be subject to a civil penalty of anywhere between double and quintuple the amount contributed or received. Failure to file reports will result in penalties of $50 per day. Furthermore, any person who believes that a violation of certain sections of the amendment has occurred may file a complaint with the Secretary of State's office within 180 days of the alleged violation. The complaint is then referred within three days to an administrative law judge who conducts a hearing and rules on the complaint within 30 days of the referral. There are no provisions for filtering complaints and no "frivolousness" penalties to discourage the filing of frivolous or harassing complaints. A filed complaint, even if frivolous, must still be defended. If the Secretary of State fails to enforce the decision of the administrative law judge, a private right of action or civil lawsuit may be brought in a state district court. The prevailing party in such a lawsuit is entitled to recover its reasonable attorney fees and costs. Colo. Const. Art. XXVIII § 9(2); C.R.S. § 1-45-111.5.

> ***TIP:*** The above requirements of Amendment 27 and Article 45 of Title 1 do not apply to home rule counties or municipalities, *e.g.*, Denver and Boulder, if they have adopted charters, ordinances or resolutions that address campaign finance rules. The municipal laws may be more, or less, restrictive than the state laws. 8 CCR 1505-6 27.1; Opinion of Attorney General, issued January 15, 2003.

RESOURCES: Colo. Const. Art. XXVIII; full text of Amendment 27 is available from The New Rules Project; http://www.newrules.org/gov/coloradocfr.html.

Amendment 27 Regulations adopted June 2003 are available from the Colorado Secretary of state web page; http://www.sos.state.co.us/pubs/info_center/main.htm.

Colorado Fair Campaign Practices Act, C.R.S. §§ 1-45-101 through 118.

8 CCR 1505-6, Rules 21 through 27.

CHAPTER 11: GENERAL RESOURCES

11.01

ONLINE RESOURCES: The Internet is full of helpful resources for nonprofit organizations, their boards, and managers. The list below represents some of the websites that the authors find useful, but it is in no way exhaustive, nor should the inclusion of a website below be construed as an endorsement of a particular site or its content. The Internet is continually changing and expanding and links that are active one month can disappear or change the next. Similarly, websites that offer free information as of the date of this book's publication may begin charging for access to their resources. An attempt has been made to assure the accuracy and currentness of the links set forth below, but neither the authors nor Bradford Publishing can take responsibility for changes that will no doubt take place in the ever-evolving realm of the World Wide Web.

We encourage readers to inform us of changes to the information provided below or of additional online resources to be considered for inclusion in future editions of this book by contacting the Editorial Department at Bradford Publishing Co., 1743 Wazee Street, Denver, Colorado 80202; phone (303) 292-2500.

Charity Channel

Discussion forums, helpful articles, and resources. Widely used by some of the most prominent tax-exempt specialists including attorneys. Voluntary annual fee to become a subscriber.

30021 Tomas Street, Suite 300
Rancho Santa Margarita, CA 92688-2128
Phone: (949) 589-5938
Fax: (949) 589-4399
http://www.charitychannel.com/

Nonprofit Risk Management Center

Online advice, free technical assistance, and risk management consulting.

1130 Seventeenth Street, NW, Suite 210
Washington, D.C. 20036
Phone: (202) 785-3891
Fax: (202) 296-0349
http://www.nonprofitrisk.org/

Internet Nonprofit Center

Information for and about nonprofits, including FAQs and a document library.

The Evergreen State Society
P.O. Box 20682
Seattle, WA 98102-0682
http://www.nonprofits.org

Alliance for Nonprofit Management

Professional association devoted to improving the management and governance capacity of nonprofits.

1899 L Street NW, 6th Floor
Washington D.C. 20036
Phone: (202) 955-8406
Fax: (202) 721-0086
http://www.allianceonline.org/

Nonprofitlaw.com: The Internet Site for Tax-Exempt Organizations
Legal information from the law firm of Pfau Englund, Nonprofit Law, P.C.

3212 Duke Street, #622
Alexandria, VA 22314
Phone: (703) 304-1204
http://www.nonprofitlaw.com/

Management Assistance Program for Nonprofits
Management and Board Development services for nonprofit organizations, governmental agencies, and religious institutions. Excellent (and free!) online management library.

2233 University Avenue West, Suite 360
St Paul, MN 55114-1629
Phone: (651) 647-1216
Fax: (651) 647-1369
http://www.mapfornonprofits.org/

Don Kramer's Nonprofit Issues
A legal newsletter covering nonprofit law.

Nonprofit Issues, Inc.
P.O. Box 482
Dresher, PA 19025
Phone: (215) 542-7547 (888) NP-Issue
Fax: (215) 542-7548
http://www.nonprofitissues.com

WebNP (formerly MyNoodle.org)
Dedicated to offering the nonprofit community a central focal point to get news and information that affect their organizations and to find key resources to further their missions.

Bourassa Media Group
62 Cedar Street
Worcester, MA 01609
Phone: (508) 831-1310
http://webnp.nt5.us/

NonProfitExpert.com

The website of Minges & Associates LLC, management consultants for nonprofits.

Minges & Associates, LLC
101 W 14th Street, Suite 103
Greenville, NC 27834
Phone: (252) 758-9800
http://www.nonprofitexpert.com/default.htm

Energize, Inc.

An international training, consulting and publishing firm specializing in volunteerism.

5450 Wissahickon Ave.
Philadelphia, PA 19144
Phone: (215) 438-8342
Fax: (215) 438-0434
http://www.energizeinc.com/

CAPLAW

Legal assistance nationwide for Community Action Agencies operating under the federal Community Services Block Grant Program

Community Action Program Legal Services, Inc.
178 Tremont Street, 10th Floor
Boston, MA 02111
Phone: (617) 357-6915
Fax: (617) 350-7899
http://www.caplaw.org/

Nonprofit Genie

Information and resources for the nonprofit community provided by CompassPoint Nonprofit Services, including Board Café—the Newsletter for Nonprofit Boards.

CompassPoint Nonprofit Services
706 Mission Street, 5th Floor
San Francisco, CA 94103
Phone: (415) 541-9000
Fax: (415) 541-7708
http://www.genie.org/

IKNOW: Interactive Knowledge for Nonprofit Organizations Worldwide

Developed and maintained by Raffa, P.C., a provider of consulting, accounting, technology, and outsourcing for nonprofit organizations.

Raffa, P.C.
1899 L Street, Suite 600
Washington, D.C. 20036
Phone: (202) 822-5000
http://www.iknow.org/

Runquist & Zybach, LLP

A southern California law firm specializing in nonprofit organizations among other specialties. Useful articles.

10618 Woodbridge St.
Toluca Lake, CA 91602
Phone: (818) 760-8986
Fax: (818) 760-8314
http://www.runquist.com/

FedLaw

Legal resources for federal legal research.

http://www.thecre.com/fedlaw/default.htm

Online Compendium of Federal and State Regulations for U.S. Nonprofit Organizations

Includes online law libraries and court decisions.

http://www.paperglyphs.com/nporegulation/main.html

Cornell Law School Legal Information Institute

http://www.law.cornell.edu/

11.02

GOVERNMENT AND ORGANIZATIONAL RESOURCES:

Colorado Secretary of State
1560 Broadway, Suite 200
Denver, CO 80202-5169
(303) 894-2251
Licensing/Charitable Solicitation: (303) 894-2200
http://www.sos.state.co.us/

Colorado Business Assistance Center
1625 Broadway, Suite 1710
Denver, CO 80202
Phone: (303) 892-3840
http://www.state.co.us/oed/sbdc/bac.html

Colorado Department of Labor and Employment
1515 Arapahoe Street
Tower 2, Suite 400
Denver, CO 80202-2117
Phone: (303) 318-8000
Fax: (303) 318-8048
http://www.coworkforce.com/

Colorado Supreme Court Library
B112 State Judicial Bldg.
2 East 14th Avenue
Denver, CO 80203
Phone: (303) 837-3720
http://www.state.co.us/courts/sctlib/index.html

Colorado Civil Rights Division
1560 Broadway, Suite 1050
Denver, CO 80202
Phone: (303) 894-2997
Fax: (303) 894-7830
http://www.dora.state.co.us/civil-rights/

Colorado Bureau of Investigation
690 Kipling St.
Denver, CO 80215
Phone: (303) 239-4300
http://cbi.state.co.us/
CBI Convicted Sex Offender Registry; http://sor.state.co.us/default.asp

Colorado Department of Law/Attorney General
1525 Sherman St. 7th floor
Denver CO 80203
Phone: (303) 866-4500
Fax: (303)866-5691
http://www.ago.state.co.us/

The Internal Revenue Service
http://www.irs.gov/

United States Postal Service
http://www.usps.com/

U.S. Citizenship and Immigration Services
(formerly the Immigration and Naturalization Service)
Denver District Office
4730 Paris Street
Denver, CO 80239
Phone: (303) 371-3841
http://uscis.gov/graphics/fieldoffices/denver/aboutus.htm

U.S. Department of Labor Wage and Hour Division
http://www.dol.gov/esa/whd/

U.S. Equal Employment Opportunity Commission (EEOC)
Denver District Office
303 E. 17th Avenue, Suite 510
Denver, CO 80203
Phone: (303) 866-1300
Fax: (303) 866-1085
http://www.eeoc.gov/denver/index.html

National Council of Nonprofit Associations
A 501(c)(3) membership-based organization of state and regional associations.
1030 15th Street NW, Suite 870
Washington, D.C. 20005-1525
Phone: (202) 962-0322
Fax: (202) 962-0321
http://ncna.org/

National Association of State Charities Officials
A forum for the exchange of views and experiences relating to charitable trust and charitable solicitations issues.
http://nasconet.org/

BBB Wise Giving Alliance
Collects and distributes information on hundreds of nonprofit organizations that solicit nationally or have national or international program services.
http://www.give.org/

Guidestar
A national online database of nonprofit organizations, including 990 filings.
http://www.guidestar.org/

Idealist.org

Connects people, nonprofit organizations and resources.

http://www.idealist.org/

Colorado Association of Nonprofit Organizations (CANPO)

A voluntary association of Colorado nonprofit organizations. Has many publications, a resource library, and a home page with links, as well as FAQ's.

455 Sherman Street, Suite 207
Denver, CO 80203-4494
Phone: (303) 832-5710
Fax: (303) 894-0161
http://www.canpo.org/

CANPO ASI

The leading provider of insurance coverage for nonprofit organizations and their employees in Colorado.

455 Sherman Street, Suite 207
Denver, CO 80203-4494
Phone: (303) 894-0298
Fax: (303) 894-0161
http://www.canpoasi.org

Nonprofits' Insurance Alliance of California (NIAC)

A 501(c)(3) tax exempt liability insurance pool created to be a stable source of reasonably priced liability insurance for 501(c)(3) nonprofits in California. Has a number of useful articles regarding nonprofit insurance and risk management issues applicable to nonprofits in any state.

P.O. Box 8507
Santa Cruz, CA 95061-8522
Phone: (831) 459-0980 or (800) 359-6422
Fax: (831) 459-0853
http://www.niac.org/

Colorado Springs Chamber Nonprofit Partnership

The primary organization in Southern Colorado founded to provide assistance and foster quality and excellence within the nonprofit community.

2 North Cascade Avenue, Suite 110
Colorado Springs, CO 80903
Phone: (719) 575-4341
Fax: (719) 635-1571
http://www.chambernonprofitpartnership.org

Community Resource Center

Technical assistance, training, and consulting services to individuals, nonprofit organizations, and community-based coalitions throughout Colorado and nationally.

655 Broadway, Suite 300
Denver, CO 80203-3426
Phone: (303) 623-1540 or (800) 516-6284
Fax: (303) 623-1567
http://www.crcamerica.org/

BoardSource

A resource for practical information, tools and best practices, training, and leadership development for board members of nonprofit organizations.

1828 L Street NW, Suite 900
Washington, D.C. 20036
Phone: (202) 452-6262 or (800) 883-6262
Fax: (202) 452-6299
http://www.ncnb.org/

American Bar Association

A voluntary professional association of attorneys in the United States.

750 N Lake Shore Drive
Chicago IL 60611
(312) 988-5000 or (800) 285-2221
http://w3.abanet.org/home.cfm

Colorado Bar Association

A voluntary professional association of attorneys in Colorado.

1900 Grant Street, Suite 900
Denver, CO 80203
Phone: (303) 860-1115
Fax: (303) 894-0821
http://www.cobar.org/

OMB Watch

1742 Connecticut Avenue, NW
Washington, D.C. 20009
Phone: (202) 234-8494
Fax: (202) 234-8584
http://www.ombwatch.org/

Alliance for Justice

11 Dupont Circle, NW, 2nd Floor
Washington, D.C. 20036
Phone: (202) 822-6070
Fax: (202) 822-6068
http://www.afj.org/

11.03

PUBLISHERS AND PUBLICATIONS:

Bradford Publishing Company
1743 Wazee Street
Denver, CO 80202-5920
(303) 292-2590
http://www.bradfordpublishing.com/

Don Kramer's Nonprofit Issues, Inc.
P.O. Box 482
Dresher, PA 19025
Phone: (215) 542-7547
Fax: (215) 542-7548
http://www.nonprofitissues.com/

John Wiley and Sons, Inc.
Customer Care Center/Consumer Accounts
10475 Crosspoint Blvd.
Indianapolis, IN 46256
Phone: (877) 762-2974
Fax: (800) 597-3299
http://www.wiley.com/WileyCDA/

Nolo Press
http://www.nolo.com/

Guidebook for Directors of Nonprofit Corporations (2nd Ed. 2002); available from the American Bar Association; (800) 285-2221;
http://www.abanet.org/abapubs/nonprofit.html

J. BLAZEK, **990 HANDBOOK: A LINE BY LINE APPROACH** (2001), for use with both Form 990 and Form 990EZ; available from: John Wiley & Sons, (877) 762-2974;
http://www.wiley.com/WileyCDA/WileyTitle/productCd-0471417815.html

J.D. DEWITT, **VOLUNTEER LEGAL HANDBOOK** (6th Ed. 2001);
http://www.iciclesoftware.com/vlh/

J.S. OTT, **UNDERSTANDING NONPROFIT ORGANIZATIONS: GOVERNANCE, LEADERSHIP AND MANAGEMENT** (2001); available from Westview Press, (800) 386-5656;
http://www.perseusbooksgroup.com/perseus-cgi-bin/display/0-8133-6787-5

B. HOPKINS, **STARTING AND MANAGING A NONPROFIT ORGANIZATION,** (3rd Ed. 2000; available from: John Wiley & Sons, (877) 762-2974;
http://www.wiley.com/WileyCDA/WileyTitle/productCd-047139727X.html

A. MANCUSO, **HOW TO FORM A NONPROFIT CORPORATION** (National Edition) (5th Ed. 2002); available from Nolo Press;
http://www.nolo.com/

G.C. Grissom, A. Sparkman, & P. Zwanzig, ***An Overview of the Colorado Revised Nonprofit Corporation Act,*** The Colorado Lawyer, (Sept. 1997), Vol. 26, No. 9, pp. 5-20; available free to Colorado Bar Association members;
http://www.cobar.org/tcl/tcl_articles.cfm?ArticleID=1526

The Colorado Revised Nonprofit Corporation Act: With Commentary by the Revision Committee (1997); available from Continuing Legal Education in Colorado, Inc.;
http://www.cobar.org/cle/

11.04

COLORADO NONPROFIT EDUCATIONAL RESOURCES:

Regis University

School for Professional Studies
Department of Nonprofit Management
3333 Regis Boulevard
Denver, CO 80221-1099
Phone: (303) 458-4100 or (800) 388-2366
http://www.regis.edu/regis.asp?sctn=apg&p1=gp&p2=mnm

University of Denver

Institute for Public Policy Studies
2199 S. University Blvd.
Denver, CO 80208
Phone: (303) 871-2468
Fax: (303) 871-3066
http://www.du.edu/ipps/

APPENDIX 1

Tax-Exempt Organizations Recognized by the IRS Under Section 501(c) of Title 26, Subtitle A, CHAPTER 1, Subchapter F, PART I

Internal Revenue Code Section 501(c)(1): Corporations organized under an act of Congress, *e.g.*, the Federal Deposit Insurance Corporation, Federal Reserve Banks, and the American Red Cross.

Internal Revenue Code Section 501(c)(2): Title holding companies wholly owned by a tax-exempt parent organization.

Internal Revenue Code Section 501(c)(3): Charitable, religious, scientific, literary, educational, and other similar organizations.

Internal Revenue Code Section 501(c)(4): Civic leagues, community organizations and other social welfare organizations.

Internal Revenue Code Section 501(c)(5): Labor, agricultural, and horticultural organizations.

Internal Revenue Code Section 501(c)(6): Business leagues including professional associations, chambers of commerce, real estate boards.

Internal Revenue Code Section 501(c)(7): Social and recreational clubs, including hobby and country clubs.

Internal Revenue Code Section 501(c)(8): Fraternal beneficiary societies, including fraternal lodges that provide benefits to their members.

Internal Revenue Code Section 501(c)(9): Voluntary employees' beneficiary associations including labor unions.

Internal Revenue Code Section 501(c)(10): Domestic fraternal societies, including fraternal lodges that do not provide member benefits and the net earnings of which go to religious, charitable, educational or similar causes.

Internal Revenue Code Section 501(c)(11): Teachers' retirement fund associations.

Internal Revenue Code Section 501(c)(12): Benevolent or mutual organizations, *e.g.*, local life insurance associations, irrigation companies, and cooperative telephone companies.

Internal Revenue Code Section 501(c)(13): Certain cemetery companies.

Internal Revenue Code Section 501(c)(14): Certain credit unions and mutual reserve funds.

Internal Revenue Code Section 501(c)(15): Certain insurance companies or associations.

Internal Revenue Code Section 501(c)(16): Crop operations finance corporations.

Internal Revenue Code Section 501(c)(17): Supplemental unemployment benefit trusts.

Internal Revenue Code Section 501(c)(18): Pension plan trusts.

Internal Revenue Code Section 501(c)(19): Post-1982 veterans' organizations.

Internal Revenue Code Section 501(c)(20): Legal services organizations.

Internal Revenue Code Section 501(c)(21): Black Lung benefits trusts.

Internal Revenue Code Section 501(c)(22): Multi-employer benefits trusts under the Employee Retirement Income Security Act of 1974.

Internal Revenue Code Section 501(c)(23): Pre-1982 Veterans' Organizations.

Internal Revenue Code Section 501(c)(24): Single-employer pension plans under the Employee Retirement Income Security Act of 1974.

Internal Revenue Code Section 501(c)(25): Multi-parent title-holding corporations or trusts.

Internal Revenue Code Section 501(c)(26): High-risk individuals health care coverage organizations.

Internal Revenue Code Section 501(c)(27): Workers' compensation reinsurance organizations.

Internal Revenue Code Section 501(c)(28): The National Railroad Retirement Investment Trust.

APPENDIX 2A

Colorado Posting Requirements

See also the Colorado Department of Labor home page: http://www.coworkforce.com/

SUBJECT	STATUTE	POSTER	ORDER FROM
Minimum Wage Law	C.R.S. § 8-6; Colorado Wage Order #23	Colorado Minimum Wage Poster	Division of Labor, Labor Standards, 1515 Arapahoe St., Tower 2, Suite 375 Denver, CO 80202-2117 303 572-2241 http://www.coworkforce.com/LAB/
Wage Payment Law	C.R.S. § 8-4	Employers shall post a notice specifying the regular paydays and the time and place of payment.	Employer prints own notice
Civil Rights	C.R.S. § 24-34	This establishment complies ... with Colorado's anti-discrimination laws. (employment, housing, accommodations)	Colorado Civil Rights Division 1560 Broadway, Rm 1050 Denver, CO 80202 303 894-2997
Unemployment Insurance	C.R.S. § 8-70	Notice to Employees ... Colorado Employment Security Act	Colorado Division of Employment & Training Liability Section 1515 Arapahoe St., Tower 3, Suite 200 Denver, CO 80202-2117 303 603-8231
Workers' Compensation	C.R.S. § 8-40	WC 49 – Notice to Employees ... Workers' Compensation Act WC 50 – Notice to Employer of Injury	Obtain from WC insurance carrier or purchase from: Bradford Publishing 1743 Wazee St. Denver, CO 80202 303 292-2590

APPENDIX 2B

Federal Posting Requirements

A customized list of required federal posters may be obtained by completing an online questionnaire at: http://www.dol.gov/elaws/posters.htm

SUBJECT	STATUTE	POSTER	ORDER FROM
Minimum Wage	Fair Labor Standards Act	Minimum Wage (WH-1088)	U.S. Dept. of Labor Wage & Hour Division 1801 California, Rm. 935 Denver, CO 80204 303 844-4405
Polygraph Tests	Employee Polygraph Act	Notice-Employee Polygraph Protection Act (WH–1462)	Same as Above
Family and Medical Leave	Family and Medical Leave Act of 1993	Your Rights Under the Family and Medical Leave Act of 1993 (WH-1420)	Same as Above
Equal Employment	Civil Rights Act of 1964	Equal Employment Is the Law	EEOC 303 E. 17th Ave. Suite 510 Denver, CO 80203
Age Discrimination	Age Discrimination in Employment Act	Equal Employment Is the Law	EEOC Same as above
Workers with Disabilities	Other Civil Rights Titles; Rehabilitation Act of 1973; Americans with Disabilities Act	Equal Employment Is the Law	EEOC Same as above
Veterans	Vietnam Era Veterans Readjustment Act of 1974	Equal Employment Is the Law	EEOC Same as Above
Safety	Occupational Safety and Health Act (OSHA)	Job Safety & Health (OSHA-2203) Log of Occupational Illness/Injury (FORM-200)	OSHA Administration 1999 Broadway, Suite 1690 Denver, CO 80202-5716 303 844-1600

INDEX

BRADFORD PUBLISHING COMPANY

Founded in 1881, Bradford Publishing Company is Colorado's oldest and most trusted publisher of legal forms, law books, and legal information.

Other publications of interest from Bradford Publishing:

Colorado Land Planning and Development Law, 6th Edition

The Lawyer's Winning Edge: Exceptional Courtroom Performance

Employment Law: An Essential Guide for Colorado Employers

Web Law: A Field Guide to Internet Publishing

Managing Your Wired Workforce: A Practical Guide

Friendly Divorce Guidebook for Colorado, 5th Edition

Ordinary Issues—Extraordinary Solutions: Legal Guide for the Colorado GLBT Community

Bradford's Colorado Revised Statutes Field of Practice Desk Reference Volumes

- ***Family Law and Domestic Matters***
- ***Real Property Law***
- ***Probate, Trusts, and Fiduciaries***
- ***Corporations, Associations, Labor, & Industry***
- ***Colorado Court Rules***

A Legal Guide For Practicing Psychotherapy in Colorado

Living with Wildfires: Prevention, Preparation & Recovery

Preserving Your Wealth: A Guide to Colorado Probate & Estate Planning

Colorado Will and Estate Planner

Residential Real Estate Closings in Colorado

Winning Big in Colorado Small Claims Court, 2nd Edition

Landlord & Tenant Guide to Colorado Evictions, 2nd Edition

Instructions for Using the CD-ROM

The complete contents of this book and selected statutory materials are stored on the enclosed CD-ROM in Adobe PDF files. You may view these files using any version of *Adobe Acrobat* or *Acrobat Reader.* For your convenience, we have included the newest member of the Adobe software family, *Adobe Reader 6.0,* on the CD-ROM. (See installation instructions below.)

Using an older version of *Acrobat* or *Reader*

If you currently have the "full version" of *Acrobat* installed on your computer, or if your version of *Reader* includes the optional search function, you may perform keyword searches of the text on the CD-ROM using your existing software. However, if your Adobe software is older than version "6.0," you must first load the index file from the CD-ROM as follows:

1. Open *Acrobat* or *Reader.* On the menu bar, click "Edit/Search/Select Indexes... ." The "Index Selection" window will appear; click the "Add..." button.
2. The "Select Index" window will appear; click the "My Computer" button. Then select your CD-ROM drive and click the "Open" button.
3. Select the "Nonprofit Index.pdx" file and click the "Open" button. The "Index Selection" window will reappear; click the "OK" button.
4. To perform a keyword search, click on "Edit/Search/Query..." (or click the "Search" binoculars icon on the toolbar) and type your search string in the query window. You may use simple Boolean operators, such as AND and OR, in your search.
5. Click the "Search" button. The "Search Results" window will appear with a list of the documents (*i.e.*, PDF files) that contain your search term(s) displayed in order of the frequency in which the terms appear. To view the results, select a document and click the "View" button. Your search terms will be highlighted in the document.

Installing the new *Adobe Reader 6.0**

If your computer uses Windows 98SE, Me, 2000, or XP, we recommend using *Adobe Reader 6.0* to view and search the *Nonprofit Management* files on the CD-ROM. This new version of *Reader* has greatly improved search capabilities and a "friendlier" user interface. There is no need to load indexes, as described above; the program will perform keyword searches "on the fly" in every PDF file under a given path. *Adobe Reader* is "freeware." There is no additional charge to install or use the program. However, a window will pop up the first time you open *Reader* asking you to accept Adobe's end-user license. Just click the "Accept" button, and you can start using the program immediately.

The installation file for *Adobe Reader 6.0* is included in the "Adobe Reader" folder on the CD-ROM. To install the program, simply locate and right-click on the "Adobe Reader 6 install.exe" file, then click "Open" on the menu that pops up. The software will lead you through several steps and then install itself on your computer automatically. **NOTE:** You must have "Administrator Rights" to your computer in order to install this, or any other, software program. If you do not have administrator rights, you may need to contact the IT manager in your firm to install *Adobe Reader 6.0.*

To perform a search, open *Adobe Reader 6.0* and click on the "Search" binoculars icon on the toolbar. A window will appear on the right side of your screen where you can enter your keywords and your search parameters. To search the book and statute text files on the CD-ROM, click on "All PDF documents in..." and select your CD-ROM drive. **NOTE:** To use Boolean operators in your search, you must select "Use Advanced Search Options" (at the bottom of the search window) and then select "Boolean query" on the "Return results containing:" menu. For additional information, consult the "Adobe Reader Help..." file on the "Help" menu.

* You must have Windows 98SE, Me, 2000, or XP to use Adobe Reader 6.0. If you have the original Windows 98 or 95, you must use Acrobat Reader 5.05 instead, available free from Adobe at: http://www.adobe.com/products/acrobat/readstep2.html.